WINTER CLIMBS IN THE CAIRNGORMS

About the authors

Allen Fyffe has been an active mountaineer for over 40 years. During part of that time he was an instructor and guide, and now is the Executive Secretary of Mountain Leader Training Scotland, involved in the administration of mountaineering and climbing qualifications in Scotland. Allen has been involved in every aspect of mountaineering and climbing, and in Scotland has climbed over 200 new routes in both summer and winter. In the Alps he made the first British ascent of the North Face of Les Droites, an early British ascent of the North Face of the Eiger, and the first winter ascent of the Central Spur of Les Courtes. In the Himalaya he made a two-man first ascent of the South-West Flank of Kalanka and the Scottish Pillar on Bhagirathi III. He has also been a member of expeditions to Dhaulaghiri IV, Everest South-West Face and Everest North-East Ridge, Meru and Broad Peak.

Along with Iain Peter he made an early British ascent of Khan Tengri in the Tien Shan and the first British ascent of Pik Pobeda. The two wrote the highly acclaimed *Handbook of Climbing* and, more recently, with Andy Cunningham, he wrote *Winter Skills* for Mountain Leader Training UK. Allen has also climbed in Canada, Peru and on the big walls in Yosemite and Zion. He continues to be active, especially in the Cairngorms, where he has been involved in the production of several guidebooks.

Blair Fyffe has been climbing and mountaineering since a young age, and has been involved in all aspects of the sport from bouldering to big-wall and expedition climbing. He has rock climbed extensively throughout Britain and mainland Europe to a high standard (E7 and French 8b). In winter Blair has made numerous first ascents and early repeats. His first ascents include Rhyme of the Ancient Mariner (VII, 7) and the first winter ascent of Knuckleduster (VIII, 9), both on Ben Nevis.

Beyond Britain Blair has climbed new winter routes in the Lofoten Islands of artic Norway and new alpine routes in the Tien Shan mountains of Kyrgyzstan. He has also climbed in the European Alps and on the big walls of Yosemite Valley. In 2006 Blair completed a PhD in slab-avalanche release at Edinburgh University. He now works as a forecaster for sportscotland Avalanche Information Service during the winter months. During the summer he does a variety of jobs, including mountain leader, countryside ranger and research associate for Edinburgh University.

WINTER CLIMBS IN THE CAIRNGORMS

THE CAIRNGORMS AND CREAG MEAGAIDH

by
Allen Fyffe and Blair Fyffe

CICERONE

2 POLICE SQUARE, MILNTHORPE, CUMBRIA LA7 7PY
www.cicerone.co.uk

Sixth edition 2011
ISBN: 978 1 85284 622 0
Fifth edition 2000, Fourth edition 1987, Third edition 1981 (all by Allen Fyffe)
Second edition (with John Cunningham) 1976, First edition (John Cunningham) 1973
Printed in China on behalf of Latitude Press Ltd.
A catalogue record for this book is available from the British Library.
All photographs are by the authors unless otherwise stated.

Advice to readers

While every effort is made by our authors to ensure the accuracy of guidebooks as they go to print, changes can occur during the lifetime of an edition. If we know of any, there will be an Updates tab on this book's page on the Cicerone website (www.cicerone.co.uk), so please check before planning your trip. We also advise that you check information about such things as transport, accommodation and shops locally. Even rights of way can be altered over time. We are always grateful for information about any discrepancies between a guidebook and the facts on the ground, sent by email to info@cicerone.co.uk or by post to Cicerone, 2 Police Square, Milnthorpe LA7 7PY, United Kingdom.

Warning

Mountain climbing can be a dangerous activity carrying a risk of personal injury or death. It should be undertaken only by those with a full understanding of the risks and with the training and experience to evaluate them. While every care and effort has been taken in the preparation of this guide, the user should be aware that conditions can be highly variable and can change quickly, materially affecting the seriousness of a climb. Therefore, except for any liability which cannot be excluded by law, neither Cicerone nor the authors accept liability for damage of any nature (including damage to property, personal injury or death) arising directly or indirectly from the information in this book. If you need to raise the alarm, dial 999 and ask for Mountain Rescue, give your number to the police and remain switched on until the rescue team arrives or you are given the all clear to switch off.

Front cover: Neil Johnson on the top pitch of Swan Song (Fiacaill Buttress, Coire an t-Sneachda)

CONTENTS

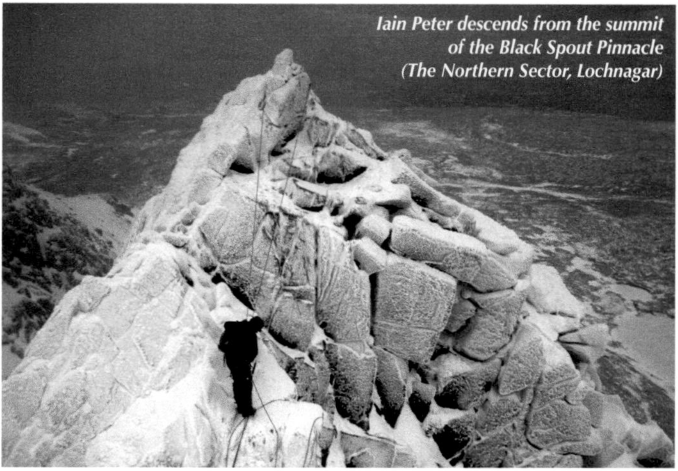

Iain Peter descends from the summit of the Black Spout Pinnacle (The Northern Sector, Lochnagar)

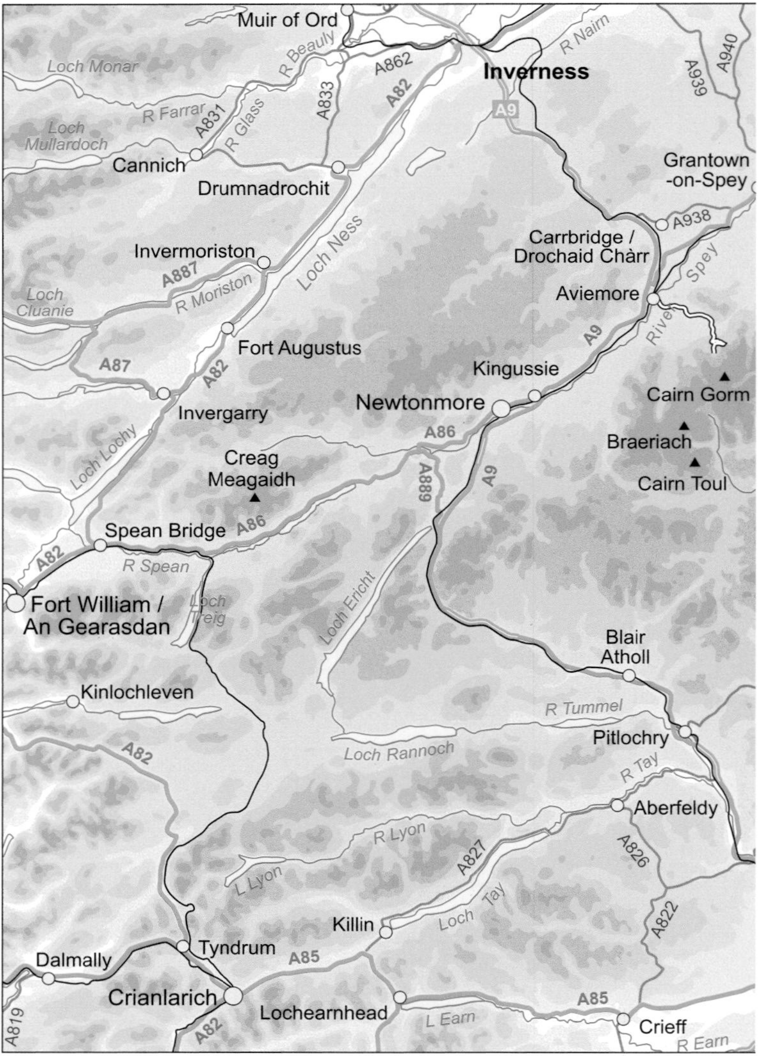
Muir of Ord
R Beauly
Loch Monar
A862
R Nairn
Inverness
A940
A939
A9
A833
A82
R Farrar
A831
R Glass
Loch Mullardoch
Cannich
Drumnadrochit
Grantown -on-Spey
A938
Loch Ness
Carrbridge / Drochaid Chàrr
Invermoriston
A887
Spey
Loch Cluanie
R Moriston
Aviemore
River
A9
Fort Augustus
A87
A82
Kingussie
Cairn Gorm
Newtonmore
Invergarry
A86
Braeriach
Loch Lochy
Creag Meagaidh
A889
A9
Cairn Toul
Spean Bridge
A86
A82
R Spean
Fort William / An Gearasdan
Loch Treig
Loch Ericht
Blair Atholl
Kinlochleven
R Tummel
Pitlochry
A82
Loch Rannoch
R Tay
Aberfeldy
R Lyon
A827
A826
L Lyon
Loch Tay
A822
Killin
Tyndrum
A85
Dalmally
Crianlarich
A85
Lochearnhead
L Earn
Crieff
A819
A82
R Earn

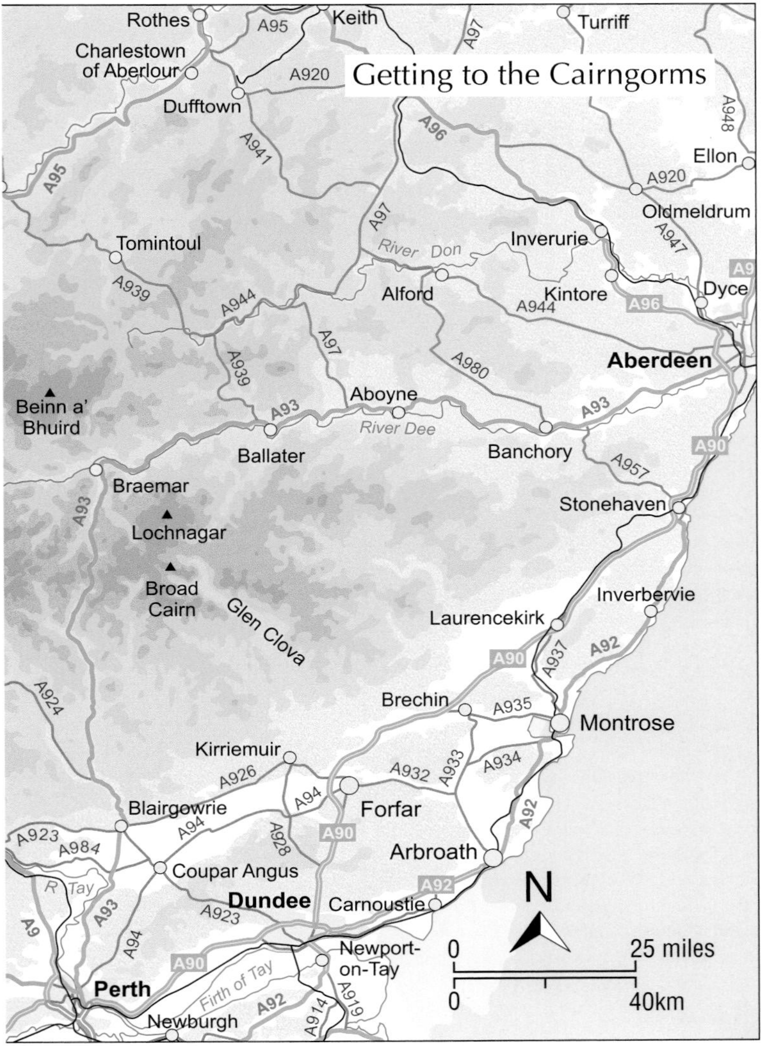
Getting to the Cairngorms
Rothes
Keith
Turriff
Charlestown
of Aberlour
Dufftown
Tomintoul
Inverurie
Oldmeldrum
Ellon
Alford
Kintore
Dyce
Aberdeen
Beinn a'
Bhuird
Aboyne
Ballater
Banchory
Braemar
Lochnagar
Broad
Cairn
Glen Clova
Stonehaven
Inverbervie
Laurencekirk
Brechin
Montrose
Kirriemuir
Forfar
Blairgowrie
Arbroath
Coupar Angus
Dundee
Carnoustie
Newport-
on-Tay
Perth
Newburgh
River Don
River Dee
R Tay
Firth of Tay
A95
A97
A920
A96
A941
A948
A947
A939
A944
A980
A93
A90
A957
A92
A937
A935
A934
A933
A932
A926
A94
A928
A924
A923
A984
A9
A914
A919
N
0
25 miles
0
40km

LIST OF DIAGRAMS

Looking west along Loch Avon to Carn Etchachan and the Shelter Stone Crag, with Stag Rocks and Stac an Fharaidh visible on the right

With easy access, reliable conditions and quality climbing, the Northern Corries always prove popular (The Mess of Pottage, Coire an t-Sneachda)

INTRODUCTION

The major climbing venues of the Cairngorms provide some of the finest winter routes in Britain. From the remote corries of Braeriach and Beinn a'Bhuird to the magnificent cliffs of Lochnagar and Creag an Dubh Loch and the readily accessible Northern Corries of Cairn Gorm, every aspect of winter climbing is to be found here. There are long, varied routes and short technical test-pieces; there are pure ice climbs as well as mixed routes to rival any in the country. Building on previous editions, this guide offers a selection of the best routes in each area – and, where possible, routes of all grades are given. Where there is a variety of routes, a number of climbs at a similar standard are detailed to allow for some choice should conditions or availability dictate a change in plan. Many of the routes follow fairly natural lines which, once embarked upon, should be relatively easy to follow, the exception being some of the more recent hard mixed routes which require a more detailed description.

Scottish winter climbing can be a hazardous pastime. The weather is often unfavourable and can change with startling suddenness, transforming a pleasant excursion into a battle for survival. Too many people have underestimated these mountains and paid the ultimate price. It is essential to be well equipped – both physically and mentally – before setting off on a winter route. Having the correct equipment must be accompanied by the ability to use it properly. When the weather, the conditions and the climb are right, then winter climbing in the Cairngorms can offer an unforgettable experience.

CONDITIONS

Good climbing conditions can occur in this area at any time between November and April, although February and March tend to be the most reliable months. In some years winter climbs can be in condition as early as October and as late as May. Winter ascents have even been made in June!

Part of the challenge of winter climbing is correctly predicting climbing conditions and choosing suitable objectives accordingly. Knowing when, for example, it is better to go for a buttress route rather than a gully, or whether to push your grade or try something well within your capabilities, can make the difference between a great day's climbing and an unpleasant and potentially dangerous expedition. However, predicting conditions can be tricky, especially for those based far from the mountains. Observing and learning how the weather affects the climbs is the first stage – how much

A pair of ptarmigan in winter plumage

thaw and refreeze is required to produce good ice, how long it takes for the turf to freeze and for the rocks to rime up, whether the ice will be hard and brittle or soft and plastic. In the past this knowledge was often hard-won, with many climbing trips ending in disappointment due to poor conditions in the chosen venue. These days, however, with a plethora of up-to-date conditions blogs, web cams and winter-climbing forums, it is easier to stay well informed on current conditions, especially for popular areas.

The Cairngorms are further from the sea than other Scottish winter-climbing areas, and many of the cliffs are very high. This has advantages and disadvantages. Early in the season the Northern Corries of Cairn Gorm, and the other higher crags, are among the first in the country to come into condition. Freezing temperatures and a northerly wind blowing cloud and snow showers onto the crags can rapidly build rime, bringing snowed-up rock climbs into condition very quickly. However, for mixed routes that rely on vegetation it is very important to wait for the turf to be properly frozen before they are climbed to minimise damage to the ground. Some routes in the Northern Corries, such as Invernookie, are getting progressively harder as the turf disappears because they are being climbed in unfrozen conditions. It can be a frustratingly long wait for the ground to freeze properly in the autumn, especially if snow falls and insulates unfrozen turf. Once frozen, however, the turf takes a long time to thaw out again.

Conditions generally do not fluctuate as rapidly in the Cairngorms as elsewhere, and this means that the build-up of good snow-ice can take longer than on other cliffs. It also means that deep soft snow can remain unconsolidated for long periods, making the approaches to the crags arduous, and then requiring a lot of clearing once on the route. In these conditions the buttresses often give better and safer climbing than the gullies. On the other hand the more consistent temperatures mean that climbing is often possible here after a large thaw has stripped the crags bare in other areas.

Routes which rely on seeps and springs for their ice tend to require a period of very cold weather to come into condition. These routes, along with the steepest of the buttress climbs which hold little snow at the best of times, may strip bare after only a short period of thaw or bright sunshine, especially those that are south facing and later in the season. Some routes require a number of melt–freeze cycles to bring them into good condition. These are often in their best condition in the middle to late in the season after a number of these cycles has built up the ice.

Winter climbing ethics are strongly held in Scotland, especially when it comes to mixed climbs on buttresses and ridges. To be in acceptable winter condition, buttresses should be generally white, there should be snow on the rocks, and turf should be well frozen. Snow on the ledges and dry rocks is generally not held to be sufficient, neither is a coating of hoar frost.

Early morning light on the approach to Creag Meagaidh (photo: Steve Fortune)

The size and scale of the crags and the approaches make the ability to navigate essential even for a visit to the closest of the cliffs. Bad weather can occur at any time, with winds of over 100mph being common, and gusts well in excess of that speed often being encountered. Gale-force winds may blow continually for days or even weeks at a time. Much of the high plateau is featureless, and in a white-out accurate navigation is sometimes needed to find the cliff – and more is often required to find the way back after the climb. To climb safely in this area requires sound winter-mountaineering skills.

Checking the weather forecast before setting off is an essential precaution. It can be obtained from most daily papers, the radio or television. However, the best source of mountain weather information is probably the internet. The Mountain Weather Information Service (www.mwis.org.uk) and the Met Office (www.metoffice.gov.uk) both provide free mountain weather forecasts, which can be accessed online and on some mobile phones.

Many climbers and instructors have a blog or conditions page. These tend to be regularly updated and can be a great source of information on climbing conditions. Less specific to climbing, but useful for an overall picture of weather and snow conditions, are the web pages of the ski areas. Cairn Gorm, The Lecht and Glen Shee ski areas all have webcam images and snow and weather reports on their pages. There is a weather station on the summit of Cairn Gorm, which can be a very useful source of real-time weather information. The SAIS avalanche reports and blogs (www.sais.gov.uk) are another useful source.

ROUTES AND GRADES

The usual winter-climbing two-tier grading system has been used in this guide. The first grade, a Roman numeral, indicates the overall difficulty of the route. This gives some indication of seriousness. The second, an Arabic number, indicates the technical difficulty of the climbing.

Grade I
Uncomplicated snow climbs that have no pitches under average conditions. However, cornice difficulties may be encountered, there can be dangerous run-outs, and the avalanche hazard is often high in the snowy confines of a Grade I gully.

Grade II
Gullies that have individual or minor pitches or high angled snow. Cornices can be difficult. Also the easiest buttresses under winter conditions.

Grade III
Gullies that contain ice in quantity. There is normally one big pitch and often several smaller ones. The buttresses are fairly sustained.

Grade IV
Routes of sustained technical difficulty. Short vertical steps or longer sections of 60–70° ice expected in gullies. Buttresses require a good range of climbing techniques or are long and sustained.

Grade V
Climbs that are difficult, sustained and generally serious. On ice climbs long, steep and sustained pitches are to be expected. Buttresses require winter techniques such as axe hooking and torquing, combined with competent rock-climbing ability.

Grade VI
Ice climbs have long vertical sections or are thin and tenuous. Buttress climbs include everything in Grade V, but there is more of it.

Grade VII
Usually buttress or face routes that are very sustained or technically extreme. If ice is involved, it is extremely steep and/or thin.

Grade VIII and above
Very hard and sustained mixed routes. By the time you are considering this sort of grade, you should have a fair idea what is involved.

The technical grades, which are given by the Arabic number, are based on the technical difficulty found on ice routes of Grades III, IV and V. The Roman number indicates the overall difficulty of leading the route, taking into account the seriousness, technical problems, protection, route finding, sustained nature, etc. The system is similar to the way adjectival and technical grades are used to grade rock climbs. In this way a V,4 would be a technically easy but serious Grade V route, probably on ice; V,5 would be a classic ice route with adequate protection; V,6 likely to be a classic buttress route – harder but better protected than a V ice route: V,7 would be a technically very difficult climb but with a short crux and good protection. It is unlikely that the technical grade will vary by more than two from the overall grade.

Grades are given for average conditions, which may or may not exist. A big build-up of snow may make gully climbs easier but buttresses harder, as more clearing is required to find holds and protection. The grades of some routes can vary dramatically, and on some of the harder climbs occasionally conditions are such that even classic routes may be one or even two grades easier than that given. The absence or presence of even one good placement can make a big difference to the difficulty of some climbs. Occasionally a split grade is used in the lower grades to indicate a climb whose difficulty varies according to the build-up – such

Brian Duthie pulling some steep moves on the first pitch of Fall-out Corner (Number 4 Buttress, Coire an Lochain) (photo: Henning Wackerage)

as when pitches disappear to give easier climbing, often later in the season.

A combination of short daylight hours and poor weather gives Scottish winter climbing an Alpine-like urgency. Because of the need for speed and the variability of conditions, the use of aid tends to be less rigid than in summer. However, these two requirements, speed and aid, are not always compatible. The more aid used, the longer it takes and the risk from approaching darkness increases.

Although pegs are still required in some situations, climbers should attempt to apply modern rock-climbing ethics as far as possible to winter climbs. Fortunately, it is often the gullies with their poorer rock that require pegs, while many of the more open buttress routes on better granite can be adequately protected with nuts and so on. Attempts should be made to limit the use of pegs on all climbs, especially those that are also popular summer climbs.

It is worth selecting a climb with conditions in mind for both safety and enjoyment. Climbing behind other parties on ice routes usually brings with it the danger of dislodged ice, and this is best avoided if at all possible. In thawing conditions there can be a very real danger from ice and rock fall, particularly in some of the easier gullies, where the rock may be of dubious quality and can be loosened by freeze–thaw action during the winter. Hooking and torquing of axes behind blocks can leaver them off, especially if the ground is not well frozen. There have been serious accidents resulting from both rock and ice fall.

ROUTE LENGTHS

Route lengths are the combination of pitch lengths. For some routes, especially easier gullies, this value is approximate, as there is often not a clearly defined boundary between the approach slopes and the start of the route. Ropes of 50m are sufficient for the majority of routes, although 60m ropes will sometimes be quite handy, especially when trying to run it out to the plateau. Pitch lengths are given on some routes to help with route finding. On many easier routes where it is possible to belay in numerous places, pitch lengths are often not given or required.

RECOMMENDED ROUTES

As this is a selective guide some routes have been excluded, and all the climbs that have been included are worthwhile and have some positive features. However, a star system has been used to indicate quality. This has been done by considering all the features which make up a climb – length, line, escapability, how sustained it is, and the quality of the climbing. Since winter is such a variable environment, climbing routes in poor conditions may not warrant their stars. The stars are pointers – something to argue about – and, above all, subjective!

Aladdin's Seat in Coire an t-Sneachda, with John Lyall standing on top (photo: John Lyall collection)

Diagrams and route numbers

In the guide all the main crags are illustrated by topo diagrams, although all routes may not be shown. For those crags without diagrams, the text should be sufficient to locate and follow the routes. Most crags have the routes described from left to right, but in a few cases, such as Hell's Lum, where the normal approach to the crag is from the right, the routes are described from right to left. In such cases this is clearly indicated. All directions refer to a climber facing the cliff unless otherwise stated, such as for descents. Not all routes are shown (numbered) on the diagrams in order to avoid overcrowding. A broken line on a diagram indicates that a section of the climb is hidden. The numbered routes offer good reference points for adjacent non-numbered climbs. Indexes of routes are given at the end of the guide.

MAPS

The climbing areas described in this guide are covered by a range of maps in the Ordnance Survey 1:50,000 Landranger series. The Lochnagar/Creag an Dubh Loch area is covered by Sheet 44, entitled Ballater & Glen Clova; the Cairn Gorm area is covered by Sheet 36, Grantown & Aviemore. Part of the area is also on Sheet 43, Braemar & Blair Atholl.

The OS Explorer maps at 1:25,000 scale also cover the area. Use Sheet 403, Cairn Gorm & Aviemore, for the Central and Northern Cairngorms; Sheet 404, Braemar, Tomintoul, Glen Avon, for Beinn a Bhuird; and Sheet 388, Lochnagar, Glen Muick & Glen Clova, for Lochnagar, Creag an Dubh Loch and Glen Clova.

Creag Meagaidh is covered by Landranger Sheet 34, Fort Augustus; Sheet 42, Glen Garry & Loch Rannoch; and Explorer Sheet 401, Loch Laggan & Creag Meagaidh. Harvey Maps produce the 1:25,000 Superwalker series maps. Three of these – The Cairngorms, Ben Avon and Lochnagar – cover most of the crags in this guidebook. Harvey also produce a series of 1:40,000 Mountain Maps, of which The Cairngorms and Lochnagar sheet covers most of the area.

The ability to use a map and compass correctly is essential for all winter mountaineers and climbers.

GPS systems can provide a useful back-up to more traditional map and compass skills, and it is recommended that they are used in this way, rather than as the sole navigational aid. Walking on the bearing obtained from a traditional compass will nearly always be steadier than following that from its satellite-driven GPS cousin. The location of the foot of some routes is given by a bearing from a prominent feature for some crags to aid their location in poor visibility.

Access rights

The Land Reform (Scotland) Act 2003 established statutory rights of responsible access to land and inland water

Loch Avon, Carn Etchachan and the Shelter Stone Crag

for outdoor recreation and crossing land. These are known as Scottish access rights. The Scottish Outdoor Access Code (available from www.snh.gov.uk) gives detailed guidance on the responsibilities of those exercising access rights and of those managing land and water. The Act sets out where and when access rights apply, and how land should be managed with regard to access. The Code defines how access rights should be exercised.

The three principles for responsible access apply to both the public and land managers.

- Respect the interests of other people – be considerate, respect privacy and livelihoods and the needs of those enjoying the outdoors.
- Care for the environment – look after the places you visit and enjoy, and care for wildlife and historic sites.
- Take responsibility for your own actions – the outdoors cannot be made risk-free for people exercising access rights; land managers should act with care for people's safety.

EQUIPMENT

Ice axe and crampons are essential for any winter outing, whether walking or climbing. For climbing it is assumed that two tools are used, with either curved or inclined picks. Climbing with leashless tools is becoming more popular at all grades – however, they lend themselves particularly to the higher grades. Unless you are very confident with these tools, lanyards connecting them to your harness are recommended.

Crampons should have front points and be adjusted accurately to fit the boots. They should be securely attached to the boots by either straps or a clip-on arrangement. The boots themselves should be rigid, with a good sole for step-kicking, and be able to take crampons. Ill-fitting crampons can be a positive danger in winter.

For any winter climbing a helmet should be considered mandatory. There is always the risk of being hit by falling ice, even from the most skilled and considerate leader. Besides, a helmet provides good insulation from the cold!

A normal rack of gear covering a reasonable range of crack sizes is usually sufficient. Camming devices can still work well on granite in winter if the interior of the cracks are ice-free, but should always be treated more carefully than in summer. A few pegs may be necessary on some routes, but the majority of climbs, especially on buttresses, can be done safely without them. Ice screws are obviously needed on ice routes. One or two drive-in/screw-out pegs such as warthogs, or bulldog-style ice hooks, are quite versatile and can be invaluable when hammered into frozen turf if nothing else is available. Try to match the gear to the climb and avoid being burdened by unnecessary weight.

A complete water- and windproof shell outer layer is necessary, as is spare clothing and food. A synthetic belay jacket that can be pulled on over a waterproof shell is also useful in a team. As the name suggests this can be worn by the belayer, who seconds the pitch wearing it and then passes it over to his/her partner before starting to lead the next pitch. Also essential is a head-torch and adequate battery power. A bivvy bag of some type is a worthwhile addition. Extra gloves are extremely useful, especially in damper conditions, when having dry and, hence, warm hands for at least part of the day is something to be savoured. Several extra pairs may be worthwhile in certain conditions. Even the best climbers will not be able to complete their route if they do not learn what to wear, and how to wear it, in order to keep warm and comfortable.

Mobile phones

Coverage is mostly good, but users should be aware of the limitations of mobile phones, especially if tucked away inside any of the corries or deeper glens. When using a mobile phone to raise the alarm, dial 999 or the local police station and ask for Mountain Rescue, give your number to the police and remain switched on until the rescue team arrives or you are given the all clear to switch off. Remember that your phone will make 999 calls on any available network, so it is worth trying even if your phone shows no coverage on your network, and whether or not there is credit on your account. Texting is often a useful of way of preserving battery life.

AVALANCHES

Avalanches occur in the Cairngorms and on Creag Meagaidh every year, often with tragic results. Anyone intending to climb or walk in the Scottish mountains in winter is strongly advised to acquaint themselves with a basic understanding of avalanches. As well as various courses and lectures which are available during the winter months, there exist some excellent books on the subject, with *A Chance in a Million* by Barton and Wright being the classic text on avalanches in Scotland. The ability to judge the likelihood and consequences of an avalanche, and to know what to do in the event of an avalanche incident, could save lives.

Snow and avalanche

A basic knowledge of how and why avalanches occur is a prerequisite for learning how to avoid them. Storm cycles and changing weather conditions tend to build up a highly layered mountain snowpack. Avalanches usually occur when the bonds between adjacent layers, or that between the snowpack and the ground, fails. Changes that occur over time both within and between these layers can increase or decrease snow stability, depending on the circumstances.

Different types of avalanches exist and are generally classified according to their physical characteristics. An avalanche can release from a single point or a whole area (loose or slab); it may be the whole snow cover or only part of it that slides (full or partial depth); and it can be channelled or not (confined or unconfined). It may also be airborne or flow along the ground.

Avalanches are initiated because of either changing internal factors, such as bonds between layers being

A full-depth avalanche on The Great Slab, Coire an Lochain

weakened by rising temperatures, or external factors, such as snowfall or a person walking or skiing on the slope. The details of the release process are complex and poorly understood. However, some basic principles are well known. Avalanches can release on slopes between about 20° and 60°, although slopes between 30° and 45° are the most likely to release, with about 38° being the optimum angle for slab avalanches. Above about 60° snow tends to slide off in small sluffs rather than building up to reach dangerous quantities. The greatest danger usually exists during and for approximately 24 hours after a period of heavy snowfall. This danger period is longer in cold temperatures, when the snow consolidates more slowly. Thaws, especially if accompanied by rain, produce a wet-snow hazard, as well as the danger of collapsing cornices. Even in the absence of snowfall or thaw, a significant avalanche hazard may be created by the wind redepositing the snowpack.

Avalanche types

There are various types of avalanche, and these tend to occur under different conditions and present different degrees of hazard.

Powder or loose snow avalanches typically occur during, or right after, a snowfall. Usually the failure begins at a point and spreads out down the slope in an inverted V shape. They are generally small in size, but in the confines of a gully they can be unpleasant and are sometimes large enough to knock a climber off.

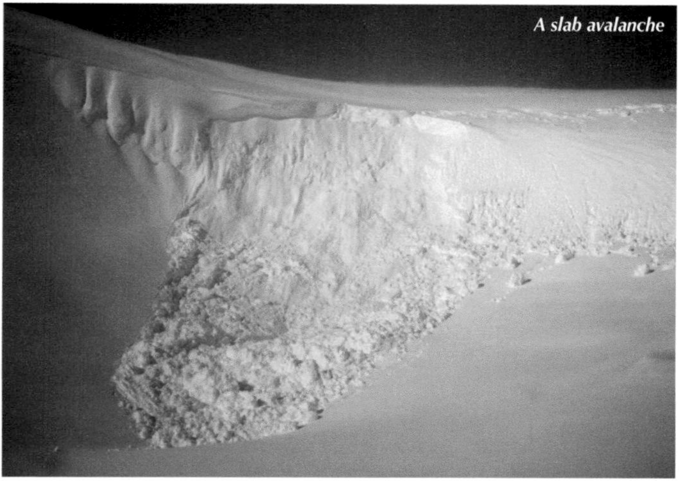
A slab avalanche

Sgor an Lochain Uiane and An Garbh Choire from Ben Macdui (Cairntoul/Braeriach Amphitheatre)

A **slab avalanche**, on the other hand, occurs when a cohesive slab of snow slides on a weak layer. They are the most common, least predictable and, therefore, the most dangerous type of avalanche. This type of snow, called windslab, is formed when wind-transported, and therefore damaged, snow crystals accumulate in sheltered areas such as lee slopes. Windslab consistency can vary from soft to hard, depending mainly on the speed of the wind that transported the snow. Hard slab, in particular, is very deceptive, as it can be firm enough to walk on without sinking in and so feel safe to the unwary. However, it does tend to have a dull, chalky appearance and may squeak or creak when walked on or probed with an axe. Although most common on lee slopes, particularly below cornices, it can build up in unexpected places, even on windward slopes.

Wet-snow avalanches usually occur during a thaw, when the snow or its top layers become saturated. The extra weight and lubrication of this water can weaken the bonds between different snow layers, or between snow and the ground, and may cause a large area to slide. Although easier to predict, this type of avalanche can be particularly descructive due to the high density of wet snow. Wet-snow avalanches can harden rapidly on settling, and so it can be extremely difficult to escape from them unless this is done immediately.

Avalanche avoidance

Before starting out

Avalanche awareness should start long before the mountains are reached. Monitoring the weather in the days prior to a climbing trip is a basic precaution, with heavy snowfall accompanied by wind being the main danger sign. Long periods of cold temperatures tend to make any danger last longer, while a freezing level that rises and falls rapidly usually quickly consolidates the snow pack. Be aware of the recent and forecast wind direction, as the greatest danger is likely to be on lee slopes, the place where windslab accumulates. Consult the snow and avalanche forecast, and consider possible alternatives should conditions turn out to be worse than expected. Seek expert local advice – avalanches tend to have local characteristics. Have the appropriate equipment and know how to use it.

In the mountains

Ongoing observations on the hill should be used to confirm, and refine or adjust, your initial hazard evaluation. Avalanches occurring or signs of recent activity are the most significant indicators of an avalanche danger and should not be ignored. On the approach observe the nature of the snow on the ground and in the air. The behaviour of snow underfoot can be very informative. Cracking and breaking away of snow blocks from beneath your feet is an indication of slab and instability. Look for signs of recent windslab deposition. Spindrift is usually a danger sign, as even fairly light winds can redistribute huge amounts of snow, packing it in as windslab on lee slopes and in other sheltered locations. Even a light surface drift can produce localised danger, especially in the tops of gullies.

Signs of a rise in temperature – such as rain, wet snow, sun balls rolling down the slope, strong sunlight, and melting snow and ice – can all be danger signs, especially if large cornices exist. If the thaw is due to strong sunshine, then different slope aspects may make a large difference, with perhaps danger on south faces but safer northerly aspects. In these circumstances, slopes of a similar aspect and altitude should be considered extremely suspect.

Although general observation is important, a simple **snow pit** can give further information about the snowpack and its stability. A snow pit dug in a safe but relevant position for the suspect slope is useful. It is dug down to ground level or, more usually, to the level of a stable consolidated layer. The back or sidewall of the pit is inspected for snow layers of differing hardness. Significant differences in hardness between adjacent snow layers can be a warning sign. A pit can be dug quickly with an axe and need not be elaborate to give relevant information. Even the resistance felt when pushing the axe into the snow may reveal much about the layers. However, due to local variations in the properties of snow, any snow pit or test will only give information about one point, and must be considered as part of the overall picture.

Route choice and safety precautions

A number of factors influence route choice in avalanche terrain (here route

In very snowy conditions, ridges and buttresses usually provide the safest and best climbing conditions – here teams enjoy the Fiacaill Ridge

choice is not limited to a climb, but includes all movement in the mountains). Ridges, buttresses and flat ground are safer than open slopes. Windward slopes are generally safer than lee slopes, but even here local variations in topography can create a localised avalanche hazard. Convex slopes are more likely to slide than concave ones, and gullies or depressions tend to concentrate avalanche depth and power. Even a very small area of windslab can represent a hazard if the run-out is into rocks, over a drop, or into a terrain trap such as a stream-bed or similar hollow where the debris can be funnelled and build up to considerable depths. Some very serious accidents have occurred where the slab that released was only about the size of a mattress.

The need to travel on a suspect slope varies according to the circumstances. For example, it is seldom if ever necessary on the way up the hill in the morning, when you can vary the route or even retreat. However, it may be forced on you on the way down, in bad weather or in the dark. Travel one at a time between islands of safety and watch the person moving. Never assume that if one person crosses safely then there is no danger – this is not the case – but all use the same track. Tighten clothing, remove wrist loops and loosen rucksack straps so that it can be abandoned if necessary. If a slope has to be crossed, then traverse it high up rather than low down to reduce the amount of snow above, and thus reduce possible burial depth should it slide. It is better to be carried further but buried less deeply.

Ross Hewitt on Tough Guy, in the Eagle Ridge and Parallel Buttress Group (The Norhern Sector, Lochnagar) (photo: Sandy Simpson)

If you are caught in an avalanche

If you feel the snow slope around you move, then shout to alert others and try to delay your departure by using your axe. Attempt to roll out to the side. If you are carrying a heavy sack, get rid of it. A light sack, however, can provide some protection and will not drag you down too much – and if you are lucky enough not to be buried, you will still have your gear with you. During the avalanche, if possible get onto your back with your head uphill and try to swim or roll in order to stay on the surface. As the avalanche slows make a desperate effort to get to the surface, or thrust a limb out of the snow. Make every effort to create a breathing space in front of your face. As the snow comes to a halt it often hardens up very rapidly, so making escape even more difficult as time passes. If buried, try to remain calm so as to conserve oxygen and energy, and do not shout as the sound will not be heard on the surface.

If you see someone caught in an avalanche

Keep them in sight and note their starting position and where they were last seen. Check for further danger, and attract the attention of other people in the area. Mark the position where the victim was last seen, so as to indicate the most likely burial area. Make a thorough search of the debris for surface clues. Probe the most likely burial spots then conduct a systematic search, probing with ice axes or walking poles with the baskets removed. If there are a lot of people in the vicinity then send someone for help, but remember the **initial search is vital**. If a buried victim is not suffering any serious trauma injuries then he/she has about a 90 per cent chance of survival if dug out in the first 15 minutes. However, after 35 minutes this drops to only about 30 per cent. Therefore the importance of the first search cannot be stressed too strongly.

Avalanche information

There is much good written material on avalanches, and some reading on the subject should be considered as part of overall mountain safety. Avalanche reports are produced by the sportscotland Avalanche Information Service (SAIS) for much of the area covered by this guide. Much useful information and daily forecasts can be found on their website at www.sais.gov.uk. This website can also be a useful source of information for assessing climbing conditions. In addition the daily forecasts are often displayed in police stations, sports shops and hotels throughout the area. They are also posted at many popular mountain access points, such as the Cairn Gorm ski area car park and Aberarder farm.

When using the avalanche report it is worth noting the date and time of issue, as the hazard is quoted for the day of issue and reflects the existing conditions. The avalanche outlook for the following day is also given, but this is **dependent on the weather forecast**.

If this forecast is not accurate, then the avalanche forecast itself may be inaccurate. Having an avalanche information service forecast does not absolve climbers of responsibility for making their own decisions and assessment of the avalanche hazard.

MOUNTAIN RESCUE

Mountain rescue teams are made up of experienced and skilful local mountaineers who undergo regular training in mountaineering and remote-care first aid skills. Rescues are co-ordinated by the police, who should be contacted by telephone on 999 in case of an accident or possible problem.

A direct line to the Aviemore or Braemar police stations may be quicker, and the numbers are as follows.

Aviemore police 01479 810 222
Deeside police 08456 005 700

The rescue organisations will require concise information about the incident, such as the name of the climb, the location, a map reference if possible, the number injured, the nature of the injuries, how they are equipped and if anyone is with the casualty. If there are only two in the party and it is not possible to contact the mountain rescue teams or attract anyone else either by shouting, whistle or torch-light, it is a difficult decision whether to go for help or stay. This will depend on the nature of injuries, the location, weather, equipment and perhaps other considerations. If the casualty is unconscious, then this decision is even more difficult. If you do go for help, make sure that the casualty is as well equipped and as comfortable as possible, and in the most sheltered and well-marked location that you can find or create.

There is a first aid box in the corrie of Lochnagar on a small flattening midway between the loch and Central Buttress. Likewise there is one in Coire an t-Sneachda near the triangular boulder by the lochans, but the contents of these boxes are likely to vary. Both these locations are favourite gearing-up spots.

CAIRNGORMS NORTH

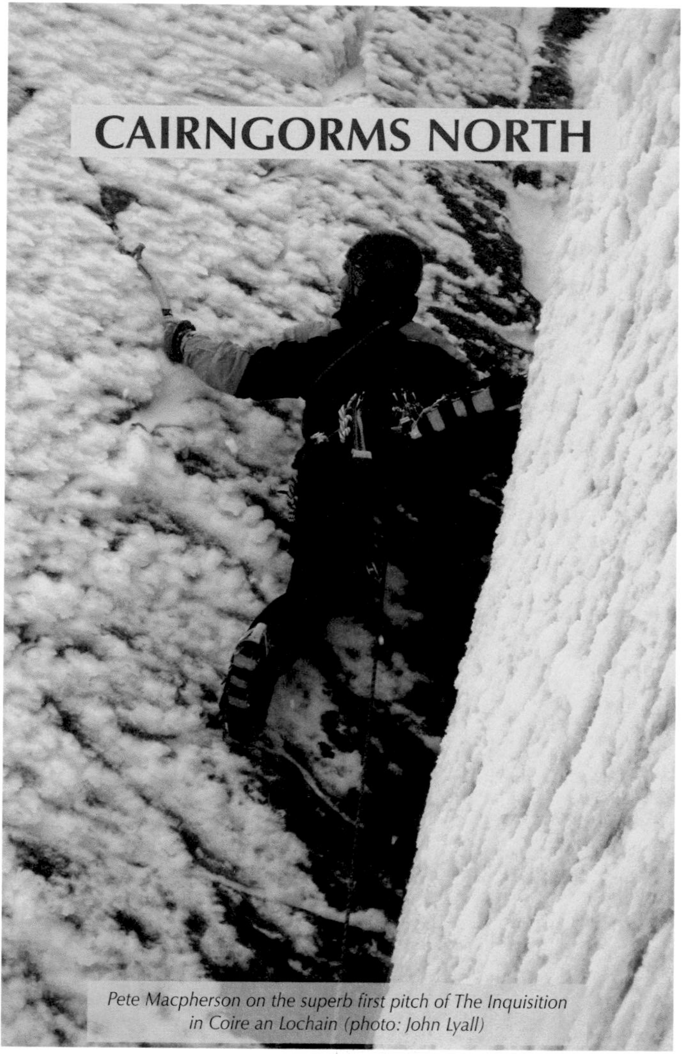

Pete Macpherson on the superb first pitch of The Inquisition in Coire an Lochain (photo: John Lyall)

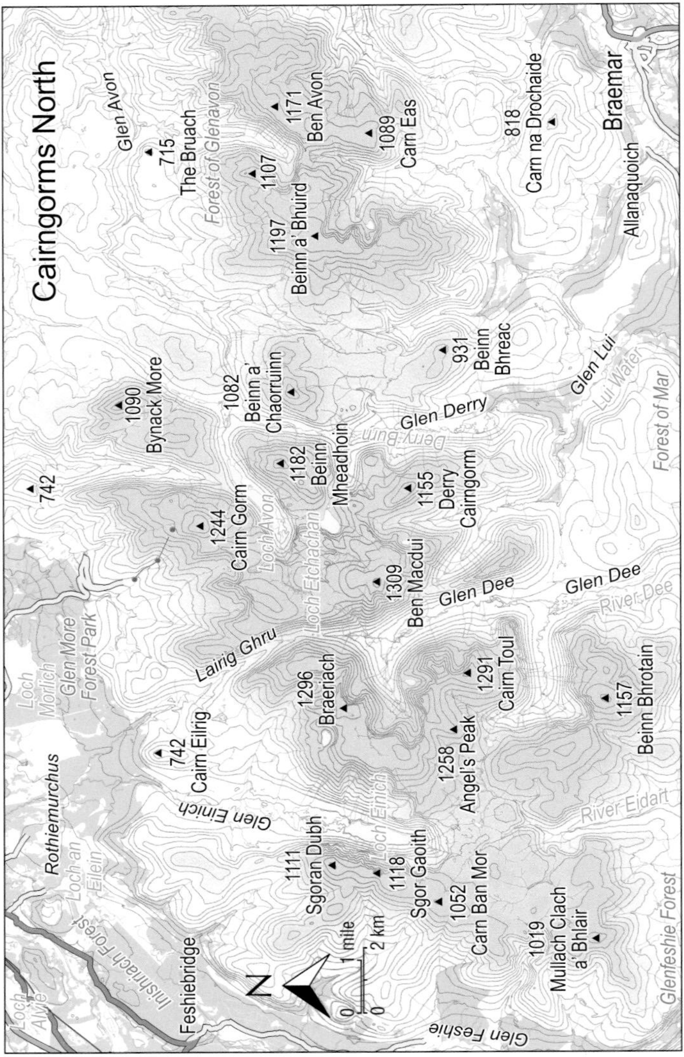
Cairngorms North
Glen Avon
715
The Bruach
Forest of Glenavon
1107
1171
Ben Avon
1089
Carn Eas
1197
Beinn a' Bhuird
818
Carn na Drochaide
Braemar
Allanaquoich
742
1090
Bynack More
1082
Beinn a' Chaorruinn
931
Beinn Bhreac
Glen Derry
Derry Burn
Glen Lui
Lui Water
Forest of Mar
1244
Cairn Gorm
Loch Avon
1182
Beinn Mheadhoin
1155
Derry Cairngorm
Loch Etchachan
1309
Ben Macdui
Glen Dee
Glen Dee
River Dee
Lairig Ghru
Loch Morlich
Glen More Forest Park
1296
Braeriach
1291
Cairn Toul
1157
Beinn Bhrotain
Rothiemurchus
742
Cairn Eilrig
1258
Angel's Peak
Glen Einich
Loch Einich
River Eidart
1111
Sgoran Dubh
1118
Sgor Gaoith
Loch an Eilein
1052
Carn Ban Mor
1019
Mullach Clach a' Bhlair
Glenfeshie Forest
Inshriach Forest
Feshiebridge
Loch Alvie
N
0
1 mile
0
2 km
Glen Feshie

Coire an t-Sneachda

NH 994 033

This is the most accessible of the climbing corries in this area. A somewhat broken and sprawling set of buttresses ringed round the corrie edge. Of the Northern Corries of Cairn Gorm this contains the widest selection of good low-grade winter routes, and as such is the most popular of all the cliffs, especially at peak holiday times, when it can be worth avoiding. However, there is a good selection of routes of all grades and of most styles of climbing. There should be something climbable most of the winter season, and some of the rockier routes come into condition very quickly.

On the far left of the corrie is **The Mess of Pottage**, with the straight gash of Jacob's Ladder on its right flank. Next is an area of broken ground, and in the centre of the corrie is **Aladdin's Buttress**, which is defined on its left by the big dog-leg gully of Aladdin's Couloir. This buttress actually consists of a lower dome-shaped mass of rock with more broken ground above. Here are a number of ridges, the right-most one, Pygmy Ridge, being the most obvious. Next is **Fluted Buttress**, which gives the longest routes in the corrie and merges into Aladdin's Buttress, and it is cut by a number of gullies and faults. On its right side it runs into the snow slopes of the Goat Track, the wide slope leading to the col at the head of Coire Domhain. Last is the **Fiacaill Buttress**, which lies in a subsidiary part of the corrie high on the right and forms the side of the Fiacaill a'Choire an t-Sneachda, usually just referred to as the Fiacaill Ridge, which separates this corrie from the Coire an Lochain.

Approaches

From the car park in Coire Cas follow the good path heading first west then south round the Fiacaill a'Choire Chais for several hundred metres to a junction, then take the left fork into the corrie. This path is not marked on some older maps. The right fork continues to Coire an Lochain. Follow the path south into the corrie, where it peters out at the start of the boulder field, and go on to the small lochans below the centre of the cliff. It is unusual if there is not a track in the snow, even when the path is buried. A less obvious alternative is to go from the car park to the White Lady Shieling, then follow the track which zig-zags up Coire Cas until the Fiacaill a'Choire Chais can be crossed and a slightly diagonal line taken down into the corrie.

Descents

From the top of the climbs the usual descent is to follow the plateau rim round to descend the Fiacaill a'Choire Chais into Coire Cas and so to the car park. The Goat Track, the slope west of Fluted Buttress, gives a steep but convenient return to the corrie floor, but can be an avalanche risk. For climbs on the left of the corrie it is possible to descend from the col east of The Mess of Pottage and go down diagonally below that buttress. For climbs on the Fiacaill Buttress, the Fiacaill Ridge or the Goat Track give convenient descents.

No Blue Skies living up to its name (photo: Henning Wackerage)

In thick and misty conditions it may be difficult to identify some of the climbs, but from the first aid box just south of the lochans, the magnetic bearings to some of the main gullies are as follows.

- Aladdin's Couloir 110°
- Aladdin's Mirror 145°
- Trident Gullies 184°
- Goat Track Gully 222°
- Fiacaill Couloir 242°

Conditions

This is a high, accessible, north-facing corrie whose buttress routes come into condition very quickly; the easier gullies do not take much longer to form either. However, the ice development mostly depends on freeze–thaw and snow-melt, so takes longer to come into condition. Because of the popularity of this corrie many routes are becoming harder as vegetation is destroyed, especially by ascents in lean or thawing conditions. However, this can mean that the route is well marked with crampon and tool placements. There can be some serious rock-fall danger in thaw conditions, particularly in the area of Fingers Ridge and Red Gully.

In windy conditions, especially with westerlies, the top of the cliffs, especially The Mess of Pottage, can be very exposed. The Fiacaill Buttress is much more sheltered then, but the approach slopes can have dangerous slab build-up in these conditions. With a northerly airstream these cliffs are often shrouded in cloud.

The Mess of Pottage

NH 998 032 *Altitude 1060m* *North-west facing*

The left-most buttress; the main section is seamed with cracks and corners, while the right side is slabby low down and easy angled above. In the centre of the main section a big stepped fault slants up slightly left and is used by several routes.

The Opening Break **100m IV,5**

A Cunningham and A Fyffe, November 1990

The obvious left-facing corner on the left of the buttress – low in the grade. Start below the corner and climb cracks up the initial slabby steps, with a detour right then back left at the first bulge. Climb the corner, which can be icy. Above, go right to easy ground and follow a fault up left below a steeper wall until twin cracks lead to more easy ground and the top. It is possible to avoid the first pitch and the crux by slanting in rightwards to the corner from higher up, making it a Grade III.

Honeypot **90m IV,6****

J Lyall and M Sclater, 25 March 1989

Lies near the left edge of the buttress and takes the obvious square-cut chimney near the left side of the top wall. Start in a recess, where awkward moves give access to a right-slanting line. This leads to easier climbing up a gully, which is followed to the upper wall. Climb the square-cut chimney, passing the roof steeply on the right wall. The left side of the wide chimney fault can also be climbed.

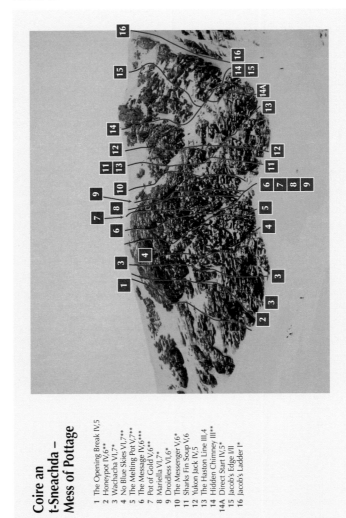

Coire an t-Sneachda – Mess of Pottage

1 The Opening Break IV,5
2 Honeypot IV,6**
3 Wachacha VI,7*
4 No Blue Skies VI,7**
5 The Melting Pot V,7**
6 The Message IV,6***
7 Pot of Gold V,6**
8 Mariella VI,7*
9 Droidless VI,6*
10 The Messenger V,6*
11 Sharks Fin Soup V,6
12 Yukon Jack IV,5
13 The Haston Line III,4
14 Hidden Chimney III**
14A Direct Start IV,5*
15 Jacob's Edge I/II
16 Jacob's Ladder I*

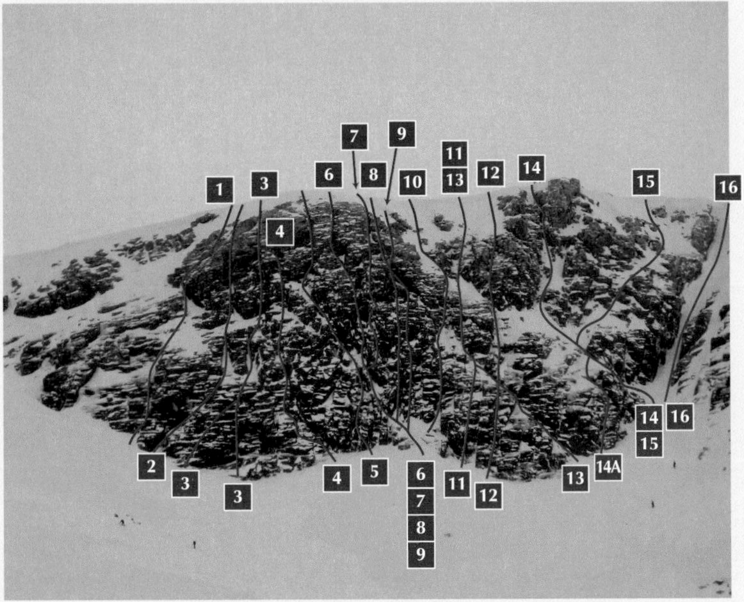

Honeypot

Wachacha **90m VI,7***

J Lyall and A Nisbet, 6 January 1990

Takes a line to the right of Honeypot and has two possible starts. Either begin about 6m right of Honeypot and climb a right-slanting crack to gain easy ground that leads to the steep top wall, or climb an obvious right-facing corner further right again. Where it steepens, swing onto the left rib then continue up the crack line to the top wall (this is the summer line). Follow a crack and left-facing corner system, then trend left to below the upper roof and come back right to the crack going through the roof and follow this to the top.

No Blue Skies (photo: Henning Wackerage)

No Blue Skies 110m VI,7**

A Fyffe and L Healey, 20 December 1990

A good but somewhat devious climb. Start left of the lowest point of the buttress, where an obvious diagonal line slants left. Climb the diagonal corner until a traverse left to gain a right-facing corner can be made. Climb this, then exit left onto a ledge by a horizontal slot. Continue up the crack line above to easier ground below the upper walls. Climb up to a fine right-facing flake crack, which is climbed to a ledge. Go to its left end (at this point it joins Wachacaha), then through the walls above by the crack, which is followed to the plateau.

The Melting Pot 90m V,7**

A Cunningham and A Nisbet, February 1987

The main feature of this route is the steep groove in the middle of the upper wall, which is gained by a fairly direct line. Start midway between No Blue Skies and the main diagonal fault taken by The Hybrid. Climb leftwards into a short, obvious groove with a tall, steep left wall. Leave the groove over a bulge and go left round an arete to more broken ground leading to the diagonal fault, which is followed to a large bay. Climb the overhanging groove then continue up the crack line to finish.

The Hybrid 100m IV,5*

Makes use of the diagonal fault. Start as for The Message and climb the obvious diagonal stepped fault for a pitch. Continue up and left as for The Melting Pot to the ledge system below the top wall. Move awkwardly up right to a higher ledge or traverse out right at a lower level to gain the front face and go left and up to the big ledge. This is the crux. Finish up the top pitch of The Message.

The Message 90m IV,6***

A Cunningham and W Todd, 23 January 1986

A good, popular and well-scarred route which takes the deepest groove in the centre of the face right of diagonal fault. Start at the top of a large bay right of the lowest rocks and climb the stepped diagonal fault until the deep corner can be gained. Climb a short wall into the corner (this can be difficult) and follow the corner to the top, then go left then up to the upper ledge. Climb the right-facing corner to a bulge, then swing left onto the edge to climb cracked slabs to the top. Alternatively, climb the crack in the slab to its right.

George McEwan on The Hybrid

Sharks Fin Soup

Pot of Gold — 90m V,6**

J Lyall and S Spalding, 26 November 1988

An interesting if escapable route up the edge of the buttress right of The Message. Climb the first pitch of The Message until a traverse right gains cracks and a narrow chimney on the buttress edge. Climb up until near The Message then climb up right to a large ledge. Climb the wall above by shallow corners and flakes to finish up a shallow chimney.

Mariella — 80m VI,7*

C Forrest, G Ettle and A Nisbet, 6 January 1991

Takes the deep red groove capped by an overhang and is high in the grade. Start as for The Message and climb into the groove. Follow this to a swing left below the roof and continue up a crack line to a ledge shared with Droidless (30m). Continue up the crack line (15m). Move left and climb walls and slabs to the plateau.

Droidless — 85m VI,6*

C Forrest and G Ettle, 21 December 1990

The parallel crack line 3m right of the deep red groove of Mariella. It has a sustained first pitch. Start just on the right of Mariella and gain the main fault by a slanting corner just on its left, then follow the fault over the bulge to a ledge below parallel cracks (30m). Continue up the cracks, a difficult start, to an easing in angle in a bay below an obvious right-facing corner (20m). Climb the corner then easier ground (35m).

The Messenger — 80m V,6*

G Ettle and C Campell, 15 November 1991

Takes the obvious left-facing corner some 10m right of the previous routes. Climb the corner, pulling left past the obvious roof with difficulty (30m). Trend right into an open fault and climb this and then a steep right-facing corner (30m). Easier climbing leads to the top (20m).

Sharks Fin Soup — 90m V,6

J Preston, G Ettle and I Taylor, 10 December 1999

Between the lines of The Message and Yukon Jack are two crack lines. The left one has an obvious huge flake at its foot (the right crack in Despot, V,7). Climb up onto this huge fin and up the crack line above. Continue in the same line to join The Haston Line and finish up that.

Yukon Jack — 90m IV,5

M Sinclair and C Schiller, 30 December 1993

Takes the main right-facing corner in the lower slabs leading to the end of the diagonal fault of The Haston Line. It can ice up to give an amenable Grade III, but is usually a harder mixed pitch. Gain the obvious right-facing corner via a crack. Climb the corner and cross The Haston Line to the steep upper rocks and finish up a wide chimney in the same line.

The Haston Line — 100m III,4

D Haston and party, 1965

The obvious lower left-slanting fault starting from the right corner of the buttress. There is an awkward corner moving up to easier ground and a choice of finishes on the upper snow slopes.

The Slant — 150m I/II

A diagonal snow line running left across the buttress. Start a pitch up Jacob's Ladder at a big recess. Climb up and left by the obvious line to open slopes on the front face and continue going left to finish up the big upper snow field.

Hidden Chimney — 110m III**

Climb The Slant for about two pitches to gain the right side of the most continuous upper buttress. Climb the chimney on its right side to the top, passing over a prominent chokestone.

Direct Start — 40m IV,5*

A good pitch that can be climbed for its own sake. Climb the prominent right-facing corner starting from the toe of the buttress. Ice makes a difference to the grade, and it is getting harder as vegetation goes.

Jacob's Edge — 90m I/II

Start up The Slant for about a pitch and a half then slant back rightwards to finish up snow slopes overlooking Jacob's Ladder. Alternatively, go almost to the foot of Hidden Chimney and slant back right towards the edge.

Jacob's Ladder — 100m I*

A Henderson and F Mitchell, Easter 1939

The straight gully defining the right edge of The Mess of Pottage is steepest at the top and the cornice can be large. In lean conditions there may be a short chokestone pitch.

Neil Johnson on The Lamp

Coire an t-Sneachda – Aladdin's Buttress

1 Aladdin's Couloir I
2 Original Route IV,5**
3 The Lamp V,6*
4 The Prodigal Principal V,5
5 Doctor's Choice IV,5**
6 Doctor Janis V,7*
7 The Genie V,7***
8 Salvation VI,7*
9 Patey's Route IV,5**
10 Terms of Endearment III
11 Honour Among Thieves IV,4
12 Aladdin's Mirror Direct IV,4**
13 Aladdin's Mirror I
14 Pygmy Ridge IV,5**

AS Aladdin's Seat

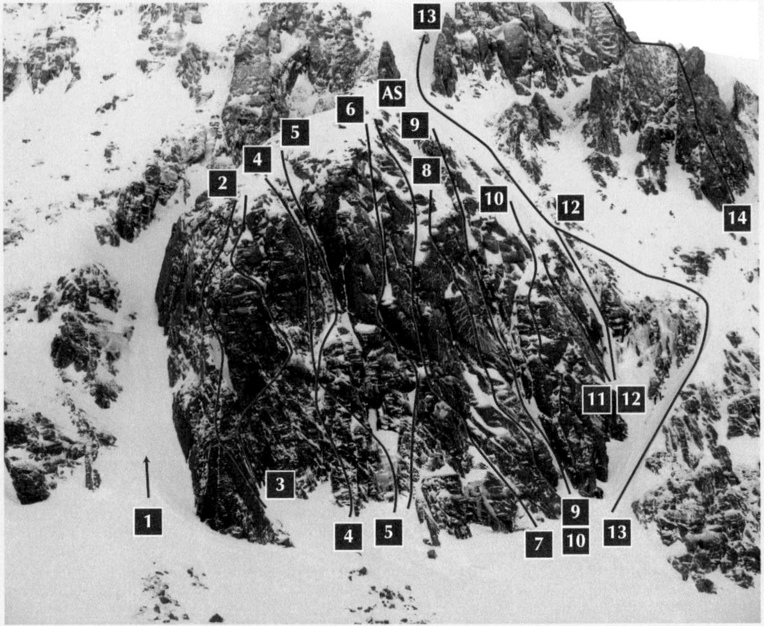

Aladdin's Buttress

NH 995 031 *Altitude 1000m* *North facing*

This is the obvious buttress in the centre of the corrie and consists of a lower dome-shaped mass of rock, which is cut by a series of left-facing corner lines. Above and to the right is an easier section of ground topped by a several roughly triangular ribs, Pygmy Ridge being the rightmost rib. The chimney fault of Patey's Route on the right side of the buttress is very obvious. Aladdin's Seat is the 10m pinnacle above the lower buttress. For routes on the lower buttress either continue up, or descend, Aladdin's Mirror or Aladdin's Couloir. Alternatively, independent finishes can be found through the upper rocks at a choice of grades. There may be an equipped abseil point in some huge boulders at the top of Original Route; a single abseil runs down into Aladdin's Couloir below the smooth wall by the bend.

Aladdin's Couloir — 180m I

A Henderson and EM Davidson, 24 March 1935

The large dog-leg gully which flanks the left side of Aladdin's Buttress. There may be a small ice pitch at the bend. Sometimes a good ice pitch develops on the left wall just by the bend. Above this the gully widens, and at a col above Aladdin's Seat is joined by Aladdin's Mirror.

Original Route — 100m IV,5**

W March and B Manson, 13 February 1972

Lies on the left side of the buttress and overlooks Aladdin's Couloir. Start 5m above and right of the toe of the long narrow rib that forms the lowest rocks on the left of the buttress. Climb a shallow corner with a couple of moves on its right to a prominent flake, well seen in profile from the right, and continue to a large snow ramp running up the flank of the buttress. From the top of the ramp climb up to some big blocks, then take the obvious line going up and left in a series of steps on the wall overlooking Aladdin's Couloir. An alternative start begins at the foot of the lowest rock and climbs a groove onto the crest V,6.

The Lamp — 100m V,6*

A Liddell and party, January 1988

A zig-zag line up the left side of Aladdin's Buttress. Start at an open corner just right of the long rib of rock. Climb the open corner, some time moving onto the right wall, to its top. Go diagonally right on the obvious ramp to gain the large central bay. Take the diagonal fault leading left to easier ground and the top of the buttress and a choice of finishes.

George McEwan on The Prodigal Principal, Right-Hand Start

The Prodigal Principal 100m V,5

G Reid and J Lyall, 19 November 1985

An ice route dependent on freeze–thaw for its formation. Start left of Doctor's Choice at ice runnels going up slabs and ramps before moving leftwards to a snow bay where Doctor's Choice is joined. Ice lines can also develop at either side of the usual first pitch, which give alternative starts. From the main bay climb the narrow chimney left of the big corner of Doctor's Choice, a good pitch.

Doctor's Choice 105m IV,5**

W March and N Dilley, 12 February 1972

A good climb which takes a huge detour to reach the largest left-facing corner in the upper part of the buttress. Start below this upper corner and climb the fault up to just below the big cave, sometimes on ice, and belay in top-left corner of the cave. Move down and go left onto the rib and follow the diagonal break left for a pitch into a snow bay. Leave this first bay on the right and gain easy ground. Go right and finish up the big corner, which is better with ice. If there is little ice, the narrow chimney of The Prodigal Principal provides a fine alternative finish.

Doctor Janis 130m V,7*

J Grosset, J Lyall and A Nolan, 4 April 1987

Takes a series of corners on the right of the big fault of Doctor's Choice. Start on the right side of the bay below Doctor's Choice. Climb the main groove slanting right, cross an overlap and continue up to the steep wall at about mid-height. Take a slanting groove/ramp cutting back left to a ledge. Return right and gain the upper groove, which slants back rightwards.

In icy conditions a combination of the lower groove of Doctor Janis and the upper groove of The Genie gives a very fine icy climb at about V,6.

The Genie — 110m V,7***

G Smith and G Ball, 1979

The central of the three main corners right of Doctor's Choice gives a good climb. Start at the foot of Patey's Route and follow the lower of the slabby ramps going left and then open corners to where the cliff steepens up. A short crack running up to below a roof leads into a left-facing corner. This is climbed to a stance below the main corner, which is followed to the top of the buttress.

The Magic Crack — 90m VII,7**

A Huber and A Mullin, 10 March 1999; A Cunningham and A Nisbet, 7 December 1985 (White Magic)

Takes the eye-catching thin crack right of The Genie. Climb The Genie for two pitches to the belay below its main corner (50m). Traverse right to gain the finger crack and follow it to the overlap and a belay on the left (20m). Strenuous but well

The finger crack of The Magic Crack

protected. Gain a right-slanting crack over the overlap, then another crack leading back left to thin moves onto the final slab (20m). Finish easily or descend in two abseils from *in situ* gear. The original winter line (**White Magic,** VI,7) climbs the first three pitches as described. The fourth pitch traverses right under an overlap to a ledge, and then finishes up a narrow chimney.

Salvation — 100m VI,7*

S Aisthorpe and J Lyall, 27 December 1987

This route is on the cracked slabs right of The Magic Crack and main corner of Damnation, VI,6, the rightmost left-facing corner. Start at the foot of Patey's Route and climb about 10m up the higher slabby ramp going left. Leave the ramp via a short chimney/groove then pass left of a short wall to a broad ramp. Break through the overlap above at some flakes and climb thin cracks up the slab. The overlap can also be climbed about 3m right of the flakes. Move up right to a block, then follow the continuation crack to the top.

Patey's Route — 120m IV,5**

TW Patey, February 1959

The wide chimney on the right side of the buttress is very popular and a fairly reliable route. Generally, the more ice, the easier it is. There is bulge at about mid-height which is difficult, and a top chokestone is usually turned by going out left then returning right by a long move back right into the chimney line.

Terms of Endearment — 100m III

A Liddell and party, 1981

The buttress edge overlooking Patey's Route. Climb the start of Patey's Route a short way to just above the initial narrows, then traverse the ledge right to its end, then make a slabby move onto the front of the buttress, usually the crux (there has been a recent substantial rock fall just to the right). Once on the crest follow the easiest line to join Aladdin's Mirror, which can be followed up or down.

Honour Among Thieves — 35m IV,4

A Fyffe, H Redfern and A Johnson

The clean-cut left-facing corner right of Aladdin's Mirror Direct can give a good ice pitch, but it is generally thin and poorly protected.

Aladdin's Mirror Direct — 25m IV,4**

A direct start which climbs the ice pitch on the right of the buttress. An easy chimney then leads to the parent route. The difficulty and length varies with build-up, and it is extremely popular. There may be other short ice pitches to its right.

Aladdin's Mirror 180m I

EUMC party, Easter 1946

An exposed snow route which skirts the right edge of the steeper rocks. Climb the open gully slanting right to turn the steep rocks, then trend back left above them to join Aladdin's Couloir above Aladdin's Seat. Finish up the couloir.

Pygmy Ridge 90m IV,5**

Above the easy snow of Aladdin's Mirror are several roughly triangular buttresses. This is the most defined right-hand buttress gained from Aladdin's Mirror or Central Left Hand. Start at a wide crack at the toe of the buttress and follow the crest of clean rock. Go across a horizontal section and finish up the final tower, although it is easy to escape right.

Central Left Hand 135m I*

This ascends the broad open rib on the left of Central Gully to finish up the defined gully right of Pygmy Ridge. A choice of lines is available, and the left side of the upper gully may contain a steep, but avoidable ice pitch.

Fluted Buttress

NH 994 030 Altitude 1020m North facing

This buttress is separated from Aladdin's Buttress by Central Gully, the left-hand of the three Trident Gullies which spring from a large snow bay extending high into the cliff. Right of this the cliff is steeper and slabbier, and the pinnacles of Fingers Ridge are very distinctive. Right of Fingers Ridge are more gullies before the buttress diminishes in height and ends by the Goat Track. Because of the slabby nature of the foot of this buttress, much can be buried in some conditions and the length of the routes varies.

Central Gully 135m I

TE Goodeve and AW Russell, 1 April 1904

The leftmost of the Trident Gullies starting from the snow bay. It slants left and the cornice is easily avoided. Can be interesting in lean conditions when short pitches may be encountered.

The Runnel 135m II**

EUMC party, Easter 1946

The central straight, well-defined gully. High up there is a steeper narrow chimney which constitutes the crux. The grooves on either side are climbable at about the same grade.

Coire an t-Sneachda – Aladdin's and Fluted Buttresses

1 Aladdin's Couloir I
2 Doctor's Choice IV,5**
3 Patey's Route IV,5**
4 Aladdin's Mirror I
5 Pygmy Ridge IV,5**
6 Central Left Hand I*
7 Central Gully I
8 The Runnel II**
9 The Grooved Rib III,4*
10 Crotched Gully II
11 Spiral Gully II**
11A Direct Finish III
12 Fluted Buttress Direct IV,5***
13 Broken Gully III
14 Red Gully II/III**
15 Western Rib II/III
16 Goat Track Gully II*

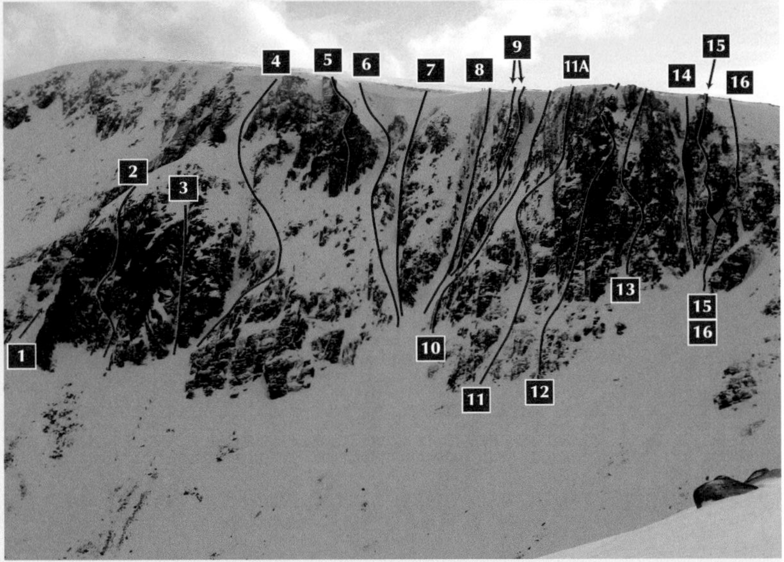

The Grooved Rib **135m III,4***

This is the buttress between The Runnel and Crotched Gully. Start at the base of the rib and climb the prominent groove to easier snow fields. There is an easy finish parallel to The Runnel from here. The route takes either of the two steep grooves in the crest of the buttress. The left groove has a smooth start and is entered from the left and followed past a small chokestone. The right-hand groove is climbed direct and steepens to an awkward bulge which leads to a platform overlooking Crotched Gully. Step left into a narrow chimney leading to an easy finish.

Crotched Gully **135m II**

EUMC party, Easter 1946

From the snow bay go up the right branch, which has a steep section near its top. This leads into a broad but well-defined upper gully, which can have a large unavoidable cornice.

Vortex **60m IV,5***

G Ettle and J Lyall, 10 January 1992

The rib between the top part of Crotched Gully and the Direct Finish to Spiral Gully, reached by climbing Spiral Gully to the slanting gully and the foot of the rib. Climb the shallow groove up the rib and turn the roof on the right or left. Finish up a well-defined arete.

Spiral Gully **150m II****

TW Patey, February 1959

The main feature of this route is the right-slanting narrow gully cutting the upper rocks. Start up broken ground on the left of the buttress, heading for twin deep grooves which lead to easier ground and the foot of the slanting gully. Climb this to a small col, then a short pitch to the top.

Direct Finish **III**

The wide groove above the start of the right-slanting upper gully gives a good mixed pitch, although sometimes it can be very icy. Other harder finishes are possible up other grooves further right.

Wavelength **130m III,4****

A Fyffe and D Bowen, 13 February 1985

Takes the left branch of the Y-shaped fault taken by Fluted Buttress Direct on the left side of the steepest slabby rocks, and becomes more defined with height. Climb up to the foot of the twin grooves of Spiral Gully and climb diagonally up and right, taking in a short steep corner to gain a diagonal fault, which goes right into the main fault, where it splits. Climb this left fault to an open corner at the top, which can be climbed or turned on the left (easier). Continue up the ridge to finish or cross Spiral Gully and climb the groove opposite.

Fluted Buttress Direct 135m IV,5***

A Fyffe and S Crymble, 18 March 1978

A good route up the narrow but prominent Y-shaped chimney system on the left of the steeper slabby rock. Climb a pitch of easy broken ground to the chimney and follow this to the fork, where the fault gets bigger – can be harder under powder conditions. Take the right fork, which leads on to the crest, and follow this to the plateau.

Broken Gully 130m III

TW Patey, J McArtney and J Cleare, February 1967

The gully between the main part of the buttress and Fingers Ridge is good to start, then the upper section is wide and straightforward. Start from the top of the first bay right of the lowest rock. Climb steeply up and right until it is possible to go left by a short wide crack onto the top of a slabby pillar near the top of the pitch. Move left into the main funnel-shaped upper gully, which is easy and offers a choice of lines. The Left-Hand Start climbs directly into the upper gully by a narrower fault and is generally harder, but needs ice.

Fingers Ridge 140m IV,4**

JR Dempster and J Wallace, 19 January 1969

The slabby ridge between Broken and Red Gullies has two prominent pinnacles high up where the buttress narrows. It is a popular route, although the upper part of the ridge has some loose blocks and is best avoided in thaw conditions. Start just at the foot of Red Gully and go diagonally left for a pitch to a good ledge by a short deep corner on the left side of the buttress. From the left side of the ledge climb the blunt rib very close to Broken Gully, trend right and climb a flake to gain the obvious open groove. Climb the right-facing groove (escape in to Broken Gully is possible here), then the pinnacled ridge to a narrow col, then to the top. The short wall at the end of the col may be the crux if climbed direct, but can be avoided on either side.

Broken Fingers, 135m, III,4, starts up Broken Gully but follows the fault all the way to finish up Fingers Ridge and is a worthwhile variation.

Red Gully 120m II/III**

The gully on the right of Fingers Ridge is narrow, well defined at the bottom and often very busy. Climb the initial chimney, usually on ice, then follow the

Topping out on Fingers Ridge (photo: Rik Higham)

funnel-shaped upper gully to finish. Again, in thaw conditions the blocky nature of the upper gully can provide a serious rock-fall danger.

Western Rib — 120m II/III

The rib on the right of Red Gully is usually gained from above the mushroom-shaped pinnacles a pitch up Goat Track Gully. Climb the blocky and escapable broad rib to the top. It is sometimes possible to climb the rib all the way from the bottom if icy.

Goat Track Gully — 120m II*

Starts close to Red Gully and slants right below a big vertical left wall. At the steep section climb the right corner, which can be awkward but well protected if bare of ice. Above the gully is less defined and open to variation.

Coire an t-Sneachda – Fiacaill Buttress

1 Escapologist IV,6
2 Men in Black VI,8
3 Houdini VI,7**
4 Stirling Bomber V,7**
5 Smokestack Lightnin' VI,7*
6 Fiacaill Couloir II/III**
7 Rampant IV,5*
8 Burning and Looting V,6*
9 Belhaven V,6**
10 Invernookie III,4**
11 Short Circuit III,5*
12 The Seam IV,5***
13 The Hurting XI,11

M Midway Ledge

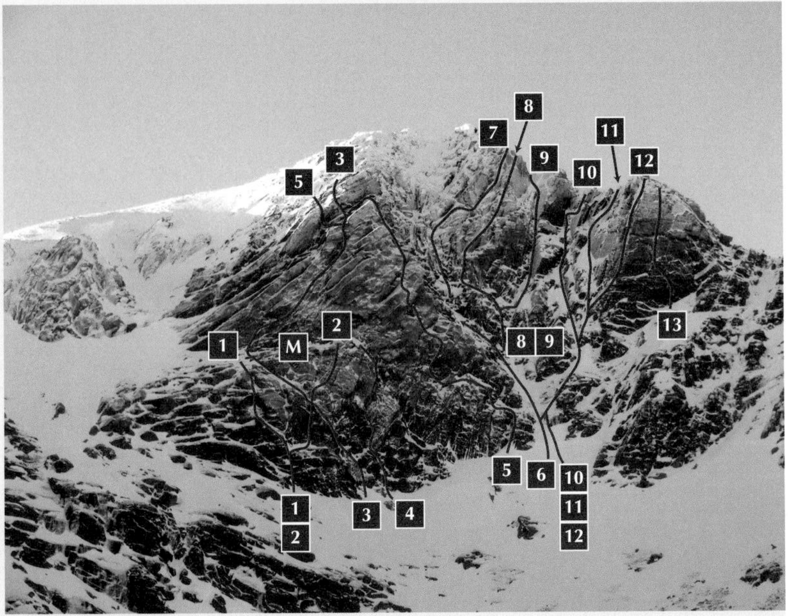

Fiacaill Buttress

NH 989 029 *Altitude 1060m* *North-east facing*

This lies high on the right of the corrie flanking the Fiacaill Ridge, which itself gives a pleasant route of Grade I–II, depending on the line taken. The Fiacaill Couloir, which is hidden from many angles, slants up leftwards, dividing the buttress into two contrasting parts. The left section is split by the midway ledge, above which are some prominent, slabby ramps. The right section is more blocky, with several large vertical features and obvious snow ramps. As the highest cliff in the corrie it may be in condition when other buttresses are not, and can also be sheltered from westerlies. However, the open lower approach slopes can be avalanche prone.

The following three routes finish on the midway ledge. Therefore they can be a good choice for a short day or in windy conditions.

Escapologist 55m IV,6

G Ettle and J Lyall, 10 March 1992

Start 8m left of the main left-slanting groove of Houdini. Slant up left before moving right over a slab to an obvious ledge. Climb up left to a large block (30m). Stretch (or jump) from the top of the block to reach turf and continue up a corner and easier continuation to the terrace (25m).

Fiacaill Couloir from above

A busy day in the Northern Corries

Straight to Jail 50m V,5*

D Jarvis and B Ottewell, April 1996

The steep groove above the start of Escapologist. Follow Escapologist to above the obvious ledge. Move right to gain a steep groove and climb this to the midway ledge. Needs good ice to be at this grade.

Men in Black 50m VI,8

G Ettle and M Garthwaite, 31 January 1998

This climb takes the wide corner crack left of Houdini to finish on the midway ledge. Start up Escapologist for 10m, then move right to a left-facing corner crack (15m). Climb the wide crack past two essential chokestones to easier climbing and a good ledge (15m). Move right into Houdini – there is a wide crack splitting the wall on the right, and the route climbs the thinner crack on its left to the ledge (20m).

Houdini 160m VI,7**

A Cunningham and A Fyffe, February 1990

An intricate but excellent line up the left face. Start in the middle of the lower tier and climb the main left-slanting groove, then trend left to the midway ledge. Climb a short wide corner to a big ledge with flakes and traverse delicately right to gain ramps, which are followed a short way to reach the left side of a big block. Go right and climb the groove/ramp going right, and above the chokestone head up by thin climbing to below the final wall. Climb this wall by going left into a niche then up to gain the step.

Stirling Bomber 55m V,7**

A Cunningham and A Fyffe, 4 January 1990

The obvious right-facing crack and chimney line on the lower buttress give a good but unusual climb finishing on the midway ledge. Start right of the chimney and climb up and left to gain and follow the flake crack into the chimney. Climb the chimney, which gradually widens (difficulty can be height dependent) and curves over to form a roof, above which a ramp is gained and followed to the midway ledge.

Jailbreak 110m VII,7*

A Fyffe and A Liddell, 31 January 1986

Takes the obvious ramp leading to the midway ledge, and then has a serious and intricate pitch leading to the more featured upper part of the buttress. Start about 15m left of Fiacaill Couloir and climb the stepped ramp to the ledge. Go left about 10m and climb up and right until moves left lead to short groove-cum-ramps running right (this is fairly direct and shares some of the upper part with Houdini). At

Fiacaill Couloir

their top, move left to the right side of a large block (Houdini also belays here then goes rightwards.) Climb the obvious ramps and corners above to below the vertical top wall. Move right of the obvious chimney (this is the final pitch of Fiacaill Buttress, which can be used to give an easier finish). Climb this diagonally left via a niche to finish by the step in the top wall (as for Houdini).

Smokestack Lightnin' 100m VI,7*

A Cunningham and A Fyffe, 16 February 1990

A fine but escapable route which zig-zags up the buttress to the left of Fiacaill Couloir. Start in a bay just left of the base of Fiacaill Couloir and climb this to a ledge. Traverse left to some large blocks. Climb a corner on the left, and then trend back rightwards to another ledge. Traverse left to below a deep overhung corner. Either climb this corner (strenuous but well protected) or gain a hanging flake on the left and use it to pull left round onto the front face. Either way, a slanting corner above gives access to the crest of the ridge. Climb this to a barrier wall and make a descending leftward traverse for about 10m (crossing Houdini) to a chimney, which is climbed to easier ground.

Fiacaill Couloir 150m II/III**

TW Patey, 17 January 1958

The big diagonal gully offers a choice of lines to the top, where the final chokestone can be hard if the build-up is poor. It can be interesting and icy or steep snow. Above the col go diagonally left to gain the plateau.

The next routes all climb the wall above Fiacaill Couloir and are accessed by climbing this, almost to the top in some cases.

Trampled Underfoot 60m IV,4

G Ettle and J Lyall, 13 January 1992

Starts about 8m up Fiacaill Couloir from the big ledge at the foot of Rampant. Climb steeply up on vegetated ledges, then move left to a short corner. Follow a ledge right and climb a large right-slanting ramp to the ridge (or, more easily, up a gully).

Rampant 75m IV,5*

A Fyffe and T Walker, 1 March 1979

Takes the narrow left-leaning ramps, then a big right-facing corner. It starts about two pitches up Fiacaill Couloir, where the left end of a large ledge system is gained by a short wall (as for the previous route). Climb the ramps, initially going up left, then up a corner to gain a ledge below a steep wall. Go right round the edge and follow the main corner, passing under a huge chokestone at the top.

Physical Graffiti — 70m IV,6*

A Fyffe and J Lyall, 7 February 2007

A fairly direct line up the vague buttress below the big top corner of Rampant. Start as for Rampant on the big ledge and go straight up to a V-shaped niche. From the top right-hand corner make awkward moves to exit left, then follow the fault passing the left side of a block roof to a ledge (35m). Climb up to the foot of the main groove of Rampant and take a short chimney on the left to gain a pinnacle. From its top, move up to a niche below an overhang and climb the slanting groove on the right leading to blocky ground and the top (35m).

Swan Song — 70m V,6*

G Ettle and J Lyall, 17 February 2007

Takes a line parallel to Physical Graffiti to finish up cracks in the side of the pillar between Rampant and Burning and Looting. Start on the big ledge and climb the fault left of the big block and continue up into a curving corner. Go up a thin crack in a slab to gain an awkward short slot leading to a ledge (35m). Climb the ramp on the right (below Rampant) and pull out right and climb the crack left of the sharp rib (35m).

Burning and Looting — 75m V,6*

Pitch 1, G Reid and J Hepburn, January 1988; as described, A Cunningham and A Fyffe, 13 February 1991

The rib between the corners of Rampant and Belhaven. Start at the big ledge as for the previous routes, and from near a big block on the ledge go up to a ledge leading right, then go into a hanging groove capped by a block. Enter the slot, strenuous but interesting, or turn it on the right. Climb the rib above by cracks and blocks, mostly on the right.

Belhaven — 75m V,6**

A Fyffe and K Geddes, 19 February 1979

The main corner system in the wall directly above the bend in the Fiacaill Couloir gives interesting climbing. Climb the couloir until big ledges lead right into the corner, which is then followed throughout. If there is a good build-up the corner can be gained direct.

Invernookie — 120m III,4**

K Spence and J Porteous, 4 January 1969

A good, popular and well-marked route that takes the main left-slanting ramp line on the wall overlooking Fiacaill Couloir. Start just right of the couloir and go up and right to gain the ramps. Climb these with some short, steep steps to where they end

The Seam from high on Fiacaill Buttress

below an impending wall. Go up the corner into the chimney-cave, and near its top traverse the ledge right and finish up the short groove.

Short Circuit **110m III,5***

S Monks, G Reid and A Fyffe, 9 February 1987

This route takes the snow ramp above and parallel to Invernookie. Start up Invernookie, but go further right to gain the higher ramp. Climb this to its top, then climb thin ice in the corner or go left and climb the cracked edge to a snow patch. Climb a short wide crack into the right of two grooves. Climb the crack in the slab to its right to finish.

The Seam **100m IV,5*****

J Grosset and J Lyall, 2 January 1986

An excellent route up the obvious chimney fault immediately left of the steep triangular wall on the right of the buttress and right of a long white streak. Climb Invernookie for a pitch, then trend up right into the chimney, which is followed to the top.

The Hurting **35m XI,11**

D McLeod, 19 February 2005

One of the hardest routes of its type anywhere, it takes a line up the centre of the triangular wall left of The Seam. It is exceptionally hard, strenuous and serious, with ground-fall potential and tenuous and blind climbing. Not one for the faint-hearted. Start at the obvious detached flake and climb the faint groove line for 10m to a ledge and runners. Continue straight up some hollow flakes, then go right to the roof. Climb the left-hand side of the roof and traverse right to a hidden flake crack. Go to the top of this, then move left, then diagonally right into a niche and the finish.

COIRE AN LOCHAIN

NH 985 025 *Altitude 1100m* *North facing*

This is the most westerly of the Northern Corries of Cairn Gorm and consists of a compact headwall of cliffs lying below the summit of Cairn Lochain and overlooking a huge pink slab – The Great Slab. This is a slope prone to avalanches and should be treated with caution.

The buttresses themselves are numbered 1 to 4, from left to right, and are separated by obvious gullies. On the left is The Vent, initially narrow but opening out into a wide funnel above; in the centre of the cliff is the wide diagonal of The Couloir; and tucked into the right-hand corner of the corrie are the two branches of Y Gully, separated by a narrow rock pillar. The rock in this corrie is very blocky and split by a succession of prominent crack and corner lines, which give some very fine mixed buttress routes.

Approaches

From the ski area car park in Coire Cas contour the Fiacaill a'Choire Chais, initially as for Coire an t-Sneachda, but take the lower track at the fork after a few hundred metres. Cross the stream and continue on one of several paths (not all shown on the map) which lead roughly south into the corrie. It is surprisingly easy to miss the corrie in bad visibility, and careful navigation is recommended in bad conditions.

Coire an Lochain (overview)

1 Iron Butterfly III
2 Ventriloquist VII,7*
3 The Vent II/III*
4 The Milky Way II/III**
5 Andromeda IV,4**
6 Central Crack Route IV,5*
7 Snow Bunting IV,5
8 Ewen Buttress III**
9 The Vicar VIII,8**
10 Grumbling Groove VI,6*
11 Oesophagus III,4**
12 Sidewinder III,4**
13 Western Route IV,6**
14 Torquing Heads VII,7*
15 Western Slant IV,4

C The Couloir
GS The Great Slab

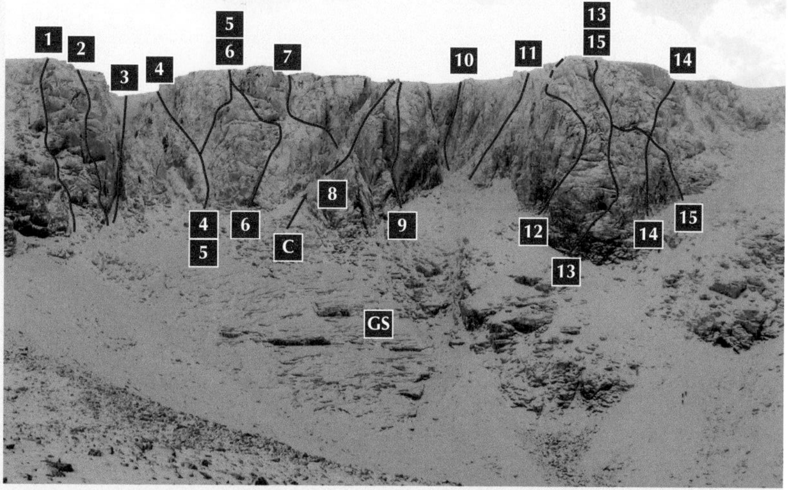

Coire an Lochain on a busy day

To gain the foot of the routes it is best to ascend the slope to one side or other of The Great Slab, depending on where your chosen route lies.

Descent

Follow the corrie edge, going roughly south-west, and descend back into the corrie to the north of the lochans or continue northwards down the ridge. The latter is safer when there is any avalanche risk. Alternatively, the Fiacaill Ridge can be descended or the plateau rim followed to eventually descend into Coire an t-Sneachda by the Goat Track or continue round and down the Fiacaill a'Choire Chais.

Conditions

This is a high cliff with its base at around 1100m. It comes into condition very quickly with snow and cold weather. However, good conditions can also extend well into the spring. Mixed routes are the first to be climbable, with the snow and ice routes taking a little longer to form. With a huge area of snow-collecting plateau above the cliff, there can be a substantial build-up of snow. This, combined with its northerly aspect and height, may mean that occasional routes, such as the branches of Y Gully, are climbable into June some years, while some of the buttresses may be good in October. Avalanches can be real hazard both below the cliff and from cornices and build-up at the top. The Great Slab is a notorious avalanche slope, and a huge full-depth avalanche occurs here each spring. At other times it becomes sheathed in ice, and it is worth avoiding this slope most of the time.

Coire an Lochain – Number 1 Buttress

1 Coronary By-pass V,7*
2 Auricle VI,7*
3 Ventriloquist VII,7*
4 Ventricle VII,8**
5 Daddy Longlegs VIII, 9**
6 Inventive IV,5
7 Adventure V,5
V The Vent II/III*

Number 1 Buttress

This buttress, the left-hand one, is cut by some deep and prominent corners; the right side is a steep wall overlooking The Vent. The front face is also steep, but merges into broken ground on the left.

Iron Butterfly — 150m III

S Docherty and B Gorman, 31 December 1969

Climbs the more broken ground bounding the left side of the more continuous rock. Start in a huge open corner about 40m below and left of The Vent. Climb a groove in the corner to a ledge below an obvious crack in a steep wall. Go right and up snow to below another steep wall, then turn this on the left to reach more snow, which is climbed to the next steep wall. Go diagonally right to gain a wide gully, which is followed to the top.

Coronary By-pass — 110m V,7*

A Fyffe and J Hepburn, 20 April 1994

Takes a line right of the upper gully of Iron Butterfly and left of Auricle. Start on the right, about 5m above the lower corner of the buttress. Climb the chimney line and slant diagonally left to below the big corner of Auricle (35m, as for Auricle). Go left below a steep wall into an open corner (10m). Climb this, crux (10m). Ascend a narrow flake chimney, move right, then go up a deep corner crack. Continue up the same line, passing a rock crevasse (30m). Climb the crack in the corner and continue up the slot and corner, or slant right in the rock crevasse to easy ground (25m).

Auricle — 90m VI,7*

C MacLean and A Nisbet, 29 November 1984

Lies on the front face of the buttress and takes the big right-facing corner. Start about 5m up from the corner of the buttress and climb a corner/chimney to reach easier ground slanting up left to below the main corner (35m, as for the previous route). Climb this strenuous groove passing several chokestones (15m). Continue up the corner above to a large flake. From the top of the flake climb an overhanging recess to the top of the buttress and cross the rock crevasse to finish (40m).

Ventriloquist — 80m VII,7*

J Lyall and A Nisbet, 21 December 1990

A fine sustained route climbing cracks in the wall just right of Auricle. It is strenuous and well protected with big cams if not verglassed. Start as for Auricle and climb the chimney crack, then move right to climb a bulging crack into a recess.

Hannah Burrows-Smith on Coronary By-pass (photo: John Lyall)

Pull steeply out of this up to the wide crack (30m). Climb the crack line (crux) into a recess and pull out right to below a wide crack 3m right of Auricle's groove (10m). Climb the crack, then move up right by two short corners to a ledge (10m). Climb the thin crack on the right, making a short detour on the right at the steepest section, cross the crevasse and finish up the deep crack (30m).

Ventricle **95m VII,8****

C MacLean and A Nisbet, 27 December 1984

Very hard but well-protected pitches separated by big ledges taking prominent grooves and cracks on the left wall of The Vent. Start about 5m right of the corner/chimney of Auricle and climb a short overhanging crack. Move right along a ledge and go up a wall near the right edge to a small mossy recess (15m). Climb a thin crack on the right and swing left into the top of an overhanging groove. Go up to a larger overhanging groove and climb this to the big corner (20m). Climb this to a big ledge (15m). In the corner is a wide crack – climb just to the right of this and step left into it and climb it (15m). Go left to finish up The Ventriloquist (30m).

Daddy Longlegs **70m VIII, 9****

B Davison, A Nisbet, 25 February 1991; (as Big Daddy) P Benson and G Robertson, 7 December 2002

Hard and strenuous climbing starting up the obvious steep groove just inside The Vent. Climb the groove, step right into a second groove and climb it to ledges (35m). Scramble up left (10m) to the base of a big corner containing a wide crack. Climb two consecutive vertical cracks in the wall right of the corner (crux) to easier ground (25m). A fine variation (**Big Daddy**, 80m, VII,8) avoids the top pitch by finishing up the wide corner crack as for Ventricle).

Inventive **70m IV,5**

A Fyffe and J Hepburn, 20 April 1994

The deepest corner in the left wall above the chokestone in The Vent. From below the chokestones climb a groove into the corner. Climb the corner to easier ground and so to the plateau. With less of a build-up, climb The Vent to above the chokestone and traverse left into the corner.

Adventure **50m V,5**

G Ettle and R Mansfield, 19 November 1996

Takes cracks and grooves in the rib right of Inventive, starting above the chokestone in The Vent. Climb a short chimney and step left to good cracks. Follow this to steep corners with precarious blocks and go up to ledges (35m). Climb the steep continuation groove to finish (15m).

The Vent — 100m II/III*

EM Davidson, RF Stobbart, M McBain, J Geddes and H Harrison, 13 April 1935

A popular route with short, although very variable difficulties, and can be even harder if very lean. The lower narrow gully has a chokestone pitch near its top; this varies with build-up and ice. Above, the gully opens out into an easy funnel.

Number 2 Buttress

This wide buttress stretches between The Vent and The Couloir. The left side has more features, while the central portion is composed of steep walls separated by ledges. The wide diagonal fault of The Milky Way is conspicuous on the left. To the right of the upper section of The Milky Way is a prominent steep tower, which is a useful landmark. There is a steep wall split by The Crack just below the plateau, which also a useful marker.

Ventilator — 100m III*

DSB Wright and party, 1969

The right side of The Vent is a defined rib. This route takes the corner on the right of the rib. Start in a snow bay about 30m right of the rib, and from its top traverse into the corner and climb it to the top of the rib. Finish up The Vent. It can be easier if there is consolidated snow on the slabbier sections.

Chute Route — 90m V,5*

M Harris, D Scott and R Shaw, 24 December 1968

The corner at the head of the snow bay can give a fine ice pitch. The left wall of the corner is distinctively smooth. Above the corner join The Milky Way to finish.

The Milky Way — 100m II/III**

TW Patey, VN Stevenson, IW Armitage, February 1959

The obvious left-slanting line on the left of the buttress. Climb this wide shallow fault over several steps. Continue up and left to finish near the top of The Vent. An alternative start is to climb the wide snow bay on the left of the fault and gain the ramp higher up by a short deep groove.

Appetite for Destruction — 100m V,6*

A Fyffe and J Hepburn, 14 February 1995

Takes the corner on the right side of the upper tower. Climb The Milky Way to below the tower, then slant back left to gain and climb the corner to belay below a roof. Continue up the corner and move right at the top. Finish direct.

Coire an Lochain – Number 2 and Number 3 Buttresses

1 Ventilator III*
2 Chute Route V,5*
3 The Milky Way II/III**
4 Appetite for Destruction V,6*
5 Demolition Man IV,5
6 Andromeda IV,4**
7 Astroturfer III*
8 Central Crack Route IV,5*
9 The Crack VI,7**
10 Snow Bunting IV,5
11 Crow's Nest Crack III
12 The Couloir I*
13 Ewen Buttress III**
13A Ewen Buttress Direct Start IV,6*
14 The Migrant VI,7**
14A Migrant Direct VII,8
15 The Vicar VIII,8**
16 Happy Tyroleans IX,10**
17 Grumbling Groove VI,6*
18 The Head-hunter VI,6*

GS The Great Slab

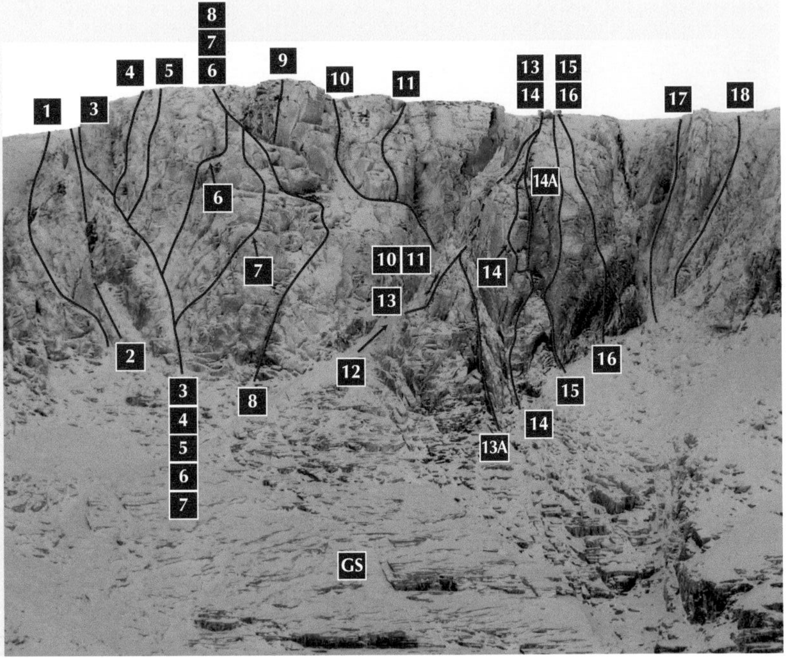

Demolition Man **110m IV,5**

I Rae and J Kerr, 3 February 1986

Right of The Milky Way in the upper section of the cliff is a prominent tower. Climb Milky Way to below the tower and trend right below it. Continue rightwards up ledges and short walls to finish with only one short awkward step.

The Andromeda Strain **110m IV,4**

J McKeever and I Dawson, 31 December 1985

Takes the fault defining the right side of the upper tower. Climb The Milky Way for about 40m to below the line of the fault. Ascend the wall above to move left into the upper fault, which is followed to the top.

Andromeda **120m IV,4****

RD Barton and JC Higham, 30 December 1970

The main corner line on the left of the more massive part of the buttress. Start up The Milky Way and climb it to the main corner. Climb either the left or the central groove, which slants up right to easier ground on the crest, and finish on the left of the conspicuous wall as for Central Crack Route.

Astroturfer **120m III***

J McKeever and I Dawson, 7 December 1985

Goes diagonally right across the buttress to finish as for Central Crack Route. Start as for Andromeda but take the lowest chimney, which leads right onto the front of the buttress. Climb the wall above on the right and continue to finish on the left of the conspicuous wall.

Central Crack Route **120m IV,5***

TW Patey, 2 February 1958

A fine route with the first pitch being the crux. It takes the obvious right slanting corner crack. Start by the lowest rocks and climb this corner crack, the start is hard and the short chimney awkward, both harder in lean or powder conditions. From its top go up mixed ground bearing slightly right to below a great square wall. Go diagonally left below it until a way through the cornice can be found, usually just on the left of the wall. Sometimes a much longer traverse is needed.

The Crack **20m VI,7****

R Anderson and R Milne, 12 January 1992

The obvious wide crack in the headwall can be reached from a number of routes.

The Inquisition 80m VI,8**

Starts up the obvious right-facing corner on the wall some way up The Couloir. Climb the superb corner then ledges to below a steep prow just left of the cul-de-sac (50m). Follow cracks on the left to the higher of two platforms (20m). Climb the overhanging crack and flake to the top (10m).

Snow Bunting 90m IV,5

R Anderson and G Ettle, 26 January 1992

This lies on the right side of the buttress starting well up The Couloir, just below the dead end of its left branch. Go up this branch, left to a ledge and along it to its end. Step left and ascend a snow bay to reach a stepped crack on the left. Climb this, then go right below a roof (with ice here the climb is much easier), then up broken ground to the top.

Crow's Nest Crack 60m III

S Kennedy and C McLeod, 18 December 1983

Takes a prominent chokestone chimney left of dead-end left branch of The Couloir. Climb this branch and move left, as for Snow Bunting, then climb the chimney to a ledge. Work up and right by easier ground to finish.

The Couloir 150m I*

The wide slanting gully is normally straightforward, with no pitches. The cornice can be large, but there is usually a way through above the col.

Number 3 Buttress

This is also known as Ewen Buttress. It consists of a slanting rib on the left, then a huge steep recess bounding a more massive section of cliff. The right side, where the cliff swings round to overlook the Left Branch of Y Gully, is seamed with corner and crack lines.

Ewen Buttress 90m III**

TW Patey and VN Stevenson, February 1959

Follows the edge overlooking The Couloir. Go up The Couloir for about a pitch until the buttress can be gained and followed to a saddle. A short, steep step (crux) leads to a gully, which is followed to the top of the buttress and The Couloir.

Coire an Lochain – Number 3 Buttress

1 The Migrant VI,7**
1A Migrant Direct VII,8
2 Happy Tyroleans IX,10**
3 The Overseer Direct V,6*
4 The Hoarmaster VI,6***
5 Hooker's Corner VI,6**
6 Left Branch of Y Gully III
7 The Head-hunter VI,6*

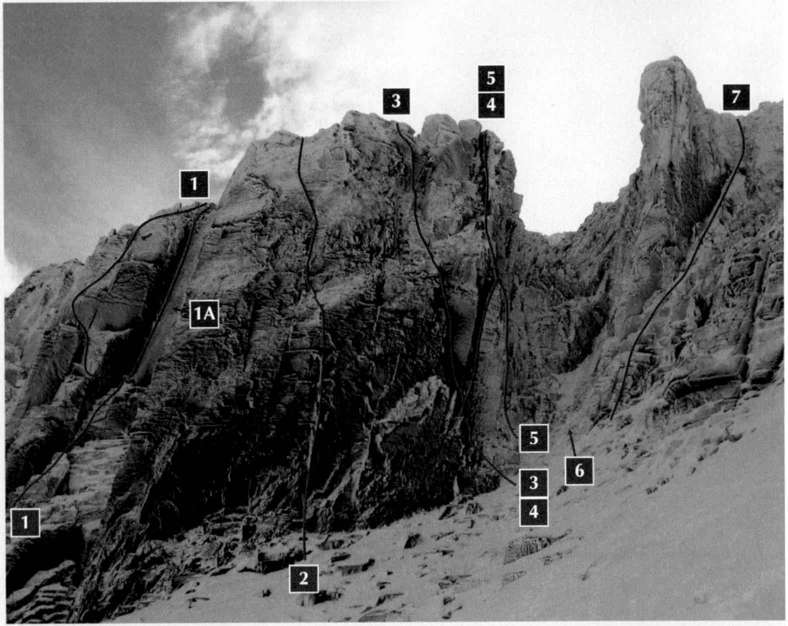

Ewen Buttress, Direct Start **45m IV,6***

The obvious corner fault to the right of the toe of the buttress is climbed to join the normal route. There is a hard move to gain the easier ground, particularly if the build-up is poor.

The Migrant **100m VI,7****

A Cunningham and A Nisbet, 13 March 1986

In the left side of the buttress is a huge alcove. This fine route climbs into this, then out on the left side. Start in a groove 5m right of Ewen Buttress Direct Start and climb this, deceptive, and make a step right to a belay (20m). Go up right under the overhanging wall, and at the first possible place go into the alcove (20m). Descend a short way and break out left onto a ledge on the arete. Follow this left, then go up over a chokestone to the top of a pinnacle. Move left to a rib leading to easier ground (40m). Go right and finish up Ewen Buttress (20m).

Migrant Direct **95m VII,8**

W Garrett and A Coull, 13 December 1996

This takes the challenge of the huge hanging groove on the left of the buttress. Start up The Migrant to gain the groove, which is climbed direct. It is sustained, with adequate but hard to place protection.

The Vicar **70m VIII,8****

G Ettle and A Nisbet, 20 December 1992

A magnificent climb taking the arete right of the huge recess. The first pitch can be split. Start up an overhanging groove, then go left towards the back of the recess. Under an overhanging groove traverse right and gain a ledge with large blocks. Climb up to a second ledge directly above the first (35m). Climb the shallow corner, moving left and climbing wall cracks where the crack becomes blind. Move onto the left wall, which leads close to the flake crack of Nocando Crack, and lasso the chokestone near the top of the flake. Move back right (thin) onto the arete and follow this to the top.

Happy Tyroleans **60m IX,10****

F Schranz, H Zak and E Netzer, 1 March 2001

A desperate test-piece originally climbed red-point style. It takes the right-hand crack line running up the steepest part of the wall and is characterised by three roofs. Start below a left-facing corner with a roof at about 10m. Climb the shallow corner with increasing difficulty to a poor stopping place just below the second roof. Beyond the third roof the corner becomes a thin overhanging crack. Climb this by some powerful moves to a desperate final rock-over onto the slabby ledge

(30m). Directly above the belay is an obvious groove with a natural fault up the slightly bulging wall above. Follow this turfy crack/groove to the top of the headwall and a series of blocky steps that lead to easy ground (30m).

The Overseer Direct 70m V,6*

A Nisbet and N Main, 20 November 1992

This takes a line up the right side of the buttress. Start at the bottom right corner of the buttress and traverse left on a ledge to gain and climb two consecutively steep corners. Continue direct to the base of a capped chimney. Pull out left and climb a vertical corner to easier ground.

The Hoarmaster 60m VI,6***

R Anderson, G Nicol and R Milne, 19 November 1988

This steep, strenuous but well-protected climb takes a chimney and crack line on the right edge of the buttress. Start at the bottom right corner of the buttress and gain a ledge, then pull into and climb the square-cut chimney (hard to start and sustained). Continue up the wide crack above for the second pitch.

Hooker's Corner 60m VI,6**

R Anderson and C Greaves, 26 November 1988

This climbs the obvious open corner right of the edge of the buttress. Start at the toe of the buttress and climb up just right of the corner. Step across, climb the corner to the top and finish up The Hoarmaster.

The Deviant 50m V,6

R Anderson, C Anderson and T Prentice, 26 November 1989

The fault immediately left of Y Gully Left Branch. Climb a line of chimneys and continue up until overhanging walls force a traverse right into the main gully.

Left Branch of Y Gully 100m III

TW Patey, G Nicol and A Wedderburn, 16 November 1952

The wide gully between the right side of Number 3 Buttress and the steep narrow pillar. Climb the gully to belay on the right of the icicle, whose presence is essential. Climb the icicle and follow the gully to the top. Rock protection can be hard to find.

Stagefright 40m VI,7**

G Ettle and R Milne, 25 January 1998

Climbs a fault on the left of the pillar between the branches of Y Gully. Start up and left of the big groove on the left of the pillar, Grumbling Groove. Climb the fine crack on the right wall to a point where it widens (big gear). Step left into a steep leftwards crack to reach a ledge (20m). Climb the wide crack above to reach good ice leading to the plateau (20m).

Grumbling Groove 60m VI,6*

S Allan and A Nisbet, 17 December 1983

The big groove on the left side of the pillar that separates the two branches of Y Gully is climbed direct, but with some suspect rock.

The Head-hunter 60m VI,6*

A Fyffe and R Mansfield, 1 December 1989

Takes the diagonal line that runs up the right side of the pillar. The groove/ramp is climbed to its top. Finish up easier ground.

Right Branch of Y Gully 100m II*

RF Stobbart, T Stobbart, Miss Harbinson and E Thompson, 14 April 1934

The wide steep gully tucked in the upper right corner of the corrie on the left of Number 4 Buttress. It is often in condition, being very high and sheltered; it can hold ice or be high angled snow. The cornice can be large.

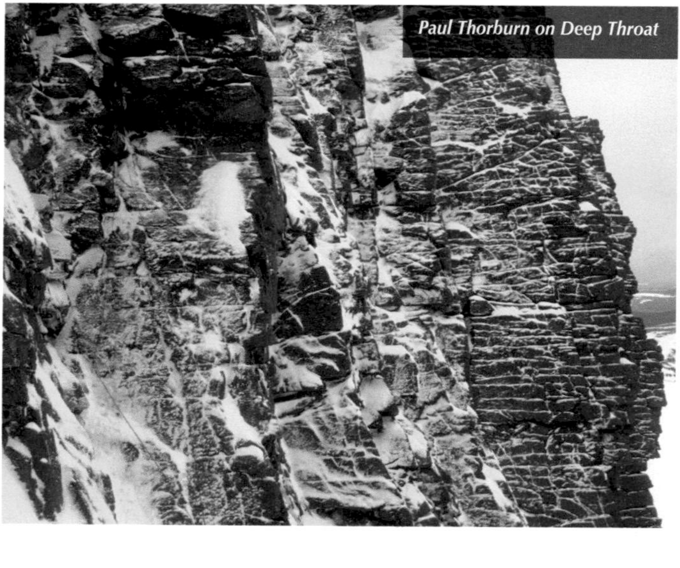

Paul Thorburn on Deep Throat

Pete Rowlands on the first pitch of Deep Throat

Number 4 Buttress

This has a steep crack- and corner-seamed face looking east and a less steep but higher front face looking north. In the centre of the side wall is the unmistakable open-book corner of Savage Slit. An ideal mixed route venue which comes into condition quickly and is very popular.

Oesophagus 70m III,4**

W March and party, 9 April 1971

About 10m right of the Right Branch of Y Gully is a groove leading to a snowy amphitheatre. The groove is often full of ice.

Deep Throat 70m V,6**

R Anderson, T Prentice and R Milne, 2 December 1989

About 20m left of Savage Slit is a pillar with a wide crack in its left side. Climb a wide groove, then the crack, which is followed over or round three roofs until a delicate traverse left below a large roof leads to a belay on a ledge (30m). Regain the crack and climb it to the top of the pillar (15m). Climb the groove onto the crest and so to the top (25m).

Coire an Lochain – Number 4 Buttress

1 Deep Throat V,6**
2 Gaffer's Groove Winter Variation V,5*
3 Bulgy VII,7*
4 Savage Slit V,6***
5 Fall-out Corner VI,7***
6 Procrastination VII,6**
7 The Third Man IV,6*
8 Sidewinder III,4**
9 Western Route IV,6**

Gaffer's Groove Winter Variation — 80m V,5*

J Cunningham and A Fyffe, February 1975

The main groove left of Savage Slit may hold lots of ice on occasion, but usually later in the season. Gain the groove direct or by traversing from the right above the rectangular roof. Above the groove climb a wide chimney leading to snow slopes and the top. Without the ice it is VI,7, and instead of the wide chimney, climb the corner running up and rightwards toward Bulgy.

Bulgy — 80m VII,7*

A Nisbet and J Preston, 27 November 1988

The groove left of the left arete of Savage Slit, finishing up a wide crack through the obvious twin roofs. Start at the foot of Savage Slit and work out left to gain the fault. Traversing out left below the first roof is the crux; large cams and no verglas are useful.

Savage Slit — 90m V,6***

G Adams, J White and F Henderson, 21 April 1957

A classic route up the wide crack in the unmistakable corner. A short but deceptive first pitch leads to the corner, which can be climbed inside or out. Because of its depth there is seldom a great deal of ice in the crack. Above the main corner finish easily up and left.

Fall-out Corner — 90m VI,7***

A Cunningham and A Nisbet, 9 December 1985

An excellent climb taking the corner right of Savage Slit. Start below the corner and climb up to below the roof at the foot of the corner, cross this and continue up the main corner, which is technical and sustained but well protected. Continue in the same line to finish as for Savage Slit.

Procrastination — 80m VII,6**

M Fowler and A Henderson, 28 December 1979

This route takes the central and thinnest of three corners, and is a serious undertaking. Climb to the start of the corner (10m), then climb the corner, turning a small roof on the right (40m). Move back left and climb the continuation of the groove to a large ledge. Climb the wall above, then go more easily to above Savage Slit, then follow this to the top (20m).

The Third Man — 100m IV,6*

S Allan and A Nisbet, 18 December 1983

Right of Fall-out Corner is a set of three corners. Start up the ramp running up right, Sidewinder, then go up to gain the right-hand corner. Climb the corner and the

Number 4 Buttress with teams on
Deep Throat, Bulgy and
Fall-out Corner

following wall to easier ground where Sidewinder crosses. Climb a shallow corner 10m right of the corner/chimney of Sidewinder and finish up a short wall.

Sidewinder **100m III,4****

A Nisbet and E Clark, 11 December 1983

A good route which uses both faces of the buttress. Start under a set of three corners and climb the ramp leading right onto the frontal face. Continue in this line crossing a short harder wall, then trend back left on easier ground to climb a corner/ chimney onto a big ledge. A short descent down a slot leads to the finish up the top of Savage Slit.

Western Route — 120m IV,6**

TW Patey, February 1959

A fine route up the front face. Start near the bottom corner of the buttress and climb the obvious right-slanting crack into a large recess. Climb the cracks in the right wall of the recess to easier ground. Continue via a short deep V-chimney, then into the big upper gully. Climb this and finish out the right wall, which can be deceptively difficult. It is also possible to finish on the left side of the capping chokestone.

Torquing Heads — 125m VII,7*

W Todd and A Cunningham, 20 January 1986

The prominent chimney on the front face is climbed over a chokestone and a leaning wall (crux, bold) to below a wide flake crack. Climb this and the bulging chimney above to easy ground. Finish up the right of the steep upper buttress.

Western Slant — 120m IV,4

R Anderson and C Anderson, 1 December 1990

Start up right from the obvious chimney of Torquing Heads at the right end of the crag, where an obvious short chimney is visible on the left. Traverse left to gain the chimney, which is climbed over a chokestone to a fault leading left to a belay beside the groove of Torquing Heads (30m). Traverse left across Torquing Heads, climb up and then left to drop down into the wide gully fault of Western Route, and move up to belay (30m). Continue up the fault to finish up the crack in the right wall, or left of the capping chokestone as for Western Route (60m).

Dave Hollinger on the first pitch of Western Slant

LURCHER'S CRAG (CREAG AN LETH-CHOIN)

NH 968 033 *Altitude 780m* *West-south-west facing*

Also known as Creag an Leth-Choin, this large broken cliff lies below the summit of the same name and overlooks the northern section of the Lairig Ghru. It is a large sprawling cliff split by three long, but fairly easy angled gullies separated by ill-defined ribs. In addition to the main gullies, which can hold large quantities of ice, a number of short, but good practice ice pitches can be found in this area, particularly to the north of the main cliff.

Approaches

From the north go to the Sugar Bowl car park, which is on the left where the road to Coire Cas and the ski area leaves the trees at the first big bend (NH 985 073). Cross the road and follow the track through the Chalamain Gap and contour round to the cliff – or, for a better view and easier walk, descend to the Lairig Ghru and reascend. From the Coire Cas car park it is possible to follow the path south-west as for Coire an Lochain, then go to the col just north of Creag an Leth-Choin (NH 969 033) and descend to below the cliffs. A flatter but longer approach is the Lairig Ghru track from Loch Morlich.

Descent

Descend northwards from the top of Creag an Leth-Choin down the ridge to reach the path leading back to the Sugar Bowl.

Conditions

This is the only cliff in this area to face west, so conditions here can be very different from those found elsewhere. Large amounts of ice can build up, and the routes, although not too steep, can become sheets of continuous ice. It can be relatively sheltered when there are easterly winds. South of the main crag is a set of blocky buttress which are not so dependent on the build-up of ice.

North Gully — 240m III

R Campbell, F Harper and MA Thompson, 23 December 1965

The big gully in the most northerly section of the crag. It usually has a couple of ice pitches. At the top it forks and either can be taken – the left may contain a good ice pitch, and the right has a short but steep iced corner.

K9 — 180m IV,4

A Fyffe and B Fyffe, 23 March 1996

This climbs two separate ice falls between North and Central Gullies. Start up the lower ice fall, which leads towards a big roof. After a pitch trend left across mixed ground, ascend easier terrain and go to the foot of the upper ice fall running down a corner. Climb this to finish.

Lurcher's Crag (north)

1 North Gully (left fork) III
2 K9 IV,4
3 Arctic Monkey III,4*
4 Central Gully III*
5 Window Gully IV,4
6 South Gully I

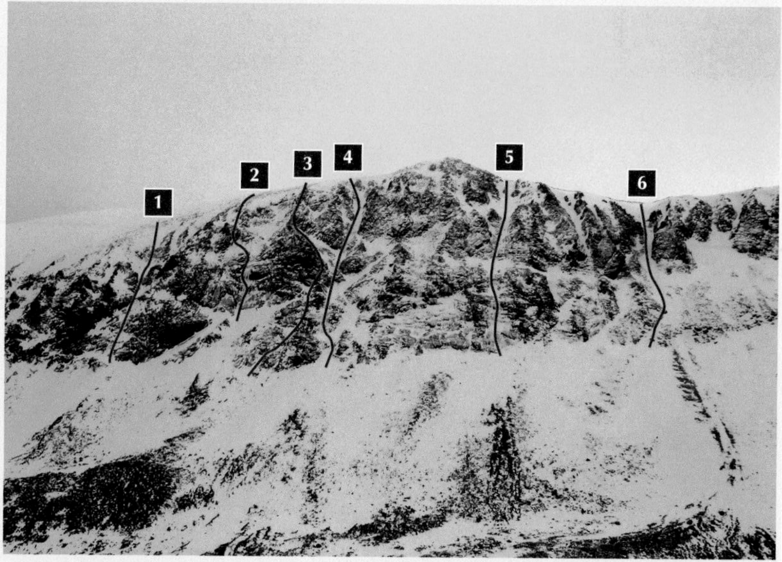

Arctic Monkey 300m III,4*

S Allan and A Nisbet, 6 January 2008

The ridge on the left of Central Gully. Start on the left of the gully and climb easy ground to where it steepens. This is passed by a line of weakness on the right, passing a smooth groove heading left, to a recess below a prominent jutting block. Pull out left through a small cave (crux) and go left up a less well-defined groove to reach the crest. Follow the crest, which becomes progressively easier.

Central Gully 300m III*

B Taplin and O Ludlow, 4 March 1970

The most obvious gully in the centre of the cliff. It may have several ice pitches low down, and either of the two branches can be followed at the top. On occasions it can be a continuous line of ice. In lean conditions it will be a grade harder.

Window Gully 220m IV,4

W March, J Cleare and J Bradshaw, 9 March 1972

Between North Gully and South Gully, the easy fault on the southern section of the crag is an ice fall. Climb iced slabs up to the ice fall, which forms down an overhanging wall. Climb behind it, cut a window and climb ice to easier ground. If the ice has to be climbed on the outside it is harder.

Eskimo Gully 240m II*

J Lyall, B Cook, and J and K Penrose, 12 March 2008

The gully left of Doorway Ridge starts as a shallow icy fault up the lower slabs, then becomes a steeper ice pitch followed by easier ground.

Doorway Ridge 200m IV,5*

J Lyall and A Nisbet, 8 December 2007

This is the second ridge north of South Gully. Start on its right and climb a subsidiary buttress to a steep corner, which leads onto the crest and then to a slight col (45m). Continue just right of the crest, over a slight pinnacle and a steeper section, to reach easy ground (45m). Finish up this easier crest over the doorway.

South Gully 150m I

The well-defined gully right of where the slabby ground at the base of the cliff disappears.

Pinnacle Ridge 150m II

A Nisbet, 9 November 2007

The ridge on the south of South Gully. Climb a right-slanting fault, then go left onto

Lurcher's Crag (south)

1 Eskimo Gully II*
2 Doorway Ridge IV,5*
3 South Gully I
4 Pinnacle Ridge II
5 Punchdrunk III
6 Drystane Ridge II
7 Wolfstone Gully VI,7
8 Quinn III
9 Collie's Ridge II
10 Hound of the Baskervilles IV,5
11 Deerhound Ridge III

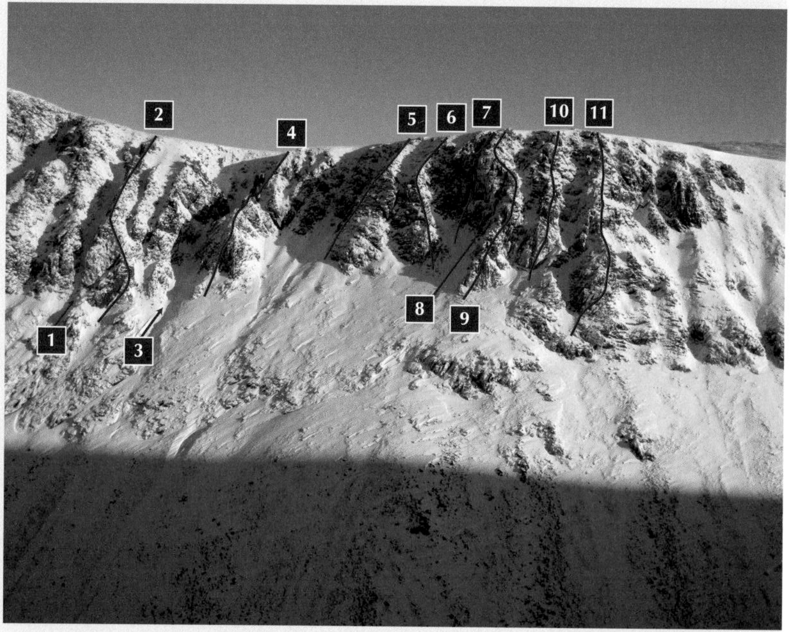

(photo: John Lyall)

the crest. Follow this over the pinnacle (avoidable) to a col and finish by a right-slanting fault.

Punchdrunk **130m III**

A Nisbet, 8 November 2008

Takes a line up the broad buttress south of Pinnacle Ridge. Start at the upper left corner of the buttress and break out right onto the face. Slant up and slightly left to a big right-facing corner. Traverse 8m right and climb a line of weakness to join the left crest higher up.

About 300m south of South Gully is an area of blocky buttresses and ribs, with a rocky amphitheatre high up that has the steep Wolfstone Gully on its back wall.

Drystane Ridge **100m II**

A Nisbet, 14 January 2007

The ridge which bounds the left side of the amphitheatre. The crux is at half-height, a steep blocky section with good flakes.

Wolfstone Gully **80m VI,7**

J Lyall and A Nisbet, 24 January 2009

The steep gully in the back of the amphitheatre. Start well right of the gully and climb turfy ledges up left to the gully below its steepest section (25m). Climb a crack in a shallow corner on the right to below a big chokestone (10m). It may be possible to climb the gully direct here if there is enough ice. Climb past the left corner of the chokestone to reach the easy upper gully (10m). Finish up this (30m).

Quinn **75m III**

B Findlay, R Ross and G Strange, 10 February 2002

The gully in the right corner of the amphitheatre and slanting up rightwards to join Collie's Ridge.

Collie's Ridge **120m II**

A Nisbet, 8 January 2007

The ridge bounding the right side of the amphitheatre and joining Quinn near the top.

Hound of the Baskervilles **150m IV,5**

A Nisbet and J Preston, 9 November 2007

The defined ridge right of Collie's Ridge. Start up grooves in the lowest rocks and climb this to a steep wall. Move left and up a small groove, a short chimney with a capstone, then a blocky corner which leads right to a level section (40m). Climb a right-facing corner on the left side of a vertical wall, then go more easily up the buttress crest to a slabby wall and a short arete (50m). Go left and back right up a blocky section to finish up a chimney (60m).

Deerhound Ridge — 180m III

I Dillon and J Lyall, 27 December 1994

This is about 150m right of the amphitheatre, and this ridge comes down lower than the others. Zig-zag up the lower part of the ridge, then go on the left to reach a col. Climb the crux groove on the left side, then finish up the crest.

SRON NA LAIRIGE

NH 967 013 *Altitude 950m* *East-north-east facing*

These cliffs lie on the flank of Sron na Lairige, overlooking the Lairig Ghru. There are a number of broken buttresses, but the most obvious feature towards the south of the crags is Lairig Ridge.

Approach

Approach as for Lurcher's Crag, but continue south down the Lairig Ghru then walk uphill to the routes. These routes are described from right to left, as this is the usual direction of approach.

Descent

The usual descent is north down Sron na Lairige to gain the Lairig Ghru.

Conditions

The routes here come into condition fairly soon, as the rock tends to be fairly broken and vegetated. There can be a substantial cornice with westerly winds, but there is usually a way through at the top of Lairig Ridge.

Polar Bear — 200m IV,5

J Lyall and A Nisbet, 7 January 2008

This is the first main buttress reached from the north. It is the right-hand of two and fairly broad and broken. Climb a turfy grooves system in the crest. The crux is a smooth section, which is climbed near its right arete.

Ghruvy Gully — 220m III**

J Lyall, 18 March 2008

The main gully between the buttresses of White Hunter and Polar Bear. A choice of two starts leads to the main gully, with the final ice pitch being the crux.

Sron na Lairige (north)

1 Polar Bear IV,5
2 Ghruvy Gully III**
3 White Hunter IV,5*
4 Ghruling Gully III
5 Ghrusome V,6
6 Ghrupie V,5**
7 Ghruve II

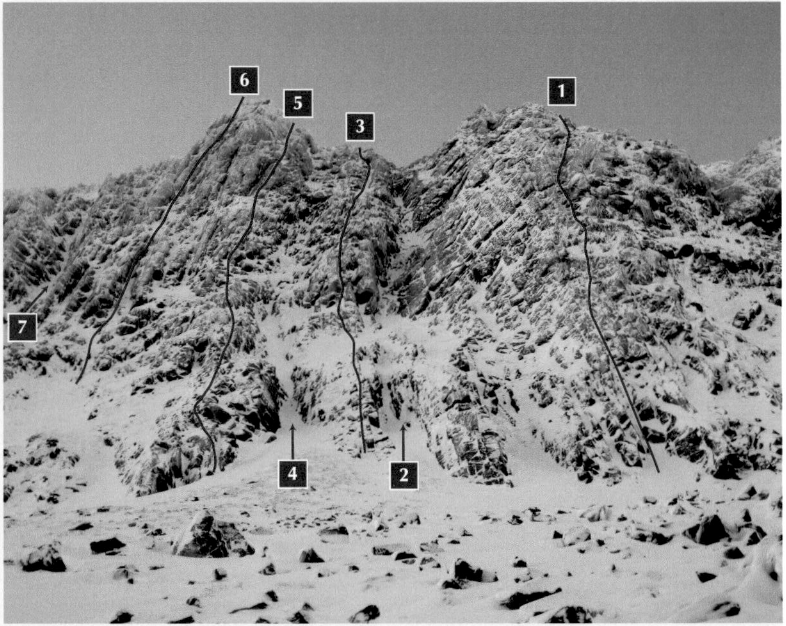

(photo: John Lyall)

White Hunter 220m IV,5*

H Burns and J Lyall, 8 January 2008

The slim pillar between Ghruling and Ghruvy Gullies. Climb the lower, easy angled crest to a steeper section (90m). Gain and climb the left-hand groove, then a cracked wall, to pass left of a prominent roof (45m). Easier climbing leads to the top.

Ghruling Gully 220m III

J Lyall, 18 March 2008

The gully on the left of the White Hunter and right of the left-hand buttress of Ghrusome. It becomes less pronounced with height and has a short mixed crux before the upper slopes.

Hamish Burns on the first ascent of White Hunter, Sron na Lairige (photo: John Lyall)

Ghrusome 200m V,6

J Lyall and A Nisbet, 14 January 2008

The left-hand of the main ridges north of Lairig Ridge. Climb the lower crest to reach a steeper section. Climb the central of three grooves to reach a steep upper tower. Climb cracks just right of the smooth right-slanting ramp that bounds the steepest section on the right. Gain a ramp, which spirals round the right side of the tower to reach its top and an easy upper ridge.

Ghrupie 150m V,5**

J Lyall and A Nisbet, 6 December 2008

Takes a groove on the left side of the buttress of Ghrusome. Climb easily up left from the lower crest of the buttress to below the central of five grooves – the one with a right dog-leg. Climb the groove, which leads directly into the most prominent groove in the upper buttress (50m). Start up this groove for about 15m, serious, then break right to more cracked terrain and follow this to join the crest at the tower (40m). Gain the top of the tower and finish up the crest.

Ghruve 220m II

J Lyall and A Nisbet, 2 April 2008

The long well-defined groove on the right of the Lairig Ridge and before the more broken buttress taken by Ghrusome. Head for two pinnacles near the top of the ridge, which is followed to the top.

The following six routes lie on the right side of Lairig Ridge, the most prominent feature here. Gormless takes the most prominent line of grooves on the right-hand side.

Braer Rabbit 130m III

J Lyall, A Nisbet and J Preston, 20 December 2006

The ridge right of Gormless. Start up and right from the base of the ridge at a steep groove. Climb the groove for 25m, then move left onto the ridge (45m). Continue up the crest to the top in two pitches.

Idiot Proof 140m IV,6*

J Lyall and A Nisbet, 2 April 2008

A line of grooves in the right wall of Gormless. Start just right of Gormless and climb a groove to a steep top that can be climbed direct or passed on the left (50m). Climb another groove, including a short crux overhanging section, until near the crest of the ridge (40m). Go diagonally left under the crest until it joined beyond its difficulties and follow the crest to the top (50m).

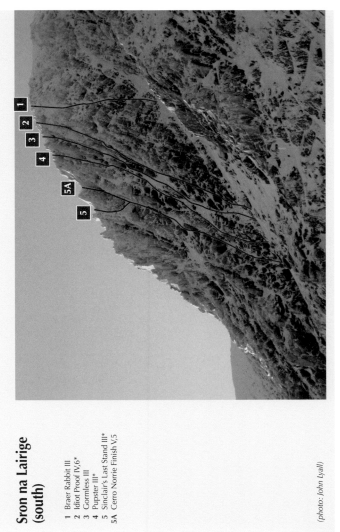

Sron na Lairige (south)

1 Braer Rabbit III
2 Idiot Proof IV,6*
3 Gormless III
4 Pupster III*
5 Sinclair's Last Stand III*
5A Cerro Norrie Finish V,5

(photo: John Lyall)

Gormless **130m III**

K Geddes and R Barton, 1982

The furthest right of the faults on this face. Start up open ramps, which develop into more defined grooves. At the fork trend right to finish near the top of the ridge.

Pupster **130m III***

D McGimpsey and S Wood, 22 January 2008

The rightmost of the three grooves starting about 10m left of Gormless. Climb a turfy groove for about 20m into the left side of a snowy bay. Follow this to its top and belay as for Gormless (50m). Go up and right on easy ground to a large rock fin and take the groove on the left (Gormless takes the groove right of the fin). Climb this left groove to the main upper groove (40m). Follow this fine groove to the top (40m).

Sinclair's Last Stand **150m III***

B Findlay and G Strange, 15 March 1992

The central groove on the large right face of Lairig Ridge. Start at an ice smear about 30m up from the lowest rocks. Climb the smear and the groove above to a short wall (50m). Turn the wall on the left, go up slightly right and climb the next groove (40m). Traverse left to a big flake on the edge, then climb the ridge crest (20m). Follow the crest to the top (40m).

Cerro Norrie Finish **40m V,5**

D McGimpsey and D Crawford, 9 March 2007

Climbs the thin groove above the traverse to gain the ridge at the top of pitch 3.

Lairig Ridge **IV,5****

G Strange and B Ross, 8 December 1985

The largest and best-defined feature. Climb the lower 30m slabby wall by its right edge, avoid an overhang on the left, and go up to easy ground. This can be avoided by a groove on the left of the wall to give an easier and more balanced route. Go up to the ridge proper and start up on the right by walls, then slabs, to a short chimney leading to the crest, which is followed direct over towers to the top.

Lairig Rib **200m II***

D Crawford, J Lyall, D McGimpsey and A Nisbet, 10 January 2007

The rib on the left side of Lairig Ridge and overlooking Lairig Gully is followed throughout. The start is quite steep, but amenable, and it improves with height.

Lairig Gully — 120m I/II

J Lyall, A Nisbet and J Preston, 20 December 2006

The narrow gully between Neon and Lairig Ridges.

Neon Ridge — 120m II

J Lyall, A Nisbet and J Preston, 20 December 2006

The ridge left of Lairig Ridge and starting higher up. Climb the steep lower wall by flakes and blocks and follow the upper crest to the top.

CARN ETCHACHAN

NJ 003 012 Altitude 850m North facing

This is the large pointed crag lying below the top of the same name. It is a complex cliff with two distinct sections – the **Main Face**, overlooking the head of Loch Avon (pronounced A'an), and the **Gully Face**, which rises out of Castlegates Gully, the huge fault that separates Carn Etchachan from the flat-topped Shelter Stone Crag on its right.

The Main Face is cut at mid-height by the Great Terrace, a series of big grassy ledges starting on the left and fading out near the junction with the Gully Face. Above the Great Terrace is the **Upper Cliff**, which is steep and complex; below is the more open and slabby **Lower Cliff**. Routes on the Lower Cliff can be used as access to the Upper Cliff or finished on the Great Terrace. The Gully Face in particular gives some very fine winter routes that can hold more ice than routes on the Main Face. Near the left margin on the Gully Face is a huge, complex vertical fault which is taken by Scorpion, and near the right side, starting well up Castlegates Gully, is the distinctive wide pink ramp of Sideslip, which is often a uniform snow slope slanting leftwards. Near the foot of Castlegates Gully is a vertical triangular rock wall about 15m high. This is the Sentinel and is a useful landmark. Below the Sentinel and running up leftwards to near the left end of the Great Terrace is the wide snow ramp of the Diagonal Shelf, the easiest means of access to the Great Terrace from the west side of the cliff.

Approaches

From the north

From the ski area car park in Coire Cas follow the main track to the White Lady Shieling. Follow the wide track up through the ski area then go up the crest of the Fiacaill a'Choire Chais to its top. Cross the plateau and descend Coire Raibeirt (avalanche risk at times). Go down either the stream bed or the rib on its right to the head of Loch Avon. Go round the head of the loch (or cross it if extremely well

Tim Chappell escaping from the Guillotine (photo: Henning Wackerage)

frozen) or cross the river further upstream (this can be awkward at times) and then head up to the cliff. For climbs on the Upper Cliff either do a route on the Lower Cliff, ascend to the Beinn Mheadhoin-Carn Etchachan col and traverse the Great Terrace, or go up the Diagonal Shelf near the right end of the lower face.

An alternative is to approach as for Hell's Lum Crag. Go into Coire an t-Sneachda, ascend the Goat Track and descend Coire Domhain (which can also be avalanche prone), then go diagonally across to the foot of the cliff. On this approach the Garbh Uisge is usually easier to cross higher up. Diagonal Gully, which splits Stag Rocks, can also be a descent to the head of Loch Avon.

From the south

The approach is for Creagan a'Choire Etchachan, from where the path is followed to Loch Etchachan and then down to Loch Avon or along the Great Terrace.

Descents

Castlegates Gully is usually a quick and convenient return to the loch side, and Pinnacle Gully can also be used. To return to the Coire Cas car park either descend to the loch then retrace an approach route, or continue across the top of the Shelter Stone Crag to gain the approach via Coire Domhain by traversing round the plateau passing above Hell's Lum Crag. Another way is to take a descending traverse west of Garbh Uisge Crag to go below Hell's Lum and ascend into Coire Domhain. From there either the Goat Track or the Fiacaill a'Choire Chais are followed back to the car park in Coire Cas.

The descent down the slopes above Loch Etchachan is awkward because of the outcrops unless conditions are good.

Conditions

This cliff has its base at around 850m and faces north. It is a big, complex face, but the buttress and chimney routes on the Main Cliff come into condition quickly with snow and cold weather. The Gully Face is much icier and the build-up here does depend to some extent on freeze–thaw action. Consequently the latter part of the season may be the best time for these climbs, which can hold their conditions until late into the spring. The Lower Cliff is slabbier and lower than elsewhere and so tends to lose its snow cover more rapidly.

The Lower Cliff, Main Face

This lower slabby face is cut by several left-trending ramps and bounded on the right by the Diagonal Shelf. Climbs here can be used to approach routes on the Upper Cliff.

Eastern Approach Route 100m IV,5*

A Fyffe and A Liddell, 4 February 1979

Near the left side of the face is a broken right-slanting fault which ends at the Great Terrace. This is the line of the route.

Carn Etchachan – Main and Gully Faces

1 Eastern Approach Route IV,5*
2 The Silent Approach IV,6*
3 Western Approach Route III*
4 Crystal Groove IV,6
5 Crevasse Route V,6*
6 Equinox VI,6*
7 Nathrach Dubh VI,6*
8 The Guillotine V,6***
9 Nom-de-Plume VI,6**
10 Pagan Slit V,6*
11 Route Major IV,5***
12 Red Guard VI,6**
13 Scorpion V,5***
14 The Sword V,5**
15 Siberia IV,5
16 Sideslip III*
17 Castle Gully III
18 Castlegates Gully I

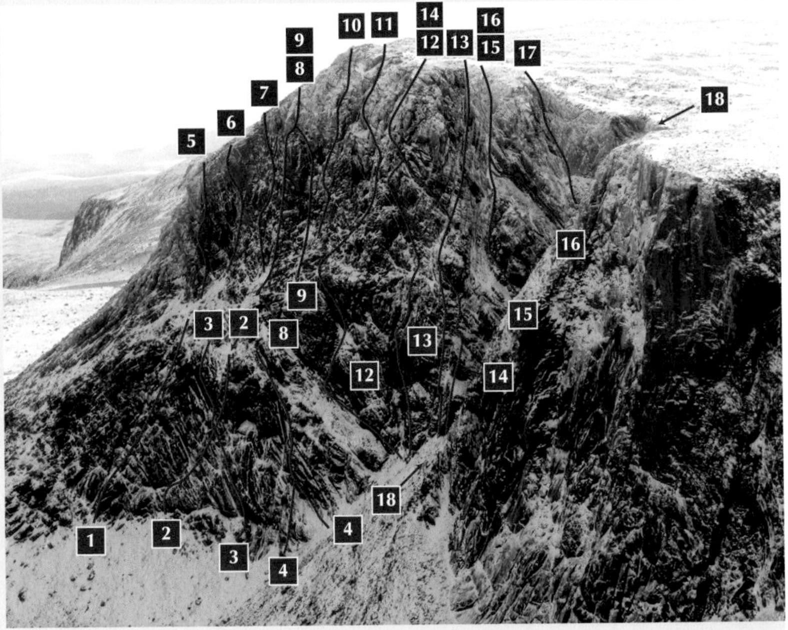

The Silent Approach 110m IV,6*

J Lyall and A Nisbet, 28 December 1989

A parallel line starting near the centre of the cliff. It slants right and crosses Western Approach Route and finishes up a trough to below The Guillotine on the Upper Cliff.

Western Approach Route 110m III*

A Nisbet and D McCutcheon, 19 December 1989

Follows a series of left-slanting ramps which reach the Great Terrace below Equinox. Start at the lowest point of the face, left of some huge blocks, and climb three narrow ramps and a short chimney to the terrace.

Crystal Groove 100m IV,6

B Davison and A Nisbet, 5 April 1996

The big groove left of and parallel to the Diagonal Shelf. Either climb direct up a shallow gully into the fault or start up a small ramp on the right. Follow the groove to an awkward finish through a chimney slot on the left. Go easily to the Diagonal Shelf.

The Upper Cliff, Main Face

This is a complex face consisting of a number of buttresses and amphitheatres. About halfway along the Great Terrace the pink rib of Python is fairly distinctive; a second and larger, but less steep pink area of rock is just to the left of the Battlements Groove. Routes here may still be in condition when the Lower Cliff is not.

Inside Edge 75m V,6

I Barron and S Kennedy, 28 November 1987

Takes the big diagonal ramp on the leftmost buttress of the upper cliff. Start as for Crevasse Route and follow this to gain access to the ramp. Continue up the ramp via a chimney to a small overhang. Surmount this and climb the corner above to a large ledge and finish up easy ground above.

Crevasse Route 75m V,6*

S Kennedy and A Nisbet, 13 January 1981

A technical and varied route up the leftmost buttress, which is characterised by a rock window above half-height and a big diagonal ramp on the left. It takes a line roughly up the centre of the buttress. Start at the lowest rocks just right of centre

Carn Etchachan – Upper and Lower Cliffs

1 Eastern Approach Route IV,5*
2 The Silent Approach IV,6*
3 Western Approach Route III*
4 Inside Edge V,6
5 Crevasse Route V,6*
6 Equinox VI,6*
7 Nathrach Dubh VI,6*
8 The Guillotine V,6***
9 Nom-de-Plume VI,6**
10 Pagan Slit V,6*
11 Route Major IV,5***

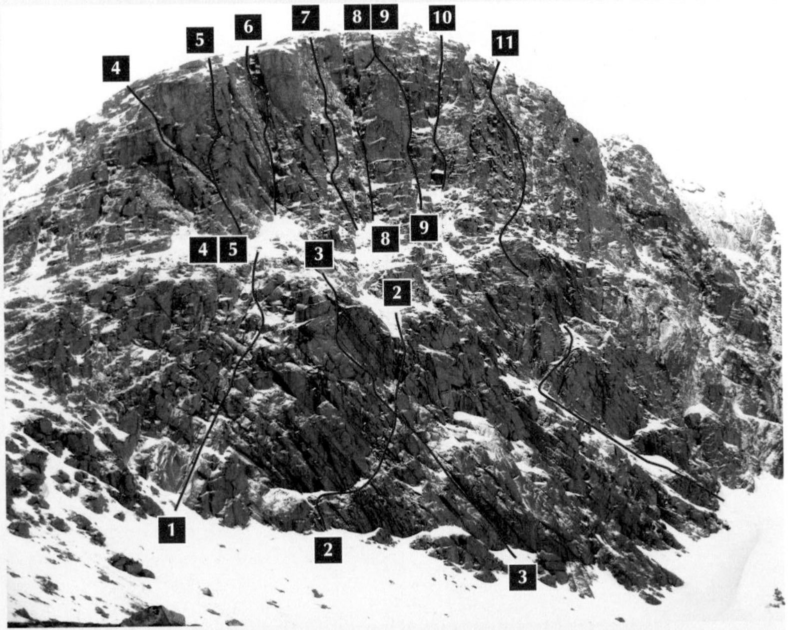

George McEwan on the last pitch of Route Major

and climb to corner on the right (40m). Climb a large leaning block, then an overhanging curving crack (crux), then step left and ascend huge flakes to a crevasse. A contorted chimney on the right leads to a fine perch. Then take the crack above for about 25m, then trend right to finish up the nose of the buttress.

Equinox — 75m VI,6*

S Kennedy, A Nisbet and N Morrison, 14 February 1981

The gully line right of the buttress of Crevasse Route and the next steeper spur is the first major fault encountered when moving right. Climb the left side of the fault for two pitches then go right to a chimney with a constricted top, which is tucked under a square-cut tower on the right. Climb this or the line on the left to finish.

Nathrach Dubh — 100m VI,6*

G Ettle, J Lyall and J Preston, 16 December 1996

A good direct route up the crack line that runs straight up the amphitheatre right of Equinox and left of The Guillotine and is distinguished by the deep obvious crack of Boa VI,6. From the terrace the finish can be seen as a W-shaped notch on the skyline. Start just left of The Guillotine and follow a ramp left until it is possible to break out right and climb the cracks up into the central right-facing corners (35m). Follow the three-tiered corners, the last being the hardest, to below the headwall (30m). Follow the groove, crack and chimney to finish just left of big roofs at the W-shaped notch (35m).

Snake Charmer 90m V,6*

J Lyall, A Nisbet and E Pirie, 23 December 1996

Takes the back left corner of the upper amphitheatre, right of the prominent wide crack of Boa. Start as for The Guillotine then trend left, crossing Nathrach Dubh at its middle corner to below the final crack of Boa (55m). Climb a turfy crack just right of the corner right of Boa for about 10m, then make a short traverse left into the corner and follow it to the top. Finish by a flake and a chokestone – a good pitch.

The Guillotine 75m V,6***

A Fyffe and A Liddell, 4 February 1979

Lies in the next bay to the right, left of the pink spur of Python. The upper wall is characterised by a deep wide crack (Boa, VI,6). Start below the upper amphitheatre and climb a groove and shallow chimney to a wide chimney (30m). Climb this to the amphitheatre (20m). Climb the second chimney on the right, passing under the huge rock guillotine blade to exit on the crest of the spur (25m). Finish up the chimney with an overhang at its top (35m, crux).

Nom-de-Plume 75m VI,6**

A Nisbet and P Langhorne, 23 December 1982

The chimney crack in the corner on the right side of the pink spur of Python is steep and strenuous. Climb series of chimneys in the corner to a huge diamond-shaped block. Pass this on the left and go onto the crest of the spur. Finish up the thin groove right of the chimney of The Guillotine or the last pitch of that route.

Pagan Slit 75m V,6*

M Fowler and A Strapcans, 27 January 1980

The right-slanting chimney right of the previous route. Initially, climb on the right of the chimney, which is broken by several ledges, then finish by the fault.

The Gully Face

This overlooks Castlegates Gully and may stay in condition well into the spring. The routes are generally long and interesting, but some depend on a good build-up of ice. Some of the rock on this part of the cliff is somewhat suspect.

Route Major 285m IV,5***

TW Patey and M Smith, 10 February 1957

A Cairn Gorm classic – long, complex and with awkward route finding. It is usually climbable under most conditions and is in condition longer than most routes here.

Looking down the penultimate pitch of Route Major, with George McEwan climbing

Mark Musgrove within the deep chimney of Red Guard (photo: Henning Wackerage)

Although it starts on the Gully Face, it finishes on the Main Face of the Upper Cliff. Start up the Diagonal Shelf, climb about 60m, then take a ramp line going up and right to reach a snow basin. Alternatively, and better, start at the foot of Red Guard and climb groove/ramps parallel to and above Diagonal Shelf directly into the snow basin. Climb the left-slanting tapered chimney, and from a ledge on its right exit on the left where it narrows (often the crux). A ramp leads to broken ground. Go about 70m, trending up rightwards below pink rock to reach the Battlements Groove. This is difficult to see from below, but is just right of the second pink rib on the Upper Cliff. Follow this groove, perhaps with a detour on the right at a steepening, to gain the main Battlements Groove, with its distinctive right wall with stepped ledges. At its top go up and left to gain a snow bay. Finish up the wide chimney with a couple of steep steps.

Red Guard — 250m VI,6**

ND Keir and M Freeman, 24 March 1978

A fine route, which is continually interesting. Initially it takes a huge chimney that cuts left into the cliff, and above mid-height it follows a wide ramp sloping left. Start just above the start of the Diagonal Shelf and climb a groove for a pitch into the main bay. Climb the partly subterranean, deep block-filled chimney. Above this climb up and right into the 'dirty continuation groove' (crux), and follow this to ledges and easier ground. Go rightwards about 10m to gain and climb the big left-slanting ramp, the lower of two. At its top continue up and left until a line of weakness going back right allows an open groove to be gained and followed to the top.

Scorpion — 240m V,5***

TW Patey, JM Taylor, AG Nicol and KA Grassick, 6 December 1952

A great route which finishes up the huge square-cut fault with the obligatory sting in the tail. Start about 15m below the Sentinel and climb a steep corner, then go left to a ledge below a steep wall. Climb this by a subterranean slanting crack (difficult to locate and a grade harder if climbed on the outside). Above this, ascend an overhanging wall then go round the corner and climb a left-slanting line. Cross a slab leftwards then go up to below the upper fault. Climb a long wide chimney with a leaning left wall that goes into the main fault. This is climbed on its right side to the top and may have lots of ice and a big cornice. Sometimes it may be necessary to exit on the left.

The Sword — 285m V,5**

JC Higham and D Wright, 5 March 1978

Takes a long diagonal to finish up the higher ramp on the upper buttress left of the huge fault of Scorpion. Start at an open groove immediately left of the Sentinel. Climb this, then a long open groove, then short walls. Work leftwards by ramps and short walls to an area of ledges. Climb Scorpion's chimney for a short way to gain a ramp (above the Red Guard ramp). Climb the ramp and finish up steps and corners.

False Scorpion — 240m V,5

W March and O Ludlow, March 1970

Climbs the main fault all the way – ice required, serious in powder conditions. Start inside Castlegates Gully above the Sentinel. Climb the main fault, keeping to the left until the main gully is reached above a narrower and steeper section. Finish as for Scorpion.

Siberia — 210m IV,5

A Fyffe and T Walker, 28 February 1979

Takes the large funnel-shaped fault in the upper cliff right of Scorpion. Needs a good build-up of snow. Climb snow ramps following the bottom edge of the buttress with the pink rock-fall scar ramp for two pitches. Where it steepens, go right and climb ramps overlooking the main gully. Where progress is halted (level with two big blocks on the right skyline) go onto the rib on the right, descend, then gain a groove that is climbed into the main funnel which leads to the top.

Sideslip — 150m III*

A Fyffe and R O'Donovan, 14 March 1975

The huge pink rock-fall-created ramp is climbed to its top edge. Go round the corner and a short steep traverse left leads into the main hanging funnel-shaped gully, which is climbed to finish. The cornice can be large.

Castle Gully — 150m III

KA Grassick and D Burnett, 5 January 1964

The gully on the right of the pink scarred buttress. Either climb the open fault leading to the better-defined upper fault, or take the fault further right and traverse left into the upper section.

Attic Rib — 100m II/III

RJ Archbold and DM Nichols, 5 March 1977

The rib near the top of the Gully Face. Start leftwards up a ramp, then move right and up a short step to the left side of the arete, which is followed to the top.

Castlegates Gully — 210m I

J McCoss, WB Meff and R Clarke, Easter 1914

The wide snow corridor between Carn Etchachan and the Shelter Stone Crag is straightforward in ascent and descent.

SHELTER STONE CRAG

NH 001 013 *Altitude 850m* *North-east facing*

This huge, flat-topped crag is the most impressive in the Northern Cairngorms. It is bounded on the left by Castlegates Gully and on the right by Pinnacle Gully, with the distinctive Fore-finger Pinnacle near its top. The crag consists of the main face looking north-east and two lesser faces overlooking the gullies on either side. On the left of the main face is the narrow, tower-like Raeburn's Buttress. The section right of this is the Central Slabs, which are massive, high-angled granite slabs defined at bottom and top by the Low and High Ledges. On the right is the Main Bastion, the most continuous rock. Near the right edge of the Main Bastion is the fault of Clach Dhian Chimney, right of which the cliff soon turns into Pinnacle Gully and diminishes in height.

Approaches

From the north

The approach is similar to that for Carn Etchachan. From the ski area car park in Coire Cas the plateau can be gained up the Fiacaille a'Choire Chais or via the Goat Track in Coire an t-Sneachda. From there descend Coire Domhain and trend diagonally to below the cliff after crossing the streams high up.

From the south

The approach is for Creagan a'Choire Etchachan, from where the path is followed to Loch Etchachan and then down to Loch Avon. This would normally be used only by parties staying in the Hutchison Memorial Hut.

Descents

Castlegates and Pinnacles Gullies are convenient descents to the head of Loch Avon. For returning to the north, either retrace the approach via Coire Domhain or Coire Raibeirt or traverse round the plateau passing above Hell's Lum Crag. Alternatively take a descending traverse west of Garbh Uisge Crag to go below Hell's Lum and ascend into Coire Domhain. From there either the Goat Track or the Fiacaille a'Choire Chais are followed back to the car park in Coire Cas.

Conditions

Most of the routes here are mixed, so cold weather and snow are the main requirements. However, with climbs over 250m in length conditions can vary considerably along the length of a route. Good conditions low down may mean too much snow in the upper sections. Many of the features on the harder routes are shallow, so snow strips quite quickly in warmer conditions. Some routes, such as Sticil Face, depend on ice. Most climbs here, however, are long, and the cliff's remote location, like that of Carn Etchachan, means that the climbs are always serious, especially if the weather turns bad.

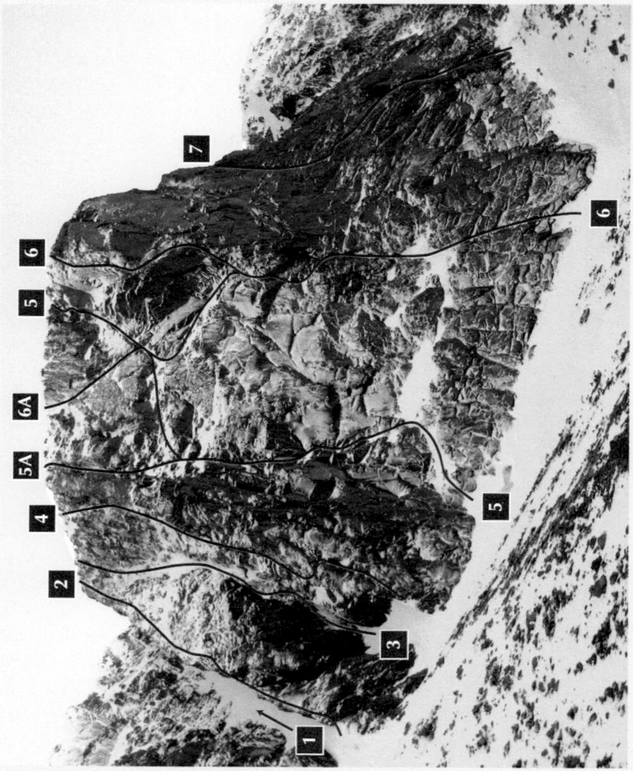

Shelter Stone Crag (front face)

1 Castlegates Gully
2 Castle Wall III
3 Breach Gully IV,5
4 Raeburn's Buttress IV,5*
5 Sticil Face V,6***
5A Sticil Face Direct Finish V,6
6 Citadel VII,8***
6A Citadel Winter Variation VI,8**
7 Clach Dhian Chimney V,5

Castle Wall — 210m III

BS Findlay and GS Strange, 31 January 1970

The well-defined arete on the face overlooking Castlegates Gully. Start some way up the gully, near the foot of the arete, and traverse right onto the crest. This is then followed to the top. The first two pitches are the most defined and difficult, and can be hard for the grade.

Breach Gully — 240m IV,5

M Freeman and GS Strange, 12 March 1977

The obvious gully between Castle Wall and Raeburn's Buttress. The first pitch can be bold. The steep blank section is turned on the right and the gully gained higher up. A through route and another right traverse then lead into the easier upper couloir. Sometimes the gully can be climbed direct on ice, in which case the grade is IV,4.

Raeburn's Buttress — 240m IV,5*

W March and J Hart, February 1971

Takes the left side of the tower-like buttress. Start in the big bay on the left, the foot of Breach Gully, and traverse right onto the front face and climb up until a line goes diagonally left to the main fault. Climb this fault to a deep, tapered chimney, which is climbed on its right edge. Above, continue to the top of the buttress and then by the easy line slanting up on the left side of the upper rocks.

Sticil Face — 240m V,6***

KA Grassick and AG Nicol, 27 December 1957

A superb, classic route up the slabby corner between Raeburn's Buttress and the Central Slabs. Start below and left of the huge corner and climb diagonally up right onto the Low Ledge. Trend back up left into the main corner below a steep wall. Climb the open corner by ice on its right wall (ice required here for the climb to be the given grade). Continue up the awkward chimney to the High Ledge, then go up diagonally right in a very exposed situation until a wide fault at its top is reached. Climb this fault until it is possible to move left into another fault and so to the top.

Direct Finish — V,6

Above the awkward chimney climb up to a corner directly above. Climb this and a short wall to easier ground and the top. This finish needs ice.

Citadel — 270m VII,8***

M Hamilton and K Spence, 23 February 1980

A hard but superb route which takes the fault on the right of the Central Slabs, then a line of weakness up the left side of the nose above. Good conditions all the way are hard to find, and many ascents have required at least one point of aid at

Jas Hepburn tackles the first pitch of Clach Dhian Chimney

the lower crux, but this is becoming less commonly the case. Start at the shallow chimney fault on the left of the main bastion and climb this, two pitches, to the Low Ledge, then a further two pitches up the fault until overhangs force an exit to ledges on the left. Trend right over slabs (ice here is a great help) to a corner with a crack in the right wall. Go up this (lower crux), then right again to gain the slab above. Climb the fault until a right traverse leads into an open corner. Climb this corner and the following one to gain a ridge. Go up the ridge, then left to a huge flake. Hand traverse this, then climb the crack and chimney above (upper crux). Continue up the crack above, then traverse right with a step down to ledges. Climb the right-slanting fault until the left of two short chimneys leads to the plateau.

Citadel Winter Variation 270m VI,8**

A Rouse and B Hall, 1975

A fine route taking a natural line. Climb Citadel to above the lower crux, then go up and left to Sticil Face. Climb that for 10m to below an obvious thin ramp trending slightly left. Climb this up the headwall to finish.

Clach Dhian Chimney 220m V,5

C Butterworth and A Frost, 4 January 1972

The obvious wide chimney line which has its crux right at the start. Climb the fault over a steep section and continue for a couple of pitches to a steepening, when an exit on the left of the chimney is taken. Go diagonally up and left, not always obvious, to gain the Slanting Crack, a fault which leads up and right. Follow this until a sensational ledge leads right to the lower step on the horizon. Continue up to below the final wall and go diagonally right to finish.

Postern Variations 245m VI,6*

M Hamilton, K Spence and A Taylor, 5/6 January 1980 (original line)

The way described has now become the usual way to do the route and the one which is most likely to be in condition. There are other, harder starts. Start just right of Clach Dhian Chimney and climb the fault a short way until the chimney can be crossed and a left-slanting ramp followed to the terrace. Climb the Slanting Crack, which runs diagonally right to where it becomes a deep chimney. Climb this chimney until unlikely moves left gain a short corner, which is climbed, followed by a traverse left with one step down into a gully. Continue left until it is possible to gain a higher ledge system above. Gain and climb the obvious right-trending line to the Second Step, the large platform on the skyline. Finish diagonally out right, as for Clach Dhian Chimney, or climb the open groove directly above the platform (much harder).

Western Union 210m IV,6*

A Cave, G Ettle, J Jeglic and A Stemfelj, 14 February 1997

A direct between Clach Dhian Chimney and Western Grooves, with some common ground in the upper section. Much of the climbing is not too difficult until the top pitch, which can be avoided on the right, lowering the technical grade. Start between these routes and follow an easy gully system for 100m to a point where

Shelter Stone Crag (right side)

1 Castle Wall III
2 Sticil Face V,6***
2A Sticil Face Direct Finish V,6
3 Citadel VII,8***
3A Citadel Winter Variation VI,8**
4 Clach Dhian Chimney V,5
5 Postern Variations VI,6*
6 Western Grooves IV,5*
7 Pinnacle Gully I
FP Fore-finger Pinnacle

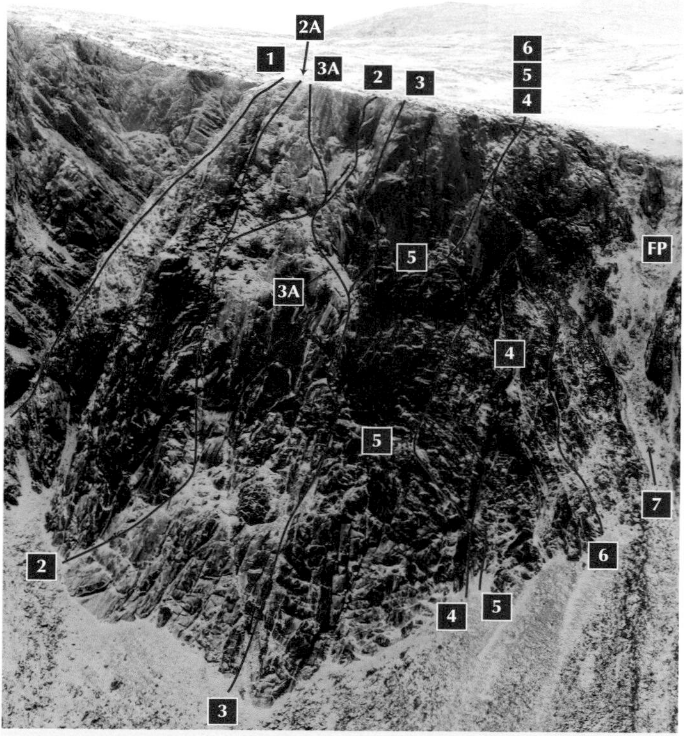

it is possible to move right into a shallow groove. Climb this direct into and up the large chimney fault which joins Clach Dhian and Western Grooves. Climb directly to a steep cracked groove just right of the deep V-groove of Clach Dhian Direct Finish. Climb this cracked groove, crux. Avoiding the final crux gives the easiest way up this part of the cliff.

Western Grooves **220m IV,5***

A Fyffe and RD Barton, March 1978

Takes a line of grooves right of Clach Dhian Chimney to finish up the top section of that route. Start about halfway between the chimney and the buttress edge and follow grooves heading for a short, deep, red chimney. Climb this and its continuation groove until a ramp leads left into the Clach Dhian Chimney and so to the first step. Finish up Clach Dhian Chimney.

Unknown Gully **150m III***

A Fyffe and party, 1979

Lies on the wall overlooking Pinnacle Gully and starts about halfway up that route. Climb the open gully which runs up to the first step on the horizon and offers a chance to sample the exposure of routes on the frontal face. Finish diagonally right as for Clach Dhian Chimney.

Shelter from the Storm **110m V,7**

A Fyffe and I Peter, 27 March 1996

Takes the steep rock right of Unknown Gully. Start in a large snow bay and climb up and right via ledges, ramps and corners to belay below a large pink slab. Go diagonally left on a hanging slab to a short right-facing corner. Climb this (crux) to a higher ramp and follow this to easier ground. Go right, then finish up a ramp sloping back leftwards.

Games of Chance **90m VI,7***

A Fyffe and R Mansfield, February 1991

A steep and varied climb which takes the wide shallow chimney in the upper part of the face between Unknown and Pinnacle Gullies. It needs ice in the upper section. Start in the big snow bay up from Unknown Gully and climb up and left to below the upper wall. Climb the steep crack over bulges to gain the main fault. Climb this wide chimney, mostly on the right side, on ice to the top.

Pinnacle Gully **250m I**

The wide straightforward gully on the right of the crag has the unique Fore-finger Pinnacle at its head.

Garbh Uisge Crag

1 Blunderbuss III
2 Garbh Gully III*
3 Crystal Crack III,4
4 Quartz Gully II*

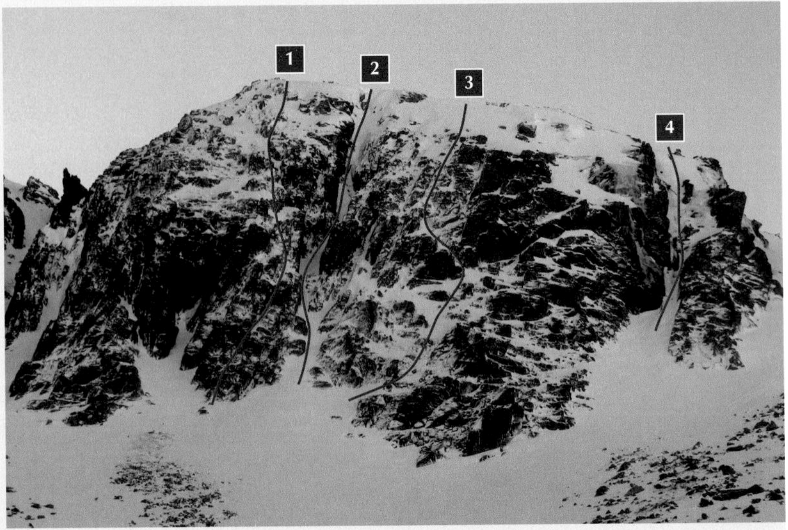

Garbh Uisge Crag

NJ 999 014 *Altitude 860m* *North facing*

This is the smaller, broken crag on the right of Pinnacle Gully and the Shelter Stone Crag. The main feature of the cliff is a Y-shaped gully which runs up the centre of the crag, Garbh Gully.

Approach and descent

As for the Shelter Stone Crag.

Conditions

A much more amenable crag than its bigger neighbour, but still with a long approach. The climbs come into condition quite rapidly and can often withstand a fair thaw. They can contain large quantities of ice, especially on the right flank in the vicinity of Quartz Gully.

Blunderbuss **135m III**

JC Higham and D Wright, 4 March 1978

Follows the buttress crest left of Garbh Gully. Start at the lowest rocks left of Garbh Gully and climb a steep chimney. Continue direct via grooves and short walls to the final snow slopes.

Garbh Gully **150m III***

A Fyffe and E Fyffe, February 1972

Climb the deep Y-shaped gully in the centre of the cliff, taking the right branch where it forks. The crux is normally a tapered ice corner after the fork. Above, easier ground leads to the plateau.

Crystal Crack **120m III,4**

D McGimpsey and A Nisbet, 5 November 2000

Climbs the left side of the wide buttress between Garbh Gully and Quartz Gully. Climb easily to a steep wall. Move right and back left to a bay below two parallel grooves, well seen from the cliff base. Climb the left-hand groove to easy ground.

Quartz Gully **90m II***

A Fyffe and E Fyffe, February 1972

The slabby open gully on the right flank, bounded on its right by a defined rib. The gully is climbed direct. Never very steep, it can contain large quantities of ice that sometimes spill over the right wall, giving some fine practice ice pitches.

HELL'S LUM CRAG

NH 995 017 *Altitude 920m* *South-east facing*

Hell's Lum Crag is one of the better cliffs in the Cairngorms for pure ice routes. It is a compact, straight-fronted crag which takes its name from the huge gully, Hell's Lum ('lum' is Scots for 'chimney'), which angles into its left-hand side but is hidden from most angles. It consists of three main sections. These sections and the routes are described from right to left, as they would normally be approached in this direction. These sections are separated by the two biggest faults, Hell's Lum, the huge deep gully on the far left, and the aptly named Deep Cut Chimney, which shows as a narrow deep gash in the upper part of the cliff.

- **The frontal face**, which has few very large features. The first is the shallow icy trough of The Escalator and then Kiwi Gully, most defined in the upper section, near the right side. Between Kiwi Gully and Deep Cut Chimney is the left-facing corner of The Wee Devil, and further right is the parallel Hell Fire Corner.
- The **Grey Buttress** right of Hell's Lum and left of Deep Cut Chimney, a narrow, deep fault with a diagonal lower section. This buttress is partially detached from the plateau, so holds less ice than other sections.
- **The slabs left of Hell's Lum**, which are steepest on their right where they angle into the gully and often hold ice in quantity.

Approaches

From the Coire Cas car park walk up through the ski area to gain the Fiacaill a'Choire Chais (NH 999 039) and ascend this to the top. Follow the plateau edge overlooking Coire an t'Sneachda over spot height 1176 and down to the col at the head of Coire Domhain. Alternatively, go into Coire an t-Sneachda and ascend the Goat Track to the same point. Follow the stream heading south until it steepens, then descend diagonally to below the cliff. This final steep part of the approach can be avalanche prone and should be treated with caution.

Descent

For those returning to the north, either retrace the approach or descend the Goat Track into Coire an t-Sneachda and return to Coire Cas that way. To return to the Loch Avon basin, either descend down Coire Domhain or the slopes well to the south of the cliff, taking care to avoid the cornice, which can extend as far as the Feith Buidhe.

Conditions

Ice is fairly reliable here because of the drainage from above and from springs, although very cold weather may freeze them at source. Snow build-up can be very extensive, especially when the winds have been from the north, and much of the lower section of cliff can bank out, shortening many of the climbs. However, because

Hell's Lum Crag (right side)

1 Auld Nick III
2 Kiwi Slabs IV,3*
3 Kiwi Gully IV,4**
4 The Wee Devil IV,5*
5 Devil's Delight V,5***
6 Hellfire Corner VI,7**
7 Salamander V,4**
8 Brimstone Groove IV,4**
9 Towering Inferno VI,5*
10 Nobody's Fault IV,6**
11 Deep Cut Chimney IV,4***
12 Hell's Lump V,6
13 Hell's Lum II/III***
14 The Chancer V,6**
15 The Gullet III*

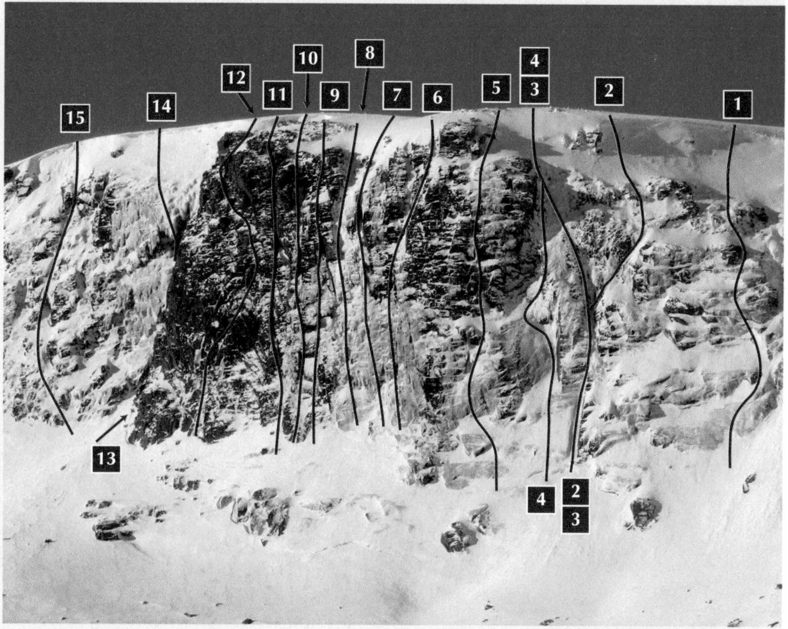

of its south-easterly aspect, in warm or sunny weather avalanches and ice falls are a real danger, as are the large cornices that usually develop above the slabs left of the Lum and on the right of the frontal face. Avalanche conditions can also develop quickly with northerly and north-westerly winds, when any snow field can be a risk.

Sneer — 120m II/III

D Haston, B Robertson and J Heron, 23 January 1966

The triangular-shaped slabs running up to the right, and right of The Escalator, often become sheathed in ice. The lower slabs usually bank out, but the upper section, above a diagonal snow ramp, gives a choice of ice lines which can often be done as individual pitches.

The Escalator — 150m II/III*

JYL Hay and A Thom, January 1960

The main fault on the right of the cliff. The lower section usually banks out, but the upper fault can be a long undulating trough of ice leading to the upper snow field and cornice.

The cliff left of The Escalator is slabby and crossed by several bands of overlaps. The lower section of much of this area can bank out with snow, making route identification difficult at times.

Auld Nick — 160m III

M Freeman and GS Strange, 20 November 1971

Based on the left-facing corner, parallel to and left of the middle section of The Escalator. It becomes more defined with height. Climb interlinked ice walls and snow slopes heading towards a steeper grey tower of rock. Climb either side of this to reach the upper snow field. The route is very variable in terms of difficulty, length and line, depending on build-up.

Kiwi Slabs — 150m IV,3*

TW Patey and VN Stevenson, February 1959

Follows Kiwi Gully to its deepest section, then breaks up rightwards on easier angled but continuous ice smears. These lead into a left-slanting corner, which in turn leads to the upper snow field. This can be extensive and heavily corniced.

Kiwi Gully — 150m IV,4**

W March and I Nicolson, 2 January 1972

The obvious gully slanting up and left gives a good ice route. Follow the slanting lower fault into the gully proper and climb this over a steepening at about two-thirds height. Above this, trend left to gain and follow the main corner on the right of the steep upper tower (as for The Wee Devil).

The Wee Devil 150m IV,5*

D Dinwoodie and J Mothersele, 17 November 1971

This route takes the well-defined left-facing corner midway up the face. Climb a vague gully system into the corner. Climb the corner to the overhang and traverse left below it. Go right on a flake to gain cracks, then continue up to the corner on the right of the steep upper tower. Finish up this corner (common with Kiwi Gully). Sometimes a line of ice leads from the corner into the upper fault, which can be followed direct.

Devil's Delight 165m V,5***

J Cunningham, W March and R O'Donovan, February 1973

A superb ice route when in condition. It takes the cascade of ice which forms in the centre of the wall between The Wee Devil and the parallel left-facing Hell Fire Corner. Start up the ice, which leads into then out of a large triangular recess. Above, the wall is steeper and is climbed by linking narrower ice runnels, which form in grooves and corners. This build-up of ice determines the degree of difficulty, but the top part normally constitutes the crux.

In the centre of the face near the highest point of the cliff lies the left-facing Hellfire Corner. Between that feature and the next break on its left lies an area of slab topped by a steeper headwall. This often forms a great sheet of ice about 30m across, up which three routes find their way. The lower slabs are open to variation, but the lines through the steep upper rocks are well defined.

Hellfire Corner 175m VI,7**

J Grosset and M Sclater, 13 February 1985

A good route up the right-bounding corner of the ice sheet that forms in the centre of the face. It is unlikely to be ice all the way, but if it is then it will be a grade easier. Climb ice in the corner to below the steepening. Climb the overhanging corner (steep but well protected) to gain the upper fault and follow this to the top.

Salamander 155m V,4**

J Cunningham, W March and R O'Donovan, February 1973

Takes a line up the centre of the ice sheet, starting near the foot of Hellfire Corner. The grade can vary with the condition and build-up of the ice. Climb the ice by the most convenient line to reach a tapered chimney in the upper wall. This is steep to start, but develops into an easier chimney leading to the top.

Sunshine and ice on the first pitch of Brimstone Groove

Brimstone Groove **170m IV,4****

S Docherty and K Spence, 27 December 1970

Climb the left edge of the ice sheet to go through the upper rocks via the wide break beside the huge beak of rock.

Towering Inferno **200m VI,5***

A Fyffe and RD Barton, 5 February 1986

This route lies on the pillar just right of Deep Cut Chimney and Nobody's Fault, and is characterised by two large rectangular roofs set one above the other. It is poorly protected in the lower section. Start as for Brimstone Groove and directly below the pillar. Above the initial easy slabs or snow fields climb up into a right-facing corner leading to the lower roof, then move onto the rib and go up into a shallow chimney. Climb the corner to the second roof and move left. Continue up the fault and follow the left-leaning fault to the top.

Nobody's Fault **150m IV,6****

G Smith and party, 1979

A fine route that follows the shallower fault parallel to and right of Deep Cut Chimney. The initial recess and the overhanging chimney provide the main difficulties.

Deep Cut Chimney **150m IV,4*****

TW Patey and D Holroyd, 19 January 1958

A classic route which takes the narrow dark fault on the frontal face. Depending on the build-up, the upper chimney can be approached by the diagonal introductory fault or directly from below. Once the fault is gained the way is obvious to the final capping chokestones, after which the finish comes with startling suddenness.

Hell's Lump **100m V,6**

A Cunningham and I Fox, 6 January 1986

A good little route based around the right-hand of two right-facing ramps that cut through the steep wall to the left of Deep Cut Chimney. Climb a left-facing corner and a groove to reach the ramp. Trend up and right to below a square roof, which is turned on the right (crux). Continue up rightwards to reach the left-slanting rake that leads to the top.

Good Intentions **125m VII,7**

A Cunningham and A Nisbet, 14 December 1986

A hard climb which takes the isolated groove on the very edge of the Grey Buttress. Start at the bottom left corner and climb broken ground and a short wall to the horizontal break below the ramp (25m). Climb the bold slabby ramp (crux) to the

Hell's Lum Crag (left side)

1 The Wee Devil IV,5*
2 Devil's Delight V,5***
3 Hellfire Corner VI,7**
4 Salamander V,4**
5 Brimstone Groove IV,4**
6 Towering Inferno VI,5*
7 Nobody's Fault IV,6**
8 Deep Cut Chimney IV,4***
9 Hell's Lump V,6
10 Good Intentions VII,7
11 Hell's Lum II/III***
12 The Chancer V,6**

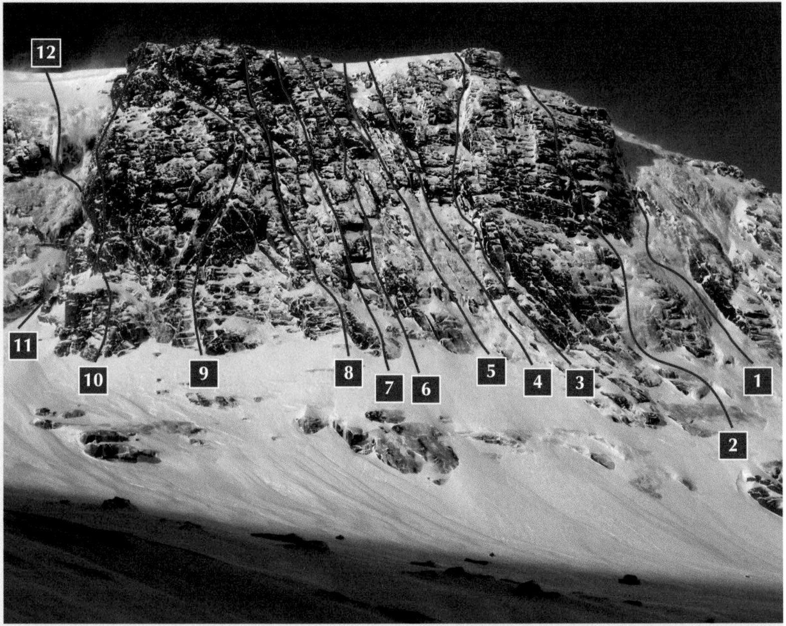

Below Hell's Lum and The Chancer (photo: Dan Caroll)

isolated groove (25m). Climb the groove, technical but well protected (10m). From the ledge at its top go diagonally left to below a wall with a prominent groove overlooking Hell's Lum (35m). Climb this groove and short walls to the top (30m).

Hell's Lum 150m II/III***

G McLeod and I Brown, March 1956

The obvious deep gully with the overhanging right wall gives a great climb in superb surroundings, although rock protection can be hard to arrange. It can vary from having up to four ice pitches to being very steep snow – in very lean conditions it can be Grade IV. The second pitch is normally the most substantial, and the cornice, which may be huge, can normally be outflanked on the right.

The Chancer 90m V,6**

J Cunningham and W March, January 1970

A short but sustained route of considerable historic importance up the ice pillar high up the face. Start at the top of the main ice pitch in Hell's Lum and climb ice on the left wall to a cave behind the ice beneath the steep section. Above is a large icicle, which is climbed onto easier ice and the final snow fields and cornice. Occasionally there is a thinner pencil of ice to the right – this is VI,6; the ice sheet on the left is the easier.

The Gullet 130m III*

J Bower and BS Findlay, 28 December 1969

This route takes the central and best defined of the three faults in the slabs left of Hell's Lum. (The other two faults are also Grade III.) Start about 20m left of Hell's

Looking up to the final chokestones in Deep Cut Chimney (photo: Richie Betts collection)

Lum and climb the fault, very shallow at first, to where it becomes deeper and better defined. Turn the steepest section on the left and continue up the corner above to the upper slopes. The cornice can be large and occasionally impassable.

Stag Rocks

NJ 003 022 *Altitude 900m* *South facing*

These cliffs, lying between Coire Domhain and Coire Raibeirt, look south over Loch Avon. They are divided into two main and one lesser section by an unnamed Y-shaped gully (NJ 000 022) and by Diagonal Gully (NJ 002 022), a long fault whose screes nearly reach the head of the loch.

The leftmost section consists of a short but very steep cliff down which ice in quantity can build-up – the Cascade area. This is left of the Y-shaped gully. Between that gully and Diagonal Gully is an area of well-defined ridges. Right of Diagonal Gully is the most substantial section of cliff, which is itself cut on the left by the straight and aptly named Amphitheatre Gully. On the left of Amphitheatre Gully is Pine Tree Buttress, which has a well-featured wall dropping into Diagonal Gully. Right of Amphitheatre Gully is the flat front face of Longbow Crag.

Approaches

From the north gain the plateau as for Hell's Lum, the Shelter Stone or Carn Etchachan and descend either Coire Raibeirt or Coire Domhain to contour round below the foot of the cliff. Alternatively, go to the top of the crag, where Diagonal Gully and the Y-shaped gully give quicker descents to the appropriate section of the cliff. The climbs on the right wall of Diagonal Gully, especially those near the top, are best approached from above, but the avalanche hazard must always be considered.

Descents

These cliffs are usually approached from the north, so the climbs finish on the plateau. Any of the approach routes can be used as a return to Loch Avon.

Conditions

Conditions vary across the different parts of the cliff. The ice routes need a period of cold weather for them to form from springs above the crags. The mixed routes on Pine Tree Buttress and Longbow Crag only need a little cold weather and snow. Northerly winds are good for this crag. However, the mixed routes strip extremely rapidly in mild weather or with strong sun, and cold weather is essential for the harder climbs. Dry rock climbing can be had on the frontal face in winter while the cliffs opposite are still clothed in snow and ice.

Left-hand Section

This is the section of cliff left of Diagonal Gully. It consists of two parts – the Cascade area, which is the short but steep section of cliff that lies in the middle of the hillside on the west of the main rocks, and the higher set of ribs and grooves between the Y-shaped gully and Diagonal Gully.

Stag Rocks (left side)

1 The Overflow III
2 Cascade V,5***
3 Cascade Right-hand IV,4
4 Afterthought Arete III*
5 Stag Route II
6 Apex Gully III
7 Deception Inlet IV,5
8 Pine Tree Route IV,4
9 Amphitheatre Gully V,6**

D Diagonal Gully
Y Y-shaped gully

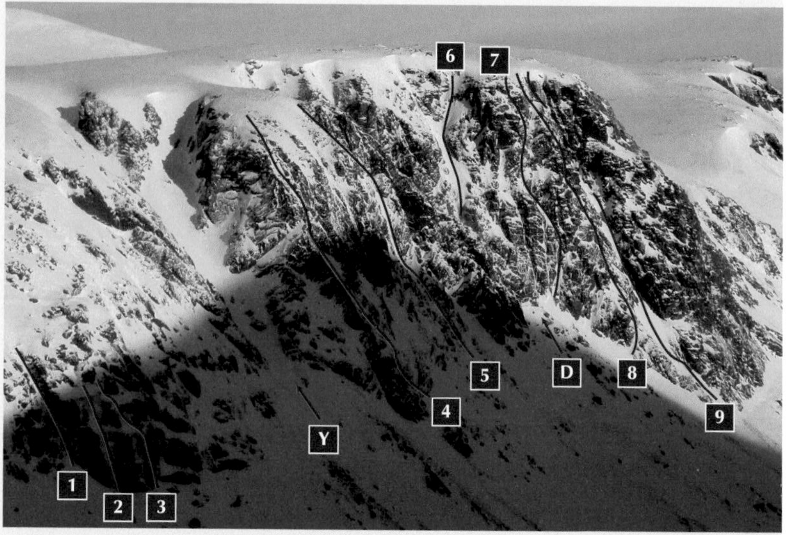

The Overflow **45m III**

A Fyffe and I Peter, 1986

The deep groove bounding the left side of the wall down which Cascade forms can give a fine ice-choked pitch.

Cascade **45m V,5*****

W March and D Alcock, February 1977

The obvious left-hand ice fall gives a pure ice climb. Although just less than vertical, it gives a sustained and serious pitch, and is not to be underestimated.

Cascade Right-hand **45m IV,4**

The ice fall that forms round the corner on the right. Not as steep as its neighbour, and it can be thicker.

Truly, Madly, Chimbley **90m III****

S Fraser, J Lyall and M Twomey, 12 February 1996

A mini Deep Cut Chimney, this surprising climb lies on the narrow diagonal buttress on the left wall of the Y-shaped gully right of Cascade. Start a short way up the gully, below a large block that sometimes banks out. Climb an ice fall left of the block and move left into a bay below the chimney (25m). The back of the icy chimney is climbed until blocked by an overhang. Pull out onto the higher set of chokestones (25m, and an excellent pitch for the grade). Follow the easy gully to the top (40m).

Afterthought Arete **150m III***

W March, November 1969

This is the rib that bounds the Y-shaped gully on its right and forms a fine narrow arete. Start on the right of the ridge and follow the crest to the plateau.

Open Caste **150m III**

A Nisbet and D McCutcheon, 20 December 1989

In the centre of the right-hand section is the deep recess of the Quartz Digger's Cave. This route lies on the buttress to its left; it is open to variation in the lower section but better defined higher up. Start at the foot of Afterthought Arete and slant up rightwards for two long pitches to below steeper ground about 20m left of the Quartz Digger's Cave. Continue rightwards below a steep corner to gain grooves in the crest, then slant back left above the steeper section. A choice of routes either by the crest or by grooves now leads to easy ground.

Jonathan Preston on Cascade, looking towards Beinn Mheadhoin

Left of the Quartz Digger's Cave there are two defined ridges, Triple Towers and Serrated Rib, which form the left side of Diagonal Gully. Both are very vegetated and are about Grade II–III.

Stag Route — 135m II

JT Campbell, B Findlay, ND Keir and GS Strange, January 1969

This follows the runnel on the left of Triple Towers. Follow the shallow gully direct over several pitches, avoiding the main pitch on the left. If the main ice pitch is climbed, Stag Route Direct, the route is Grade III, although the whole climb can be harder if not well built up.

CM Gully — 135m II/III

The gully between Triple Towers and Serrated Rib. The gully curves up left and passes below an obvious vertical rock wall to finish up the last part of Stag Route.

Diagonal Gully — 250m I

The long, easy angled gully, which divides the two sections of cliff, is very straightforward and more often used as a descent to approach routes on its true right wall. There is seldom a cornice, although the top section is the steepest.

Right-hand Section

This is divided into two main sections by Amphitheatre Gully, with Pine Tree Buttress on its left and overlooking Diagonal Gully and Longbow Crag on the right. The climbs on Pine Tree Buttress starting out of Diagonal Gully are usually approached by descending the gully.

Final Groove — 80m II/III

J Lyall and M Sclater, November 1988

The large right-facing groove near the top of Diagonal Gully is climbed direct.

Bambi — 70m IV,5

G Ettle and J Finlay, 18 December 1995

This takes the large groove immediately right of Final Selection, which is the defined ridge on the right of Final Groove. Climb up a short way, then traverse right across a slab to gain the base of the groove. Climb this until it steepens, then climb a thin crack on the slab to the right. A few insecure moves on the rib gain a good ledge (30m). Climb the corner crack on the right, moving right to easier ground (40m).

Purge — 90m IV,4*

A Cunningham and A Nisbet, 12 December 1986

Takes the narrower twin slabby ramps above Albino. Climb the ramps, heading

Stag Rocks (right side)

1 Afterthought Arete III*
2 Open Caste III
3 Stag Route II
4 CM Gully II/III
5 Final Groove II/III
6 Apex Gully III
7 Groove and Rib V,6**
8 Deception Inlet IV,5
9 Pine Tree Route IV,4
10 Amphitheatre Gully V,6**
11 Central Route VI,7
12 Stagnant Gully IV,4

D Diagonal Gully

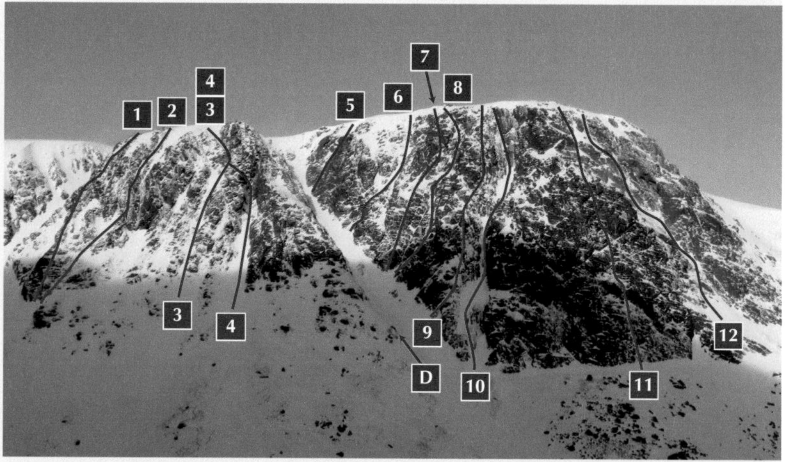

right for a full pitch, sparsely protected. Move left then go up into the deep wide groove, which has a steep section at the start. Climb the groove to easy ground.

Albino 80m IV,5*

J McKeever and G Taylor, 13 December 1986

A good route up the corner, whose slabby right wall has a distinctive blocky appearance. Climb the corner, delicate, to the steep headwall and go right to a huge flake. Go round the corner, then climb onto the crest of the buttress and follow a shallow groove. Alternatively, from round the corner, go rightwards on a steep blocky line to gain a large groove. Climb the groove and its continuation to finish up a steeper, shallower fault leading to easy ground.

Apex Gully 150m III

W March and J Hart, 18 February 1971

This is the large open fault which starts about two-thirds of the way up Diagonal Gully. The lower section is often a fine ice pitch. Above this there is a choice of routes; the left fork may contain a further ice pitch.

Light Entertainment 135m III,4*

J Lyall and D Bulmer, 25 November 1989

A good route up a set of grooves in the vague buttress. Start just below Apex Gully, where a horizontal ledge goes right. Traverse this ledge, then climb the groove at its end. Continue up grooves and chimneys to finish up a groove in a steeper tower (crux).

Jas Hepburn on the first pitch of Deception Inlet

Groove and Rib **135m V,6****

M Hamilton and R Anderson, January 1985

The left-hand of a set of three big grooves starting in Diagonal Gully at about the level of the lowest rocks on the left. When in condition it is one of the best routes on the cliff. Climb a line of ice into the main left-facing corner, climb this then continue up the rib above to the top. If there is no ice, the summer start up a corner on the left is unprotected, technical 8.

Honest Outlet **135m IV,5**

J McKeever and N Green, 15 December 1986

The central straight groove merges with Deception Inlet at its top. It is very vegetated, but can hold ice in quantity.

Deception Inlet **135m IV,5**

G Smith and K Gasely, 1979

The lower of the three grooves has a distinct curve to it. Climb the groove to its end in an amphitheatre where there is a choice of finishes – either trending back left or going right to finish near the top of Pine Tree Buttress.

Monarch of the Glen **160m VI,7***

J Lyall and R Wild, 12 January 1991

Follows a system of grooves on the left flank of Pine Tree Buttress – excellent when in condition. Start at the base of a steep wall with red streaks. Climb a groove on the right of the wall to a diagonal roof. Move left beneath it, then break through at the notch. Go up the groove above, then right to between two grooves. Climb the left groove for about 7m, then swing left into an easier groove to a ledge. Climb a steep crack in a short wall to another groove system, which is followed to a ledge overlooking Deception Inlet. Climb the obvious cracks, then the easy ridge to the top.

Pine Tree Route **180m IV,4**

J Bower and A Morgan, 7 February 1970

Follows the buttress crest that forms the left edge of Amphitheatre Gully. Start up the broad lower buttress, which may be iced up from drainage from Amphitheatre Gully. Above this there is a choice of lines, but the best stays fairly close to the right edge. Can be Grade III if well built up.

Amphitheatre Gully **225m V,6****

W March and J Hart, 17 February 1971

The gully defining the left side of Longbow Crag, the flat front face of Stag Rocks. It provides a varied and interesting climb, especially when icy. The gully is climbed

John Lyall on Stagnant Gully (photo: John Lyall collection)

into the amphitheatre, often over ice. From the amphitheatre climb the left corner by the wedge-shaped upper wall. The crux is the first pitch up the corner.

The **Right-hand Finish**, V,7, takes the corner line on the right side of the upper wedge-shaped wall.

Central Route 140m VI,7

K Spence and R Milne, November 1980

Lies near the middle of the flat front face of Longbow Crag, where a series of vegetated ledges and depressions run up slightly leftwards into some red rocks near the obvious diagonal fault taken by The Sand-Pyper. Climb these ledges and depressions, and above the diagonal fault follow the continuation of the lower line is taken through the steeper upper rocks.

Stagnant Gully 180m IV,4

G Ettle and S Kitchen, 6 January 1995

Near the right margin of the crag a large, shallow grassy gully runs up into an amphitheatre. Climb the lower gully into this upper depression, then head left into an obvious V-groove. Ascend this groove, go behind a chokestone and continue to the top. By trending left above the main face the climb is Grade II.

STAC AN FHARAIDH

NJ 014 030 *Altitude 900m* *South-east facing*

This cliff lies on the south-east side of Cairn Gorm, overlooking Loch Avon and near the Saddle at the head of Strath Nethy and consists of two sections of slabby cliff. The right-hand or **East Flank** may blank out completely, but some interesting climbing up thin smears of ice up the slabs may be had in lean conditions. Between the two sections is Rectangular Gully, a broad but shallow Grade I/II. The left-hand sector, the **West Flank**, is bounded on the left by more broken ground, which is split by several other shorter gullies. The West Flank is characterised by a long vertical diagonal wall running across the slabs at about mid-height, with the highest and steepest rocks on the left side. The routes are described from right to left, as this is the usual direction of approach.

Approaches and descents

The usual approach is from the north from the ski car park in Coire Cas. Gain the plateau via the Fiacaill a'Choire Chais and contour the south side of Cairn Gorm to reach the stream flowing south-east into Loch Avon. Descend the line of this stream and contour below the cliff to reach the routes. This bowl can be avalanche prone, and other descent lines nearer the Saddle may be preferred, even if this

Stac an Fharaidh

1 Rectangular Gully I/II
2 Apres Moi III*
3 Hoity-Toity IV,4*
4 Sermon V,6**
5 Spirit Voices VI,8
6 Not Fade Away V,6*
7 Rectangular Rib II/III
8 Narrow Gully I/II

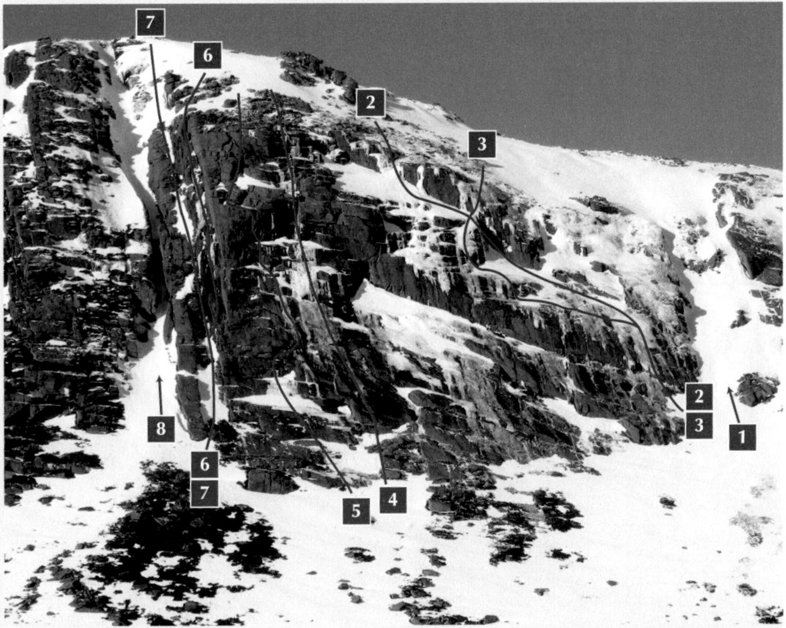

entails a longer traverse and ascent back up to the climbs. To return to the north, either retrace the approach route or skirt the summit of Cairn Gorm on the east and descend to the car park through the ski area (also a possible approach route).

Conditions

A very variable cliff; the slabby sections can bank out completely, especially the East Flank. However, on the West Flank ice in quantity can form, giving some fine climbs. As it faces south, this can strip quite quickly, so the cliff is best early in the season or in cold, cloudy conditions.

East Flank

This section of cliff can vary enormously – from banking out totally to having some thin streaks of ice running the height of the cliff. The best of these is taken by Pushover IV,4, which follows the main line running up the centre of the cliff.

Rectangular Gully 140m I/II

The shallow open gully between the two flanks may disappear under heavy snow, but can give some interesting ice pitches, particularly up the left side of the fault.

West Flank

This flank is slabby on the right, and this is cut by a long diagonal wall which increases in height leftwards. On the left is a steeper section of cliff. Ice in large quantities can build up here.

Apres Moi 150m III*

K Spence and R Anderson, 7 December 1980

This climbs a right-to-left line to gain the big right-facing corner in the upper wall. It can hold ice in quantity. Start near the right side of the lower slabs and climb to the overlap, then through it at the main break. Continue up and left to gain the ice in the corner. Climb the corner and continue trending left on the obvious shelf.

Hoity-Toity 160m IV,4*

K Spence and R Anderson, 7 December 1980

This takes the main ice fall that spills down the centre of the upper slabs. Start near the right edge of the slabs and climb up to and through the diagonal wall at the first break (as for Apres Moi). Trend left above the diagonal wall to gain the ice fall and climb it direct to the top, crossing Apres Moi at the shelf.

Eric Pirie on Not Fade Away (photo: John Lyall)

Sermon **120m V,6****

A Fyffe and I Peter, 28 January 1986

When in condition a good route up the left side of the main slab, left of the diagonal wall. Climb thin iced slabs to steeper but thicker ice that leads into the main recess in the steep upper wall. Climb the right corner/crack out of the recess to easier ground.

Spirit Voices **120m VI,8**

A Fyffe and R Mansfield, 12 January 1991

Climbs a gradually steepening line near the left edge of the slabs and is based on the summer line of Speakeasy. The first pitch is up thin iced slabs into a right-facing corner in a long overlap. Traverse right under this roof to gain thicker ice leading up and left into a large recess in the steep upper rocks. Climb up and into a short V-chimney (crux). Climb this and exit awkwardly left to a large ledge. A short, deceptive wall leads to easier ground and the top.

Not Fade Away **120m V,6***

S Blagbrough and A Fyffe, 14 February 1996

A mixed route that does need some ice. It takes the big open corner left of the vertical wall that defines the upper edge of the main section of cliff. Go up a shallow tapered chimney, as for Rectangular Rib, until the right wall can be climbed on ice smears to reach a large block (25m). Go up the slabby corner to an easing in angle (45m). Go up right into the main corner and follow this by some short deep cracks to a huge block below a steepening (40m). From the top of the block climb the short crack going up on the right to finish left of the capping block (10m).

Rectangular Rib **120m II/III**

R Anderson and A Russell, 22 February 1981

Right of Narrow Gully is an area of more broken rocks abutting the main slabs. Start up a shallow tapered chimney, then follow the slabby rib to the top.

Narrow Gully **160m I/II**

The obvious gully bounding the left side of rocks. It is narrow and very well defined to start, but opens out into easy snow slopes above a short awkward step (with a poor build-up this step can approach Grade III).

Broad Gully **140m III**

Climbs the long but shallow fault up the broad broken buttress that lies left of Narrow Gully.

THE CAIRNTOUL/BRAERIACH AMPHITHEATRE

This is a huge area of remote cliffs and corries shared by Cairntoul and Braeriach, two of the four Cairngorms summits over 1200m in height. Because of the height of this amphitheatre and its situation, cutting back into a huge high-level plateau, the cliffs share some features in common, the main one being the vast amounts of snow that accumulates here. In fact, the **Garbh Choire Mor**, the innermost corrie of An Garbh Choire, has snow fields which rarely disappear, even in summer. Another feature is the huge cornices that can stretch unbroken round the complete corrie rim. This can make the exit from some climbs difficult or even impossible, and force retreats or descents down suitable routes or long traverses below the cornice to find weaknesses through them.

Approaches

All approaches to these corries are long and arduous. The use of skis at certain times will make the approach easier, but single-day visits, especially early in the year, will usually involve much travel in the dark. The Garbh Choire Bothy (NN 959 986) provides weatherproof (?) but rough accommodation for four (possibly more, if comfort is not important). However, at busy times of the year it cannot be relied upon to be empty. The access from the bothy to the climbs is by walking uphill into the corries. Corrour Bothy (NN 981 958) in the Lairig Ghru can also be used as a base to climb from. It is larger, so there is more chance of finding floor space, but the daily approach is longer. However, it does get very busy during holiday periods.

Angel's Ridge in profile, with a figure on the skyline

From the north

From Aviemore go up the ski road towards Coire Cas to the Sugar Bowl car park (NN 985 075), which is on the left by the big bend at the upper edge of the Glenmore forest. From the car park cross the road and follow a good path down and over the bridge, then round and through the Chalamain gap and so into the Lairig Ghru. Alternatively, from the west end of Loch Morlich cross the river and continue south past Rothiemurchus Lodge and so into the Lairig Ghru. Continue past the Pools of Dee then contour south-west into the Garbh Choire hut.

From the south

Go to Derry Lodge (see Coire Sputan Dearg), then follow the path into the Lairig Ghru. Continue past Corrour Bothy to where a vague path by the Allt a Gharbh Choire heads off into the main amphitheatre and so to the bothy.

From the west

From the car park at NN 850 985 in Glen Feshie ascend Carn Ban Mor, cross the north end of the Moine Mor, ascend Einich Cairn and use one of the descents into the appropriate corrie. This is mostly used as a ski approach. The ability to navigate accurately is essential if using this approach.

From Glen Einich

The approach requires the use of a mountain bike but can be the quickest approach, although it needs no snow on the Glen Einich track. For the actual descent see the individual corrie descriptions. From the end of the public road at Whitewell (NH 915 086) go down to the main track and follow it into the glen. For Coire Bhrochain leave the track where it crosses the Beanaidh Bheag, which can be difficult to cross when the stream is high. Follow the path until it ends, cross the stream and climb the ridge between Coire Beanaidh and Coire Ruadh to the top then down into the corrie. For Garbh Coire Dhaidh climb the ridge between Coire an Lochain and Coire Ruadh and navigate to the north-east corner of the corrie. For the Garbh Choire leave the main track about 400m before the loch and follow the track up Coire Dhondail. When the plateau is reached go over spot height 1265 to reach the top of the corrie. For the Corrie of the Chokestone Gully head for the col west of Sgor an Lochain Uaine.

Angel's Peak

NN 954 977 *Altitude 1258m*

Sgor an Lochain Uaine, also known as The Angel's Peak to balance up The Devil's Point, is an attractive peak, particularly when seen from the north or the east. It provides limited climbing, but of Alpine length and appearance. The Lochain Uaine waterfall needs cold weather to form, but the upper ridge is usually climbable.

Lochain Uaine Waterfall — 100m II

A fine way of approaching the Cairntoul/Braeriach plateau if combined with Angel's Ridge. Start at the foot of the waterfall coming from Lochain Uaine, the corrie between Angel's Peak and Cairntoul. Climb the waterfall direct. The route is a little artificial as it is possible to escape in several places. It does, however, lead to the foot of Angel's Ridge.

Angel's Ridge — 300m I**

The North-East Ridge between Coire an Lochain Uaine and the Corrie of the Chokestone Gully is followed throughout, with a narrowing at the top, and makes a very fine way to ascend Sgor an Lochain Uaine. There is seldom a cornice, and it can be used as a descent.

Corrie of the Chokestone Gully

NN 954 976 Altitude 1100m North facing

This corrie, the only one on Cairntoul to give any real climbing, lies west of Sgor an Lochain Uaine, or Angel's Peak, and some way right of its shapely north-east Ridge, Angel's Ridge. The most prominent feature is the great gash of the Chokestone Gully in the centre of the corrie's back wall. To its left the ground is more broken, and on its right is a massive and well-defined buttress whose edge is taken by Bugaboo Rib. On much of the rest of the cliff the climbs are less well defined and open to variation.

Descents

Below the cliff and slanting up to the right or south-west is a large diagonal slope that gives one of the easier ways onto and off the plateau. Cornices in this area tend to be a bit smaller than elsewhere. The start can be difficult to locate in bad weather, but it slants down from a small promontory about 300m west of the top of Chokestone Gully (NN 947 976). Angel's Ridge can be used as a descent – although longer, it is easier to locate and is unlikely to have a big cornice.

Conditions

A high north-facing corrie which, in common with the other corries in the area, can have huge and extensive cornices. Because of its northerly aspect conditions here can persist well into the spring, when the routes can have an Alpine character. Unfortunately the rock in this corrie is generally poor.

South-East Couloir — 200m II

J Campbell and GR Simpson, 19 April 1970

The shallow couloir in the south-east corner of the corrie about 50m left of The

Corrie of the Chokestone Gully

1 The Shroud III*
2 Chokestone Gully III**
3 Bugaboo Rib V,7*
4 Sasquatch III*

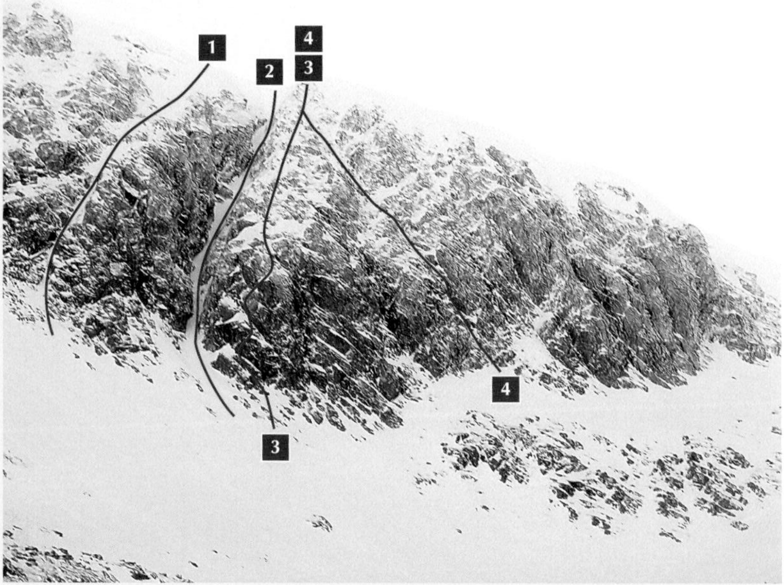

Shroud can be filled with ice or snow. In late season it can loose definition and the face can become climbable almost anywhere. Otherwise climb the gully direct to finish by a prow on the left.

The Shroud 160m III*

J Knight and I MacEachran, 9 February 1964

The narrow gully parallel to, and just left of, the Chokestone Gully. It may be necessary to climb icy rocks to gain the gully, which may contain some ice pitches.

The Flying Fox 130m IV,5*

S Richardson and R Everett, 15 February 1992

A varied route on the rocks left of the Chokestone Gully. Start at the toe of the buttress and climb awkward walls and slabs, trending right to a left-trending fault that leads to a stance (30m). Continue left on the fault to a smooth groove, step left below this and climb steeply to the crest of the buttress, slabby moves and easier ground (30m). Continue up mixed ground to the top (70m).

Chokestone Gully 150m III**

AH Hendry and party, March 1937

A remote but classic climb up the twisting fault in the steepest buttress. It can be a grade harder in lean conditions. Start near the lowest rocks in the centre of the main face. The first half of the gully is usually steep but straightforward, then it curves, narrows and steepens and there may be an ice pitch. Above a snow basin is the chokestone, which gives an ice pitch of variable size depending on the build-up. If insufficiently built up, an escape on the right is possible. The cornice is usually easiest on the right.

Bugaboo Rib 150m V,7*

BS Findlay and GS Strange, 13 April 1970

The buttress on the right of Chokestone Gully which forms a vague rib in its upper section. Start between the gully and the centre of the face and climb to a grass platform (probably banked out). Climb a steep slanting crack to an obvious block, traverse round the block and under an overhang, and go up to a large platform. Climb a crack heading right to below an overhang, then go right round a corner and along a tapering shelf to a belay. Follow the much easier ridge to the top.

Sasquatch 120m III*

RJ Archbold, D King, GR Simpson and GS Strange, 31 March 1974

Start right of the lowest rocks where they descend lower into the corrie at a horizontal ledge going left onto the face; can bank out. Traverse this to gain and climb a shallow icy depression. Continue direct or go diagonally left across another depression to finish at the top of Bugaboo Rib, where the cornice may be less imposing.

Right of Sasquatch is a series of left-trending faults and ribs that tend to peter out in the upper sections and which give a number of routes. They are generally on poorer rock and difficult to protect.

The Wanderer **100m III****

RA Smith and GS Strange, 1 March 1975

Takes the fault between the first two ribs and has a prominent steep right wall. It can be climbed direct if iced-up, but usually requires a deviation to the left before the easier upper slopes and the cornice.

The Explorer **80m III**

B Davison and A Nisbet, 26 March 1999

The next fault to the right starts up a ramp leading to a narrow chimney. Continue in the same line and finish up an arete on the right.

The Environmentalist **70m III,4***

B Davison and A Nisbet, 26 March 1999

The second-last corner is climbed mostly on ice. Climb the corner until forced left onto turf, then go back into the corner and climb it to a platform. Climb the wall on the right, then trend back left to finish as for The Explorer up an arete.

Garbh Choire Mor

NN 940 978 *Altitude 1130m* *East facing*

The innermost of the two subsidiary corries that go to make up An Garbh Choire. It is separated from its neighbouring Garbh Choire by a spur extending east from the plateau. The corrie itself consists of two sections, the Lower and Upper Corries, the latter being the more important.

Descent

Descent back into the corrie floor may be difficult because of the cornice problem. These are often huge and overhang a considerable distance. The spur running east between Garbh Choire Mor and Garbh Choire Dhaidh is one possible descent. The slope between Garbh Choire Dhaidh and Coire Bhrochain is further away, but less likely to be corniced. The descent down the shelf into the Corrie of the Chokestone Gully is fairly convenient. Any descent is best checked out before starting a climb, and it must be remembered that an abseil descent or a retreat from below an insurmountable

Garbh Choire Mor

1 Coronet Arete IV,5*
2 Crown Buttress III*
3 Great Gully I
4 She-Devil's Buttress V,5*
5 She-Devil's Corner IV,5*
6 Vulcan V,4***
7 Tiara VI,7**
8 Bunting's Gully III
8A Snow Bunting II*
9 Solo Gully I*
10 Sphinx Ridge III*
11 Sphinx Gully II
12 Pinnacle Gully I
13 Pinnacles Buttress III
14 Phoenix Gully IV,4**
15 White Nile V,5**
16 Phoenix Buttress Edge V,6
17 Phoenix Buttress IV,4**
18 Forked Lightning Route III*

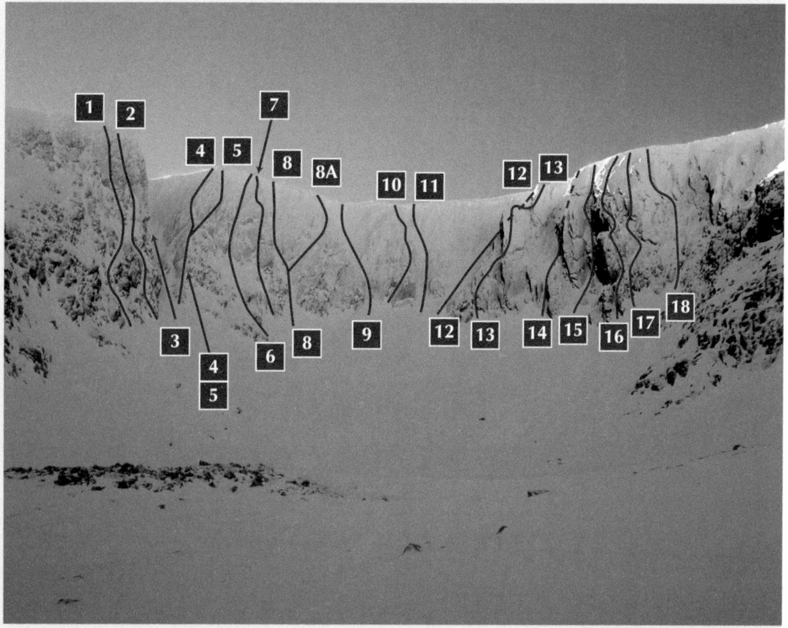

cornice may be required. When on the plateau accurate navigation is mandatory, especially in bad weather. In such circumstances it may be better to keep the rope on.

Conditions

This is probably the greatest snow-holding corrie in the Cairngorms, where immense depths can accumulate and the snow fields often last all year. They disappeared only a few times in the 20th century, but have been less extensive in recent years. This amount of snow means that many of the lower features or easy angled slopes simply disappear, and identification of routes can be difficult. Some of the easier gullies may become straightforward snow slopes. There is usually a huge and often insurmountable cornice that can be up to 10m in height. The routes possible may be determined by breaches in this cornice, and long traverses or abseil retreats from below the cornice are not uncommon.

The Lower Corrie *(NN 944 977 Altitude 1000m North facing)*

Not a well-defined area, although steep ground does continue round from here to the Corrie of the Chokestone Gully. Col Gully runs up to the col between Braeriach and Angel's Peak, West Buttress is on its right, and West Gully separates the West Buttress from the Upper Corrie. These features may nearly disappear with a heavy build-up of snow, and all the climbs are likely to have large cornices.

Col Gully 180m I

Well to the right of the Chokestone Gully face lies West Buttress, a huge broken buttress. Col Gully is to the left of this – it is obvious, easy angled and climbed direct. It can be a useful descent.

West Buttress 300m I/II

This route starts just to the right of the lowest rocks and takes the line of least resistance, zig-zagging up the face to avoid the steeper rocks.

West Gully 240m I

The obvious gully to the right of West Buttress is climbed direct.

The Upper Corrie *(NN 940 978 Altitude 1130m East facing)*

This corrie consists of a number of compact well-defined buttresses lying high under the plateau rim. Because of the build-up here, some features may be obliterated or, at least, be shortened. At times the cliff between Sphinx Ridge and Pinnacles Buttress can be a snow slope. However, the main features are, from left to right – the narrow well-defined Great Gully on the left, Sphinx Ridge, a narrow crested buttress in the centre of the cliff, and a trio of buttresses on the right. The leftmost of these is Pinnacles Buttress, and between it and Sphinx Ridge is a large slabby recess. Any of the climbs in this corrie can have impassable cornices, and this goes for the easier climbs as well. Try to check the condition of the cornices before starting on a climb.

Coronet Arete **120m IV,5***

S Richardson and C Cartwright, 15 December 1996

Takes the well-defined arete on the left of the big groove of Crown Buttress. Start 10m left of the buttress edge and climb easy grooves to where it steepens (70m). Continue up a corner system to a small platform (20m). Move up to a ledge, step left and climb a short wall to a steep groove on the left of the headwall. Climb the groove and its continuation to the top.

Crown Buttress **120m III***

J Bower and P Kale, 26 January 1967

This is the buttress on the left of the corrie that flanks the left side of Great Gully. The Crown is a rock flake on top of the arete. The route takes the big V-groove between two aretes at the top of the buttress. Start at the bottom left corner of Great Gully and climb iced slabs and ribs to a large block, keeping close to the gully edge. Continue up to the big groove, which starts as an icy chimney (crux). Easier ground leads to the plateau.

Great Gully **120m I**

The well-defined gully on the left is a fairly steep snow climb that can be heavily corniced.

She-Devil's Buttress, Original Route **120m V,5***

R Everett and S Richardson, 28 November 1993

Takes the crest of the buttress right of Great Gully. Start at the foot of the crest and climb slabby grooves up the crest to where it steepens (50m). From the top of a point of rock go left onto a slab and up and right to a crack leading to a belay (25m). Ascend the vertical wall above, move left into a shallow groove, then climb grooves to the top (45m).

She-Devil's Corner **120m IV,5***

G Boyd, BS Findlay, GR Simpson and GS Strange, 19 April 1969

This is the buttress on the right of Great Gully. On the right of the crest are two corners. This route takes the left of these twin corners. Climb iced grooves and snow aretes on the edge overlooking Great Gully (60m). Traverse right over a flake to gain the leftmost of the twin corners. Climb this to the top and, hopefully, a snow prow breaking the cornice line.

Vulcan **100m V,4*****

J Bower, J Ingram and K Turnbull, 1 March 1975

The rightmost of the twin corners gives a very fine icy climb. Start in the bay right of the lowest rocks and climb the prominent V-groove over a series of ice pitches. The lower section constitutes the crux, and the upper part may be a snow arete forming a break in the cornice.

Tiara **80m VI,7****

A Nisbet and E Clark, 22 February 1984

A sustained route following icy grooves and cracks. Just left of the buttress crest is a long narrow groove with an overhang at mid-height. Climb the groove until about 6m below this overhang and traverse right for 5m. Go up and slightly left to a smaller groove, which starts at the right end of the overhang. Follow this over a steepening to the crest, and then follow a 5m vertical wall to a belay. Descend 3m on the left and move delicately onto the upper slab, very exposed. Climb the crack near the edge, then a groove a little left. Follow this to the crest, which is climbed to the top at the same point as Vulcan.

Bunting's Gully **100m III**

JJ Light and OJ Ludlow, 9 January 1964

The shallow gully right of Great Gully is Bunting's Gully, which has on its right a buttress consisting of twin ribs that meet at a col near the top. The initial gully is easy and climbed to a fork. Climb the left branch to about 15m below the overhang, go on to the right wall, and go up and right until near the right crest. Traverse left into an upper corner, which leads to the cornice.

Snow Bunting **100m II***

JJ Light and J Vigrow, 15 March 1966

This is the right fork, which runs up to the col where the twin ribs meet. Above is a shallow gully and probably a giant cornice.

Solo Gully **100m I***

JJ Light and OJ Ludlow, 8 January 1964

Right of Bunting's Gully and left of the shapely Sphinx Ridge is Solo Gully. It is narrow at the bottom and straightforward, but it does, however, offer a descent from other routes which may have impassable cornices.

Helen Rennard on the upper part of Vulcan (photo: Henning Wackerage)

Sphinx Ridge 100m III*

JJ Light and J Vigrow, 14 March 1966

A shapely well-defined buttress in the centre of the cliffs rising between Solo Gully and a snow field. There is a steep triangular wall at the foot of it. Start in Solo Gully and climb a small gully to reach the knife-edge at the top of the lower wall. This leads delicately to a shallow groove then a short chimney (crux) on the left. Follow the arete above, often with a double cornice, to a platform and a col. Steep snow and the usual cornice to the plateau.

Sphinx Gully 100m II

A Watson and PD Baird, 31 October 1954

Between Sphinx Ridge and Pinnacles Buttress is a recessed area. This is the gully on the left of the recess below Sphinx Ridge. Climb the gully; the main pitch is climbed by a short groove and ridge on the right.

Pinnacle Gully 100m I

The gully on the right of the recess, left of Pinnacles Buttress. It curves right and steepens behind Pinnacles Buttress.

Pinnacles Buttress 100m III

J Bower, GR Simpson and GS Strange, 12 April 1968

On the right of the corrie is a trio of buttresses. The route climbs the leftmost one, which consists of two distinct pinnacles. Start just left of centre and climb to blocks near Pinnacle Gully. Climb a crack in a slab to more blocks, and at their top climb a short wall to a broad ledge. Go to its right end, then to the top of the first pinnacle. Ascend the second pinnacle, above which a snow arete leads to the top.

Phoenix Gully — 100m IV,4**

JJ Light, G McGregor, M McArthur and D Halliday, 19 March 1967

This is the steep icy gully between Pinnacles Buttress and the Tower of Babel, the first and second of the trio of buttresses. It is climbed direct to the usual problematic finish.

White Nile — 120m V,5**

RJ Archbold and M Hillman, 12 March 1977

The classic of the corrie up the steep ice between the Tower of Babel and Phoenix Buttress, the second and third of the buttresses. Climb the ice more or less direct, except for a deviation left and back right at about two-thirds height to turn an iced wall. Tends to be produced by freeze–thaw and may be better in March, but by April it catches the sun.

Phoenix Buttress Edge — 120m V,6

A Cunningham and A Nisbet, 21 January 1990

The right-hand of the three buttresses has a narrow leaning wall overlooking White Nile and easier ground to the right. The climb follows the crest, starting about 30m up from the lowest rocks. Climb a short chimney right of a corner to gain and follow a left-slanting line of slabs and grooves close to the edge to a large platform. Climb the right edge of the slabby wall above, with a mantleshelf onto a perched block. Above this return left and continue by a corner and slabs to easier ground.

Phoenix Buttress — 150m IV,4**

MG Geddes and JS Robinson, 21 December 1971

The large rightmost buttress of the three gives a fine climb. From the base of the buttress crest go up and right to a steep nose. Traverse left round this to a good ledge. Go up the groove above and go to piled blocks under a steep wall, which is climbed by a short steep corner on the right. Above, go up and right into a groove leading to the plateau.

Forked Lightning Route — 100m III*

RJ Archbold, D King, GR Simpson and GS Strange, 30 March 1974

The grooves on the right edge of Phoenix Buttress are often icy late in the season. Start at the top-right corner of the snow bay, right of the buttress, and climb ice in the second groove to the right of the buttress. Climb a left-slanting groove to gain the nearest groove to the buttress, which leads to the top.

Garbh Choire Dhaidh

NN 946 992 *Altitude 1100m* *South facing*

This is the right-hand corrie of An Garbh Choire and is separated from its companion by a spur running roughly eastwards. The Dee waterfall divides Garbh Choire Dhaidh (pronounced 'yay') into two sections. That on the left, running round to the dividing spur, is undistinguished. In fact, this whole section can bank out into a long, steep snow wall easily climbable anywhere. However, in leaner condition there are some long gullies of Grade I and II standard.

Right of the Falls of Dee are the main rocks, which are divided centrally by The Great Rift, which is seen well only from the left side of the corrie. Near the right margin, where the rocks are less massive, is the obvious fault of The Chimney Pot. The leaning buttress of Pisa next to it marks the end of the cliff proper.

Descents

The slope between Garbh Choire Dhaidh and Coire Bhrochain is straightforward and rarely corniced all the way round. The spur between the two Garbh Choires is less easy and normally corniced.

Conditions

Although some fine routes are to be found here, its south-facing aspect makes conditions less reliable than elsewhere, as the sun can rapidly strip the rocks of their cover of snow and ice. The ice routes are best early in the season.

Billabong 150m III

G Boyd, BS Findlay, GR Simpson and GS Strange, 18 April 1969

This climbs the obvious ice fall near the left margin of the main face and is based on the leftmost corner. This may, in heavy snow years, virtually disappear. Start below a corner well left of The Great Rift. Climb the ice fall to reach a platform. Continue up the ridge crest to finish via a narrow chimney in the final wall.

The Culvert 125m V,4*

A Nisbet and P Barass, 17 December 1981

Left of The Great Rift is a series of ramps and corners that usually form a fine ice fall. The ice is climbed by the best line.

The Great Rift 140m V,4*

JJ Light and AG Nicol, 21 February 1965

This defined chimney in the centre of the face is the classic climb of the corrie. Once committed to the rift, the route is easy to follow. It is best early in the season before it is too affected by the sun.

Garbh Choire Dhaidh

1 Billabong III
2 The Culvert V,4*
3 The Great Rift V,4*
4 Pommie Granite V,6
5 Boomerang IV,4*
6 Twilight Gully II*
7 Helicon Rib III
8 The Chimney Pot II*
9 Pisa II/III

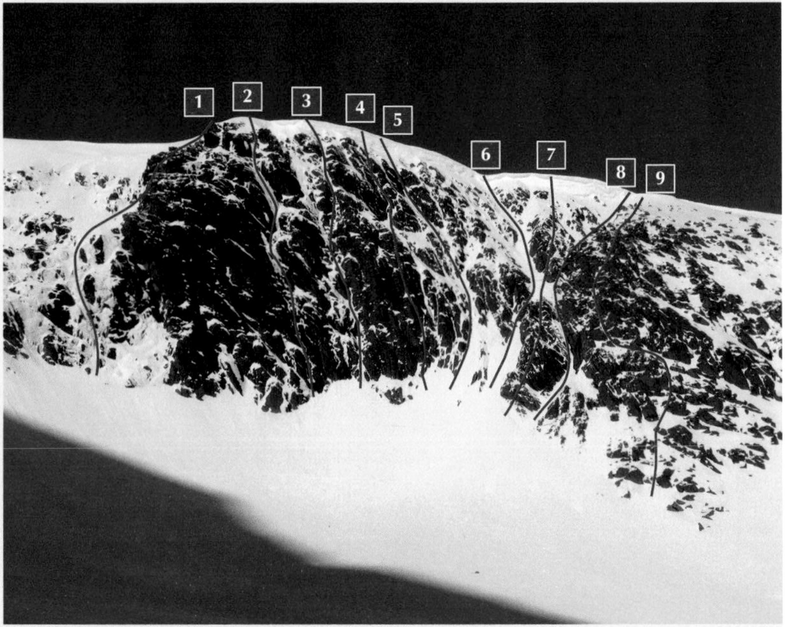

Pommie Granite **130m V,6**

G Ettle and J Lyall, 13 February 2007

Takes the rib on the right of the prominent corner of Koala, V,6. Start at the base of the rib and climb cracks on the right to gain the crest, then step right and follow wider cracks (30m). Continue up steps with wide cracks and blocks to the top of the rib (40m). Head up to a left-facing corner in the upper wall, move right into a groove and follow this, curving back left to rejoin the main corner (50m).

Boomerang **150m IV,4***

D Pyper and D Reid, 23 February 1962

Lies on the right side of the main cliff, right of The Great Rift. This route starts behind a small arete and curves up left. It can contain several ice pitches, but these may shorten and bank out at times.

Twilight Gully **150m II***

J Bower, BS Findlay, GS Strange and D Stuart, 11 April 1971

The bow-shaped gully left of Helicon Rib and right of the main mass. It may contain ice and have a huge cornice, but is the climb most likely to be continuous in marginal conditions. A better climb when in lean conditions.

Helicon Rib **130m III**

DW Duncan and AJD Smith, March 1964

The next main break right of The Great Rift is The Chimney Pot, a deep dark fault. The rib on its left is the route. Start at the foot of the well-defined rib and climb its crest for about 100m to a small col, where the difficulties end.

The Chimney Pot **140m II***

RH Sellars and KA Grassick, February 1959

The deep chimney is climbed direct. There is usually an ice pitch at the great chokestone. Above, the chimney widens to an amphitheatre, which may have a huge cornice.

Pisa **150m II/III**

DW Duncan and SP Hepburn, April 1967

The buttress forming the right side of The Chimney Pot. The route takes the line of least resistance. Start from the lowest rocks and work up, keeping close to the edge overlooking The Chimney Pot. Higher up, trend right to easier ground which leads, by way of a ridge, to the cornice.

Graeme Ettle on the first ascent of Pommie Granite (photo: John Lyall)

Coire Bhrochain

NN 954 998 *Altitude 1150m* *South facing*

This is the huge south-facing corrie lying directly below the summit of Braeriach. For convenience it is divided into three main sections by West Gully, the widest fault, and East Gully, which begins narrow and funnels out. This gives, from left to right, West, Central and East Buttresses.

Descent

The easiest descent back to the corrie floor is down the slope between Coire Bhrochain and Garbh Choire Dhaidh. The ridge on the east of the corrie leading back to the Lairig Ghru also gives a descent. Depending on the cornice, West Gully can also provide a way back down to the corrie floor.

Conditions

Again this corrie is remote and isolated, and can hold huge amounts of snow and have big cornices, although probably not as much as An Garbh Choire. The more easterly and southerly aspect make it better as an early season corrie before the sun can strip the buttresses.

West Buttress

This is the area between the left or southern end of the cliff and West Gully, the largest gully in the corrie. The main mass is slabby low down, but steepens and develops more features with height. On the right side of the main mass is the long, defined Great Couloir. Between that and West Gully are several more ridges and gullies. This buttress holds snow very well, but can have large cornices.

Pioneers' Recess Route — 200m III

GR Simpson and GS Strange, 20 April 1969

Gains, then climbs, the open chimney on the left. It passes between a square tower and detached buttress characterised by a hooked fang. Start at the lowest point of the left-hand rocks and climb up iced slabs and snow to gain the main fault. Once in the chimney, short steep pitches lead to steep snows, where the chimney widens. These lead to the cornice, which can be large; the usual exit is on the left.

Direct Route — 200m IV,5*

J Bower, GR Simpson and GS Strange, 13 April 1969

Takes the line of the most obvious grooves on the main rock mass to the right of centre. Start up the left-hand of the two ramps and climb up right to a short chimney. Continue up by a choice of lines towards the bottom of the right side of the

Coire Bhrochain – West Buttress

1 Pioneers' Recess Route III
2 Direct Route IV,5*
3 Vanishing Shelf III
4 The Great Couloir III**
5 Ebony Chimney VI,6***
6 Domed Ridge III
7 Campion Gully II
8 West Gully I

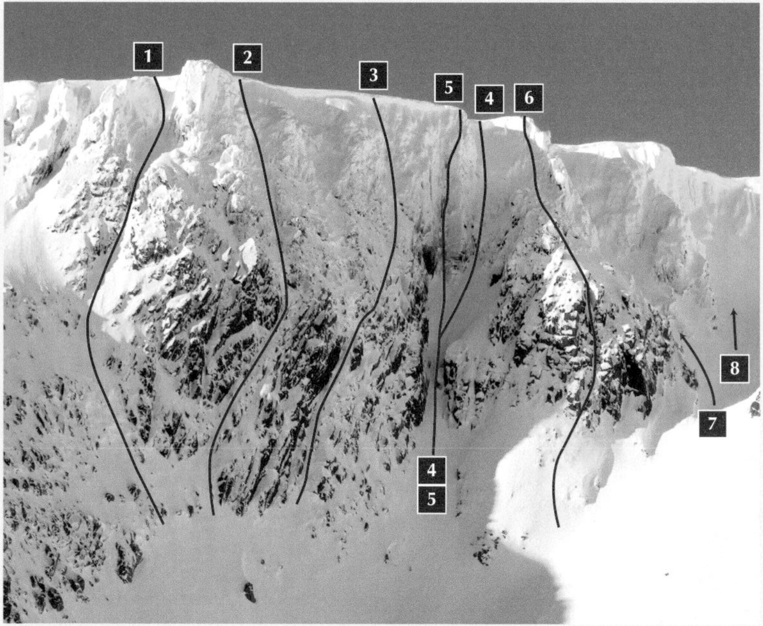

large square-topped tower at the top of the buttress. Finish by the right of the two chimneys and the rib on its right.

Vanishing Shelf **200m III**

RH Sellars and K Grassick, February 1959

The right-hand of the two ramp lines is followed to a platform overlooking The Great Couloir. Go to the end of the platform, go left on a ledge, then trend up and left to a scoop leading to the top and perhaps a huge cornice.

The Great Couloir **200m III****

JYL Hay and H Ross, 28 December 1957

The defined gully on the right of the main rocks. Climb the gully direct – the difficulty depends on the build-up on the chokestones, and the cornice can also be a problem.

Ebony Chimney **80m VI,6*****

A Nisbet and C McLeod, February 1982

A superb short route, steep and varied, following the deep chimney that forms the left branch of The Great Couloir. Climb the chimney to above the first chokestone, where a right traverse is taken. Above, a through route may be available which leads to big roofs. Go right along a ledge and climb a wall and corner to a rib. Go up the crest, then right, then up a steep groove overlooking The Great Couloir to the top.

Domed Ridge **200m III**

AG Mitchell and WPL Thomson, 9 April 1955

The broad ridge between the foot of West Gully and The Great Couloir. It is climbed direct. Start up easy slabs and grooves that lead to a tower which is climbed by a chimney (crux). Go over this and continue directly to the top.

Campion Gully **140m II**

KS Grassick and AG Nicol, 5 April 1954

Right of the upper section of Domed Ridge is a small buttress called Azalea Rib. Campion Gully lies between these two. Start at the foot of West Gully and climb the fault direct.

Azalea Rib **150m IV,5***

I Dillon and A Nisbet, December 1994

The rib that forms the upper wall of West Gully. Start just above Campion Gully and climb a snow trough, then a shelf on the right to a narrowing. Climb a short blocky corner to a crest on the left and follow this over a pinnacle to a steep upper wall, which is turned by a left traverse to a short chimney.

West Gully 150m I

The wide gully in the left corner of the gully. It is easy angled and provides the easiest way from the corrie floor to the summit plateau. Although the cornice can be continuous, it is usually smallest on the right.

Central Buttress

This lies at the back of the corrie below the summit of Braeriach and between West and East Gullies. It consists of several facets. In the centre, above mid-height, is the Black Pinnacle, whose base is easily reached by a line slanting in from the right. This is the Slab Terrace. Left of the Black Pinnacle are the Bhrochain Slabs; to its right is the Braeriach Pinnacle, with its top near plateau level. Braeriach Pinnacle is actually a buttress, and appears as a pinnacle only from the plateau.

Bhrochain Slabs 200m III

W Gault, D Bruce and A Milne, February 1960

Lies on the left of the Black Pinnacle. Start about 30m up and left of the lowest rocks. Climb corners and slabs for about three pitches to a platform. Here a chimney line running from West Gully to the col by the Black Pinnacle is reached. Follow the chimney to the col, then trend up and left to finish. Different lines are available and much can blank out in some years.

Braeriach Direct 250m IV,3

E Clark and A Nisbet, 30 January 1983

A direct line from the lowest rocks to the Black Pinnacle and the top. Start near the lowest rocks and climb an ice fall to reach the Slab Terrace. Continue up the slab corner on the left of the Black Pinnacle to the saddle behind it. Finish fairly direct.

Braeriach Pinnacle South Face 135m III

J Campbell and GR Simpson, 18 April 1970

An obvious line left of centre of the Braeriach Pinnacle. Climb a snowy rib to gain an icy chimney, then two steep diagonal ramps on the right. A gully finally leads to the top.

Braeriach Pinnacle Eastern Route 135m II

J Bower, J Buchanan and A Sproul, 16 February 1969

Follows the right edge of the Braeriach Pinnacle overlooking East Gully, then goes diagonally left at the top.

Coire Bhrochain – Central and East Buttress

1 Bhrochain Slabs III
2 Braeriach Direct IV,3
3 Braeriach Pinnacle South Face III
4 Braeriach Pinnacle Eastern Route II
5 East Gully I
6 Near East Buttress II
7 Tigris Chimney II
8 Pyramus I
9 Thisbe III*
10 Ninus III

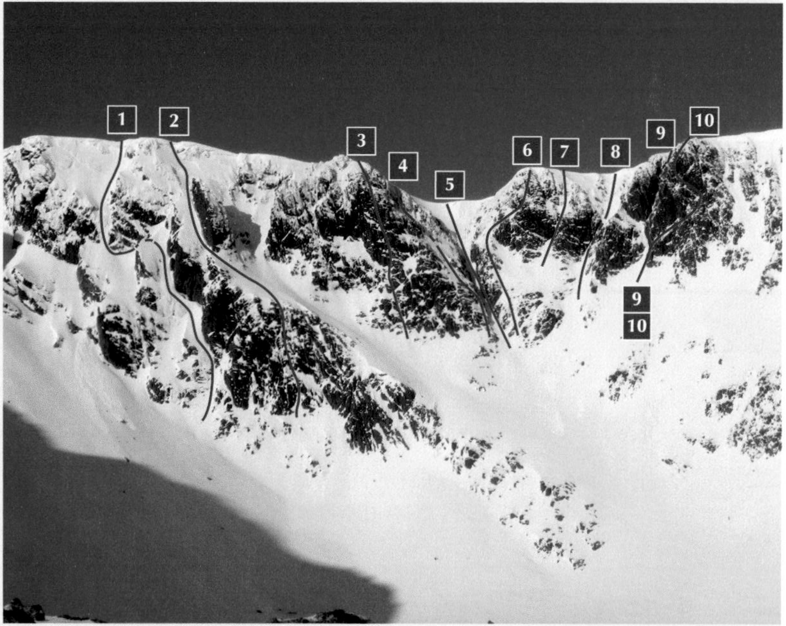

East Gully 135m I

J Drummond, T Gibson and AW Russell, 5 April 1901

The well-defined gully right of Central Buttress. It starts narrow, but widens out into a funnel in the upper half. It is climbed direct, and the cornice is usually turned on the right.

East Buttress

Stretching from East Gully to the right end of the cliff, this group is composed of a set of defined buttresses separated by gullies. These gullies, from left to right are, Tigris Chimney, Pyramus and Thisbe.

Near East Buttress 110m II

PCD Kale and CA MacIntyre, 3 February 1969

The buttress right of East Gully. The crest is followed with no special difficulty.

Tigris Chimney 100m II

PCD Kale and CA MacIntyre, 19 April 1969

This is the chimney between Near East Buttress and Babylon Rib, Grade II, a ridge in two parts. After the first pitch it opens out into a shallow scoop. If the chokestone is showing, it can be turned on the right.

Pyramus 110m I

WD Brooker and S McPherson, 12 April 1950

The next gully is characterised by a rib at its foot, giving two starts. It is straightforward, and its left branch gives a narrower start.

Thisbe 110m III*

GH Leslie and M Smith, 3 January 1955

One of the best gullies in the corrie – deep and with high walls. The gully is climbed direct and can have up to four pitches, although some can bank out. The last pitch can be turned on the right.

Ninus 150m III

BS Findlay and GS Strange, 12 April 1970

The rightmost buttress is also the largest and steepest. From the foot of Thisbe go up and right onto an obvious ramp. Continue right to a depression, which is followed to a large snow basin. Traverse left and climb a rib for two pitches to the top.

Coire an Lochain

NH 944 002 *Altitude 1100m* *North facing*

This is the right-hand of the north-facing corries of Braeriach and the only one that gives any climbing, although this is only usually available early in the season before snow completely banks it out.

Approach

The usual approach is from the north down Gleann Einich, where a mountain bike can be useful.

Descent

Easy descent to the north, but the ridge between Coire an Lochain and Coire Ruadh is the more interesting.

Conditions

Cold weather early in the year. The climb can often be seen clearly from Strathspey.

The Icefall **150m II***

A Nisbet and D McCutcheon, 4 December 1984

The ice fall at the back of the corrie can give continuous ice for its whole length, but banks out later on. Although not too steep, it can be sustained.

Following tracks into the crag

The Corries of Beinn a'Bhuird

This massive mountain, with its huge high-level plateau, holds four corries that give winter climbing. However, Coire nan Clach is more broken and does not require detailed route descriptions. The other three corries – **Coire na Ciche**, **Coire an Dubh Lochain** and the **Garbh Choire** – provide fine varied routes of all grades, while those in the Garbh Choire rank with any in the Cairngorms in one of the more remote settings to be found in this area.

All the corries are accessible from Deeside and are usually approached from the south. The Garbh Choire, however, is some considerable distance away and can also be approached from the north, but this is a long approach.

Approaches

From Deeside go on the A93 to the Invercauld Bridge, about 4km east of Braemar. Take the track about 100m east of the gates to Invercauld House (signposted Keiloch) to the car park on the right. Follow the road to just before a farm, take a signposted track on the right, and descend to gain the original road past the farm. Take the second road on the right, signposted Glen Slugain, and follow it through the forest and a gate into the glen. Continue on this track past Slugain Lodge, a ruin, where it becomes a path, then swing north and continue up upper Glen Quoich. It is possible to cycle most of this way.

- For **Coire na Ciche** leave this path when opposite the corrie and head uphill into it.
- For **Coire an Dubh Lochain** (and **Coire nan Clach**) continue up the path until near the boulder of Clach a'Cleirich, then head west into the corrie.
- For **Garbh Choire** continue past Clach a'Cleirich (NO 114 992) and go to the Sneck, the obvious col between Ben Avon and Beinn a'Bhuird, and descend and contour left into the corrie.

From the north, the Garbh Choire can be reached by going into the valley of the River Avon from Tomintoul and following it downstream to Inchrory (NJ 179 080). Continue from there to a small tin bothy (NJ 129 069), where there is a wire bridge over the River Avon and a track leads part-way into the corrie. For this approach the bothy at Faindouran Lodge (NJ 082 062) can be used as a fairly convenient base. Cycling the first part is more or less essential for this approach.

Descents

- For **Coire na Ciche** either descend the ridge running east from A'Chioch or the easy shoulder running south-east.
- For **Coire an Dubh Lochain** the same descent or the Main Rake leads back to the corrie floor.
- For **Garbh Choire** either follow the cliff edge round to the Sneck for continuing south or the broad shoulder over Stob an t-Sluichd for northerly descents.

Conditions

The corries of Beinn a'Bhuird are high and backed with an extensive snow-collecting plateau. The mountain itself is situated to the east of the main Cairngorms plateau and often experiences similar conditions to Lochnagar. The buttresses come into condition fairly readily, but the gullies and those climbs dependent on ice tend to be better in the latter part of the season. Another important consideration here is the walking conditions, as with long approaches, particularly to the Garbh Choire, any deep or difficult snow or bad weather can make remote climbing extremely serious.

Coire na Ciche

NO 098 985 Altitude 1000m East facing

A pleasant bowl-shaped corrie lying below the South Top of Beinn a'Bhuird. Because of its relative accessibility, this is probably the most popular corrie whose climbs are relatively short but technical. The majority of the climbing lies on the south wall. On the extreme left is a slabby rib which defines that end of the cliff. Some distance to its right is the huge slab taken by The Carpet. Moving right from this is the more broken Slugain Buttress, with its triangular bottom, then Twisting Gully and then the distinctive Hourglass Buttress. Right of Hourglass Buttress are three chimney faults, and in the corner of the corrie lies South Corner Gully, with the steep Grey Tower high on its left. The back wall of the corrie, right of South Corner Gully, consists of Slab Buttress, which may disappear under snow.

Neptune's Groove — 100m IV,6

A Nisbet and GS Strange, February 1982

To the right of the slabby rib on the extreme left of the cliff is an obvious 20m V-chimney with an overhung top. Climb the chimney and move out left to gain a line of ice (or grass) in the slab. Climb this, then a corner, then go left to finish up a large corner.

The Carpet — 110m VI,5*

J Bower and G Boyd, 19 March 1970

A serious route up the huge slab right of the cliff edge. The Great Slab faces south-east and catches the sun, so it thaws readily. Start below and right of a large rock alcove in a vertical wall. Climb a depression up and right to below The Great Slab. Go up this on thin ice to shelves, which go up and right to below an overhanging corner. Climb this (combined tactics may be required),

Beinn a'Bhuird – Coire na Ciche

1 Neptune's Groove IV,6
2 The Carpet VI,5*
3 Slugain Buttress III*
4 Twisting Gully II**
5 Hourglass Buttress V,6*
6 Jason's Chimney V,6**

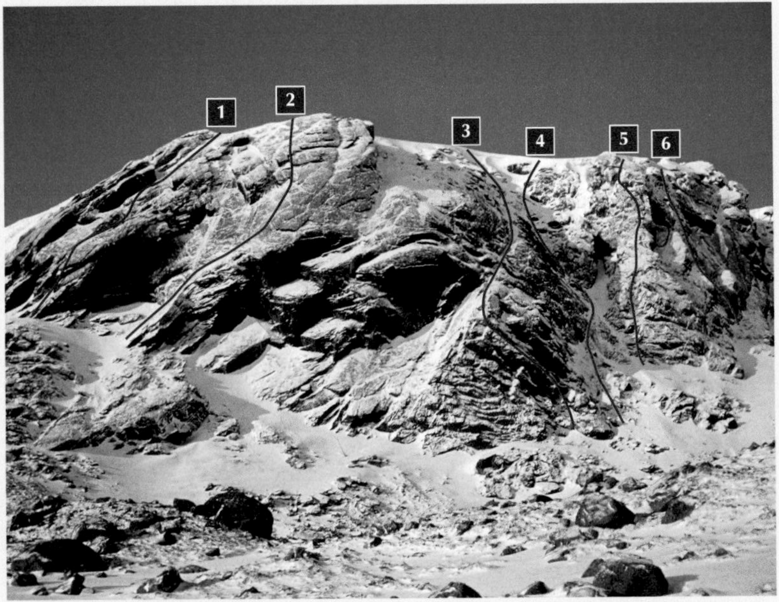

(photo: Greg Strange)

then a short chimney, then make a right traverse to a rock crevasse. Finish more easily. Above The Great Slab an ice groove on the left may provide a more natural winter finish.

Slugain Buttress 130m III*

G Adams and D Macrae, 10 February 1957

The buttress left of Twisting Gully that has a slanting groove on its left. Start on the right of the buttress and climb a chimney, avoiding the steepest rocks. Traverse left to the edge of the buttress and follow the crest to a huge block. Go up its right side, then by a diagonal chimney to easier ground.

The slanting groove itself can be good at the same grade, especially if icy.

Twisting Gully 130m II**

K Milne, J Davidson and J Reid, 28 February 1948

The best of the easier climbs lying between Slugain Buttress and the much steeper and defined Hourglass Buttress. It has a short dead-end right branch. The gully is followed throughout, the lower section being steepest, and it may contain ice, although it can bank out late in the season.

Hourglass Buttress 120m V,6*

J Bower and G Boyd, 29 March 1970

A steep climb that starts from the foot of Twisting Gully and follows a long chimney to the neck (50m). From there climb up to a big block below a steep wall (15m). Go up this wall on flakes, then go right to gain and climb a deep crack to a ledge overlooking Sickle. Take a thin crack leading left to a large platform (35m). Climb the wall above by a crack slanting left, then go left to a block. Continue left to finish up a short chimney (20m).

Sickle 110m IV,5*

A Thom and R Wiseman, March 1959

On the right side of Hourglass Buttress are three chimneys. Sickle is the leftmost and bounds the right side of Hourglass Buttress. It gives a sustained climb, which initially follows shallow chimneys and grooves and finishes by a series of chimneys.

Jason's Chimney 100m V,6**

M Freeman and ND Keir, 31 March 1974

The central of the three chimneys, which is sustained and can be icy in late season. Start just right of Sickle and climb a shallow groove into a deep chimney. Go up this and turn an overhanging block on its right, above which the angle eases. Finish below a chokestone.

Little Tower Gully **60m II**

FR Malcolm and A Thom, 17 January 1954

The narrow gully that cuts the left wall of South Corner Gully. It is climbed direct and can have a difficult capping cornice.

South Corner Gully **120m I**

The gully on the right of the main cliff and left of Slab Buttress can also be used as a descent.

Coire an Dubh Lochain

NO 090 993 *Altitude 950m* *North-east facing*

A pleasant corrie that houses two main buttresses, to the left of which is an area of more broken ground that gives some fairly obvious easier climbs. The main buttresses are the steep Bloodhound Buttress on the left and the larger slabby Glaucous Buttress on the right. They are separated by the Main Rake. The corrie may hold large accumulations of snow, which can blank out some features, particularly the lower slabs of Glaucous Buttress. On the right side of these slabs is a smooth clean slab, the Waterslide, which may be ice but can bank out.

Tantalus Gully **80m III***

GC Grieg, M Smith and K Winram, 15 March 1953

A good climb that cuts deeply into the right side of Bloodhound Buttress; it can reached by descending from the plateau. Start midway up the Main Rake. The gully is climbed direct and usually has a good long ice pitch at the beginning. There may be an awkward cornice.

Main Rake **180m I***

H Alexander, AA Longden and AM Watt, April 1911

The large diagonal ramp separating the main buttresses. It is straightforward, and the cornice usually presents no difficulties. It can be used as a descent.

Polypody Groove **200m III**

D Duncan and GR Simpson, January 1969

This route, which lies on Glaucous Buttress, gives a very variable climb, as much of the lower section can disappear under snow. Start near the left of the lower slabs and follow the main right-facing groove to the terrace at about mid-height. Early in the season this may well be iced and deserve IV,3. Above, go slightly rightwards to gain the deepest and most obvious chimney, which is climbed to the top.

Faux-pas — 200m III

J Bower, B Clarke and A Morgan, 20 January 1972

This is the right-facing corner/gully directly above the Waterslide. Start up the Waterslide, either snow or ice, to gain the gully in the upper rocks. The first pitch of the gully is the hardest.

Garbh Choire

NJ 107 015 — Altitude 950m — North to north-west facing

This is the magnificent and remote corrie lying at the head of the Slochd Mor. Routes here are serious because of their isolation, but it is worth the effort to climb in such a superb area. The main area of cliff is defined by its two finest features at either end. Nearest the Sneck, the col between Ben Avon and Beinne a'Bhuird is Squareface, and further north the unmistakable Mitre Ridge stands proud. Between the two is an area of lesser buttresses and gullies, down which the Allt an t-Sluichd pours. The easiest descent is probably to follow the cliff edge back to the Sneck.

Squareface takes its name from the superb west face that overlooks the amphitheatre known as the High Bay. On the north face, near its left end, is a large basin known as the Crucible, which can be the origin of much ice. The cornices in this area can be huge. Mitre Ridge itself is one of the finest rock features in the Cairngorms. It has a vertical, featured West Face and a slabbier, less steep but more vegetated East Face, and is topped by three towers. All the faces contain notable climbs.

Elixir — 230m III

S Richardson, 23 March 2003

The leftmost route, which sometimes has a huge cornice that forces a left traverse to avoid it. Start 50m left of the ice gully of Gold Coast and follow an open gully to an amphitheatre topped with a rock wall. Go up and left to a hidden right-slanting gully that leads to the upper snow slopes and cornice.

Alchemist's Route — 230m III

RJ Archbold and DM Nichols, 2 March 1980

Lies near the left end of the north face of Squareface, starting at an obvious ice gully. Slant up left from the foot of the ice gully to gain a snow slope. Go up this until a branch leads right and up to an obvious chimney. Climb a ramp on the left wall, then go to the top of the chimney. Follow a shallow gully above to steep snow slopes. The cornice can be huge, and it may be necessary to go right into the Crucible and exit right.

Beinn a'Bhaird – Garbh Choire (overview)

1 Alchemist's Route III
2 Gold Coast Direct V,5***
3 Crucible Route VI,5**
4 Back Bay Gully II
5 Approach Gully II*
6 Consolation Gully II
7 Nomad's Gully II
8 Comola's Ridge II*
9 The Flume II**
9A The Flume Left Hand IV,4*
9B The Flume Direct IV,4**
10 South-East Gully V,4*
11 North-West Gully III*

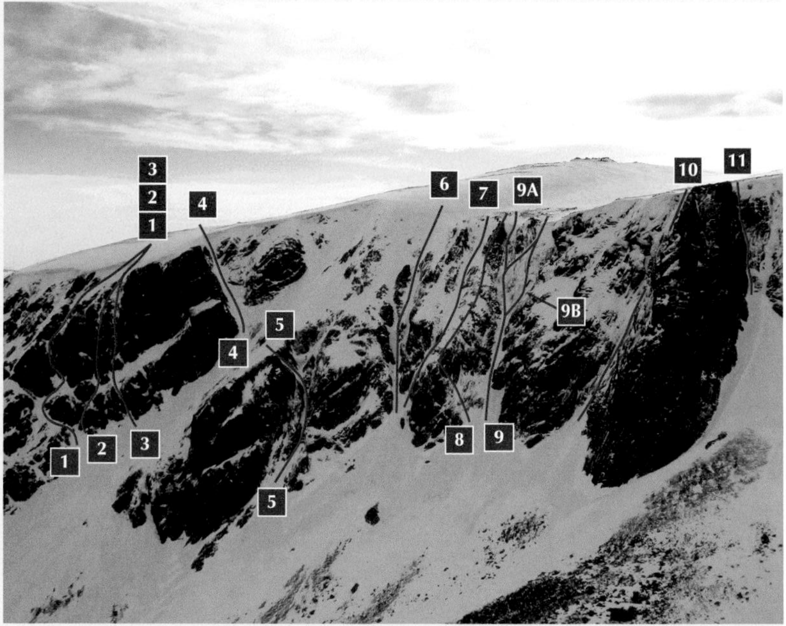

Gold Coast Direct — 180m V,5***

A Nisbet and C McLeod, 11 February 1982; as described, B Davison and A Nisbet, 10 March 1997

A fine route which climbs the left-hand ice fall. Climb a short ice gully below the Crucible, then go up to the ice fall. Climb this direct in two pitches, with a big block belay on the right below the steepest section. Climb into the Crucible and find a way out, most likely to the right. Needs a good build-up of ice.

Crucible Route — 210m VI,5**

RJ Archbold and D Dinwoodie, 7 April 1978

A route based on the right-hand ice fall, but which does not need as much ice build-up as the previous climb. Start up the ice gully of the Gold Coast to the ice falls. Go slightly left, then back right across it on a ramp. Go back up onto the ice and gain a pedestal on the rock separating the two ice falls. Traverse left on the left ice fall. Climb this into the basin and exit right.

Crucible Route Direct — 180m VI,5**

B Davison and A Nisbet, 10 March 1997

A direct version, but with fat ice. Climb two consecutive iced grooves up slabby ground right of Gold Coast that lead to the right-hand Crucible ice fall, which is climbed direct.

Back Bay Gully — 100m II

TW Patey, GB Leslie, AG Nicol and JM Taylor, 31 March 1954

This starts from the High Bay, the amphitheatre below the west face of Squareface, where an easy rake goes rightwards to the plateau. The gully, which is initially narrow, runs below the impressive west face of Squareface. At the top both forks are the same grade, although the left is generally steeper, but with a smaller cornice.

Approach Gully — 100m II*

TW Patey, GB Leslie, AG Nicol and JM Taylor, 31 March 1954

The left-hand gully leading into the High Bay can be combined with Back Bay Gully.

Consolation Gully — 180m II

TW Patey, RH Sellars and R Harper, 15 April 1956

This is the first full-length gully right of the easy rake from High Bay. It starts well defined, then opens out above. The gully is climbed direct and may contain one ice pitch.

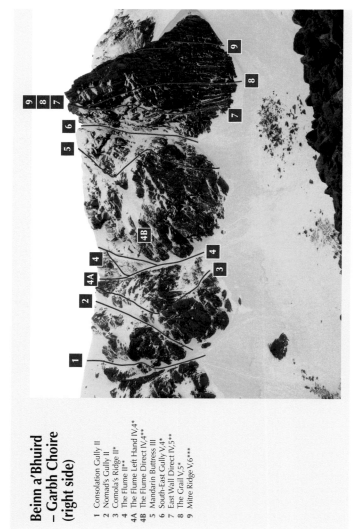

Beinn a'Bhuird – Garbh Choire (right side)

1 Consolation Gully II
2 Nomad's Gully II
3 Comola's Ridge II*
4 The Flume II**
4A The Flume Left Hand IV,4*
4B The Flume Direct IV,4**
5 Mandarin Buttress III
6 South-East Gully V,4*
7 East Wall Direct IV,5**
8 The Grail V,5*
9 Mitre Ridge V,6***

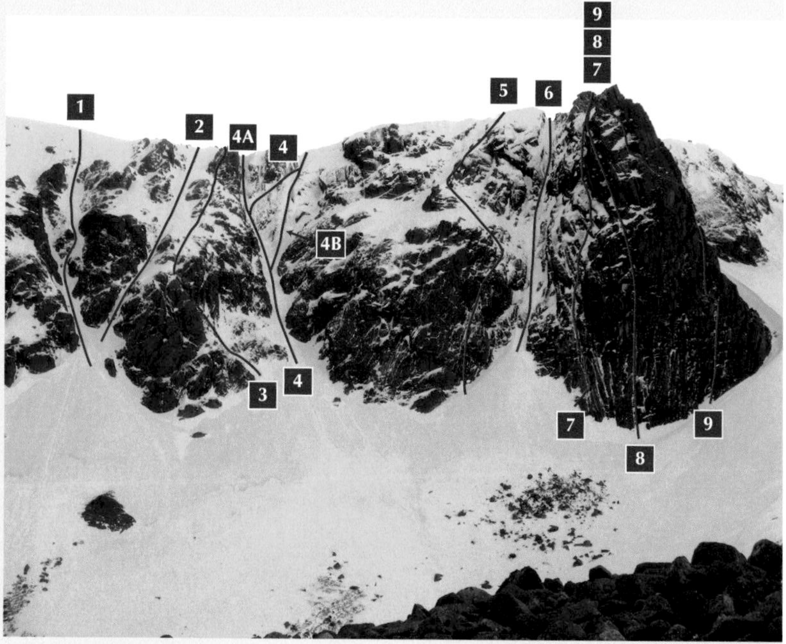

Nomad's Gully 200m II

M Mowatt and A Corbett, 13 March 1966

Start from the foot of Consolation Gully and climb the right-slanting gully, which leads to a shallower fault.

Comala's Ridge 200m II*

GR Simpson and G Boyd, 27 March 1971

The rib between Nomad's Gully and The Flume. Start at the foot of The Flume and climb grooves left to the crest. Climb this to the final tower, which is the crux, but can be avoided by taking Nomad's Gully.

The Flume Left Hand 200m IV,4*

W Moir, 31 January 1987

Left of The Flume Direct is an ice fall draining from a bowl below the plateau, which is the line of the route.

The Flume 200m II**

JM Taylor and GB Leslie, 31 March 1954

A good climb, which is in fact the bed of a stream, the Allt an t-Sluichd. It lies at about the centre of the cliffs. It is straightforward until near the top, where it may be awkward working between the ice pitches formed by the waterfall.

The Flume Direct 200m IV,4**

DF Lang and N Quinn, 15 December 1974

Climbed direct, the route is very worthwhile. The cornice may be huge, but is usually avoidable on the left.

Mandarin Buttress 200m III

WA Christie and WB Gault, March 1959

This is the large buttress which lies between The Flume and South-East Gully of Mitre Ridge. Start at the foot of South-East Gully and gain a fault on the right of the buttress. When it ends, go back left to a terrace at mid-height. Above, follow the defined upper ridge to the plateau.

South-East Gully 200m V,4*

RH Sellars and G Annand, February 1959

The shallow gully bordering the left side of Mitre Ridge gives a fine winter route, although protection is poor when the snow is unconsolidated. It climbs a series of ice pitches, the crux being the narrows about mid-height.

Robbie Miller on the final easy pitch of Cumming-Crofton route, with the steep Mitre Ridge West Wall behind (photo: Henning Wackerage)

East Wall Direct **220m IV,5****

ND Keir, J Mothersele and RA Smith, 23 February 1974

A fine sustained climb. Start about 20m left of the lowest point of the slabs. Climb up for 30m, then traverse left into a chimney system that leads to about mid-height. Then follow a series of ramps below a vertical wall to gain an ice couloir. Climb this, and at its top overhangs exit left to finish up the final tower from the col.

The Grail **250m V,5***

A Nisbet and A Clifford, 15 February 1984

A direct line up the middle of the East Wall, starting just left of the lowest rocks. Go up the vegetated fault to reach a terrace after three pitches. Climb up to the steep wall and go left to gain a ramp overlooking the ice couloir of East Wall Direct. Climb the ramp for two pitches (crux) to reach the col between the First and Second Towers.

Mitre Ridge **220m V,6*****

WD Brooker and TW Patey, 2 April 1953

A classic winter climb up the crest of the ridge and then via the towers to the plateau. Start on the right of the East Face and climb the largest groove, if there is ice. Alternatively, climb a weakness at the right corner of the ridge. Above the groove continue by a shelf running round to the West Face. Here, a deep chimney followed by a shallow gully leads to a shoulder on the ridge. Above is a short wall; traverse right and climb the wall (crux). A platform on the left is then gained by going left across a slab and up a splintered chimney. Climb the wall above and go to the col between the First and Second Towers. Turn the latter on the left and finish over an impressive arete.

Beinn a'Bhuird – Garbh Choire Mitre Ridge West Wall

1 The Grail V,5*
2 Mitre Ridge V,6***
3 Cumming-Crofton Route VI,6***
4 Commando Route IV,5*
5 North-West Gully III*

Starting up Cumming-Crofton route (photo: Henning Wackerage)

Cumming-Crofton Route — 160m VI,6***

R Renshaw and GS Strange, 26 February 1977

A superb route up the left corner that defines the cuneiform buttress on the West Face. Start below this right-slanting fault, which is parallel to the ridge crest. Climb a prominent chimney, passing a flake on its right, to a cleft at its top. Traverse right for 10m via a groove to a vertical wall, then return left by a traverse across a wall and over a bulge into the main corner. Climb this to a platform. Climb a crack in its left wall, then traverse right and go up a sloping ledge to a short wall. A gully then leads to the ridge between the First and Second Towers, the latter being turned on the left to gain the final arete.

Commando Route — 140m IV,5*

PF McDonald and IG Rowe, 9 March 1969

This climb takes the corner on the right of the cuneiform buttress on the West Face. Start up a small gully right of the main fault, then make a difficult traverse left (tension) to gain the foot of the main corner. This fault is then climbed, and the right fork, which leads to the col on the summit ridge, followed.

North-West Gully — 150m III*

RH Sellars and G Adams, 16 December 1956

The gully in the corner between the West Face and the back wall, North-West Buttress. It gives a good climb, which may have a very fine ice pitch. If the ice has not formed, then the climb will be much harder.

North-West Couloir — 120m III

M Rennie and D Duncan, February 1967

This is the shallow gully in the slabby buttress starting about 10m right of North-West Gully. It can be Grade II if the ice pitch at the start is buried.

COIRE SPUTAN DEARG

NO 000 988 *Altitude 1100m* *South-east facing*

This corrie lies high on Ben Macdui, looking southwards down Glen Luibeg. It is an open bowl with a rim of defined buttresses and several large, easy angled gullies. The routes tend to be quite short but very enjoyable, and the descents back into the corrie floor generally easy. There is not a wealth of hard climbing here, but a good range of fine easier routes. Although a more light-hearted place to climb than many of the Cairn Gorm cliffs, it is still a long walk in, especially in poor conditions.

Approaches

From the south

From Braemar go to the Linn of Dee and continue on the north of the river to a car park, where a path leads to the track to Derry Lodge, as for Creagan a'Choire Etchachan. Follow the Lairig Ghru path for about 3km until a lesser path cuts off before the Luibeg burn. This can be followed into the corrie.

From the Hutchison Memorial Hut

Approach the hut as for Creagan a'Choire Etchachan then go up the slope by the stream behind the hut. This leads south-west over the col north of Derry Cairngorm and into the corrie.

From the north

This is a long approach that goes over Ben Macdui to the corrie rim, then goes down either by descent gully or by the col at the north-east corner.

Descents

There are three main descent gullies which lead back to the corrie floor. These are Red Gully, between Pinnacle Buttress and Crystal Ridge; Glissade Gully, very easy angled, in the centre of the cliff and right of Grey Man's Crag (the largest buttress); and the Main Spout, on the extreme right of the cliff, but left of Terminal Buttress. The last is the easiest to locate and descend.

Conditions

The base of these cliffs lies at over 1100m above sea level. Because of its situation snow accumulations can be large, banking out many lower and slabbier features. However, the southerly aspect also means that the buttresses can loose their cover rapidly in thawing or sunny weather, especially later in the season. Conditions here and at nearby Creagan a'Choire Etchachan can be very different. However, some buttress routes come into condition quickly with cold weather and fresh snow.

Grey Man's Crag Area

This is the largest and best defined of the buttresses. On its left is Slab Chimney, above which is a very steep wall. The front face is cut by a series of grooves, and the right side is defined by Anchor Gully, so named for the shape of the spring snow at its foot.

Pinnacle Buttress 110m II**

WD Brooker and JW Morgan, 5 January 1950

The leftmost buttress provides an enjoyable route. Start at its foot and climb into and up a long groove left of the buttress crest. This may contain ice. Above, easier ground leads to the top.

Red Gully — 120m I

A straightforward gully between Pinnacle Buttress and Crystal Ridge can be used as a descent.

Crystal Ridge — 90m IV,4*

WD Brooker and M Smith, 5 January 1949

The next buttress on the right and separated from Pinnacle Buttress by Red Gully. The main feature is a large slab on the right, whose left edge forms a very narrow crest. Start at the buttress foot, climb to the narrow crest and follow it to its top. Above, climb an arete to a shelf and another pitch on the right to easier ground.

Slab Chimney — 120m II/III**

A Parker and J Young, 17 March 1949

The best gully in the corrie. It is Y-shaped, and the left branch, running up the right side of Crystal Ridge, is Grade I. The right branch, the route, cuts into the side of Grey Man's Crag. The gully is climbed direct, the difficulties depending on the build-up on the two chokestone pitches.

Pilgrim's Groove — 120m V,7*

S Kennedy, A Nisbet, E Clark and N Morrison, 22 February 1981

A natural winter line that climbs the groove and chimney line on the left side of the crag. Start just left of centre of the buttress and climb the groove, turning the overhang on its left wall. Continue by steep rock into the grassy depression. If the ice is sufficient follow the chimney line to the top. Alternatively, use the variation finish, which is the groove and chimney line on the left. Tension may be needed at the top overhang to regain the ordinary route.

Hanging Dyke — 120m V,5

J Bower and D Lang, 2 January 1971

Follows a geological dyke in the crest of the buttress. Start right of the lowest rocks and follow the dyke to where it steepens. Here it forms a rib left of a groove. Climb the rib for 20m (crux) until it returns to a chimney and finish up this.

Ardath Chimney — 120m III*

JYL Hay, 2 April 1955

This lies on the right flank of Grey Man's Crag. Start near Anchor Gully and climb the chimney, which is steep and defined for the first 45m. Above, the upper depression contains a short iced slab, which can be difficult. Usually best early in the season and when there is ice in the chimney.

Coire Sputan Dearg – Grey Man's Crag Area

1 Pinnacle Buttress II**
2 Crystal Ridge IV,4*
3 Slab Chimney II/III**
4 Pilgrim's Groove V,7*
4A Variation finish
5 Hanging Dyke V,5
6 Ardath Chimney III*
7 Anchor Gully I
8 Anchor Route III

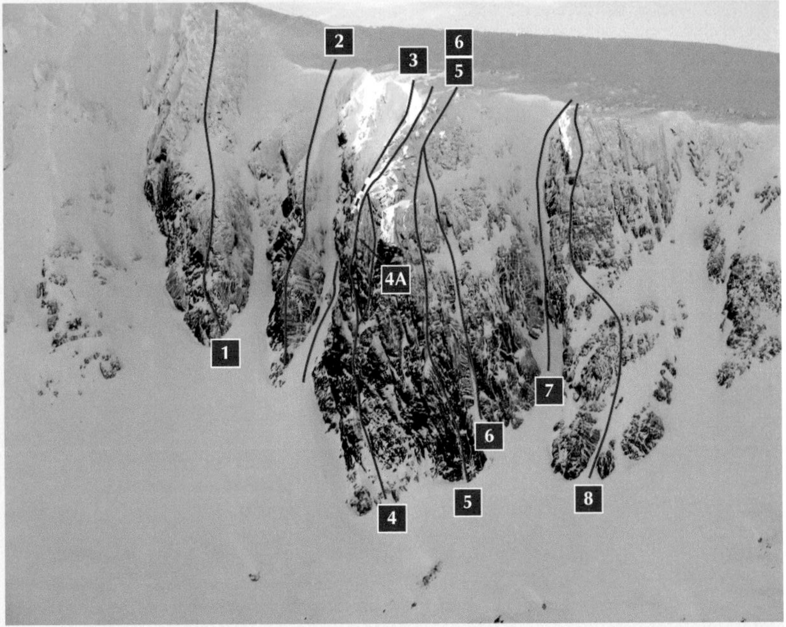

Anchor Gully **120m I**

The gully on the right of Grey Man's Crag. There may be a pitch at the narrows of the gully. Above it is easy, and the cornice is usually turned on the right.

Anchor Route **120m III**

G Adams and RWP Barclay, 25 December 1955

Lies on the two-tiered buttress right of Anchor Gully. Climb the lowest tier by the easiest line to a terrace below the upper tier (this may bank out). Follow the left edge overlooking Anchor Gully to a steepening, which is avoided by a short steep corner on the gully wall. An overhang high up is turned on the right, and above the buttress splits into two. The left-hand ridge is climbed, or both turned on the right.

Anchor Route Direct **120m III,4***

C Cartwright and S Richardson, 14 December 1997

A good direct route up the front face of the buttress. Start at the foot of the buttress crest, just right of Anchor Gully. Climb on the left side of the crest for 60m to a terrace below the centre of the upper tier. This is directly in line with the groove between the 'twin aretes' at the top of the buttress. Continue up the stepped shallow corner to the foot of the twin aretes (30m). Climb the groove between the aretes to the top (30m).

Glissade Gully

Lying near the centre of the cliff, this is a broad easy gully. The cornice is usually avoidable on the left.

Snake Ridge Area

This lies between Glissade and Narrow Gullies and consists of twin ridges, Snake Ridge being the right-hand and longer of the two.

Janus Chimney **45m III,4***

W Moir and C Whittit, 1 November 1996

The obvious chimney that splits the two ribs on left side of Snake Ridge, right of Glissade Gully.

Snake Gully **130m II***

J McArtney, T Mackie and BT Lawrie, 2 March 1963

A good route up the gully separating the two long ridges. Start up steep snow and curve left up an ice pitch. Climb this to easier ground. A short ridge and ice groove then lead to where the gully follows the right side of the upper buttress.

Coire Sputan Dearg – Glissade Gully to Terminal Buttress

1 Glissade Gully
2 Snake Gully II*
3 Narrow Gully I
4 Cherub's Buttress III
5 Flying Ridge II
6 Left-hand Icefall IV,4
7 Right-hand Icefall II/IV*
8 Flake Buttress III**
9 The Web IV,4
10 Main Spout
11 Terminal Buttress IV,5

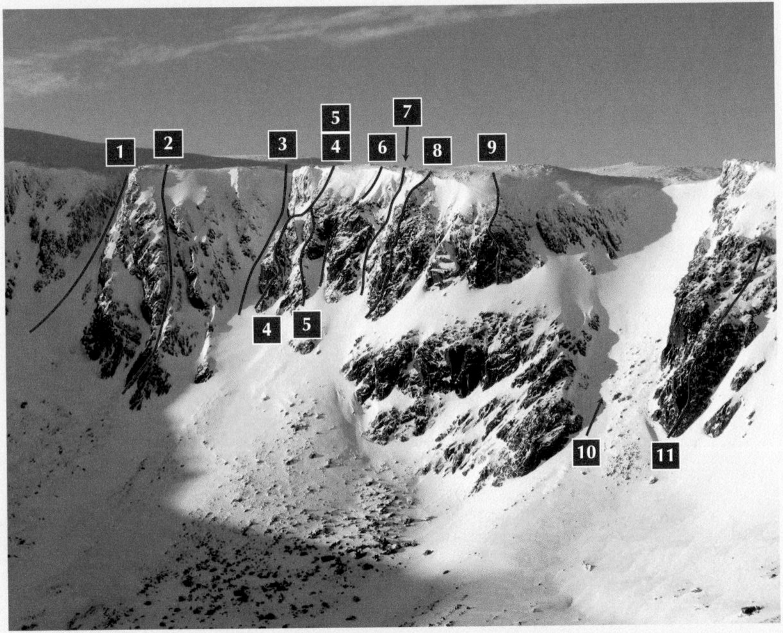

The Ladders **120m II***

GR Simpson and K Menmuir, 21 February 1971

The slim gully on the immediate right of Snake Ridge.

Narrow Gully **130m I**

A well-defined but straightforward snow climb that lies right of Snake Gully and left of a trio of buttresses.

The Central Buttresses

Right of Narrow Gully is a set of three buttresses – Cherub's Buttress, the more spectacular Black Tower, and Flake Buttress. They are separated by wet slabby depressions, which give the Left- and Right-hand Icefalls.

Cherub's Buttress **130m III**

GS Strange and D Stuart, 21 November 1970

The buttress right of Narrow Gully consists of two ridges leading into an upper amphitheatre. Start at the foot of the left ridge by Narrow Gully. Climb a flake crack and slab to below a nose. Go right into a depression and climb this to regain the crest. A chimney and arete lead into the upper amphitheatre. A level arete forms here, and above it a snow ramp going right leads to a corner on the crest and then easier ground.

Flying Ridge **130m II**

MDY Mowat and A Fyffe, 4 January 1966

The right-hand ridge is climbed into the upper amphitheatre, where the route continues as for Cherub's Buttress.

Left-hand Icefall **90m IV,4**

RJ Archbold and DM Nichols, 6 March 1974

The ice fall between Cherub's Buttress and the impressive Black Tower. The ice groove close against the Black Tower is the crux, and above easier snow leads to a col, then an arete leads to the top.

Right-hand Icefall **90m II/ IV***

A Fyffe, P Williams, M McArthur and I McLean, 3 January 1967

Between the Black Tower and Flake Buttress is a depression full of ice. Depending on the build-up and the line taken, the grade can vary considerably.

Flake Buttress 120m III**

WD Brooker and S McPherson, 10 April 1950

The right-hand buttress that lies just below the plateau rim. Start just right of the lowest rocks and follow a depression right onto the crest. Continue in the same line until a crack leads back left to a short corner. Go up left, then climb a chimney, and then follow ledges to the crest. Climb a crack behind a huge flake and go up to the gap. Climb the arete to the top.

The Web 50m IV,4

R Clothier and S Richardson, 14 November 1987

Lies on the slabby buttress right of Flake Buttress and takes a prominent corner right of a steep wall. Climb the corner, then a chimney, and above it go left to a small stance (20m). Traverse onto the crest, go round the corner, and finish up the slab or the deep crack on its left.

The Main Spout is the broad easy gully that lies on the left of Terminal Buttress, the last major rocks on the right. It is very straightforward and a convenient descent.

The Chute 50m VI,7*

J Preston and V Chelton, 29 February 2000

Lies on the steep left wall of Terminal Buttress below a shelf which slopes down into the gully. It takes the furthest left of the grooves which forms an open corner capped by a curious jammed block.

Climb the corner, going behind the jammed block, to belay on top (15m). Step left and follow an obvious left-trending crack to a shallow groove left of a prominent overhanging prow. Climb the groove to a good platform and scramble to the top (35m).

Terminal Buttress 70m IV,5

D Reid and D Pyper, 4 February 1963

Takes the prominent curved groove. Start in a short gully and climb it until a traverse round a rib gives access to a deep groove and a belay. Follow the groove until forced left round a corner onto a ledge. Go up to a broad shelf and climb the broken rib on the right to finish. The lower section can bank late in the season.

Creagan a'Choire Etchachan

NO 016 997 *Altitude 850m* *East facing*

An excellent winter cliff that compensates for its lack of length by the quality of its routes. In places the rock is wet and vegetated, and consequently many routes carry ice in quantity – in spite of the fact that the base of the cliff is only at about 850m. Although there is a long approach from any direction, the Hutchison Hut at its foot does provide accessible, if spartan, accommodation.

The cliff itself is split into several buttresses, but the two main features to aid route location are the wide gash of The Corridor, left of centre, and the narrow fault of Red Chimney, towards the right side. The Corridor bounds The Bastion, the left-hand buttress, and the Red Chimney marks the left edge of the distinctive Crimson Slabs. At the top of much of the cliff is a large snow apron, which may have a big cornice well back from the top rocks. This should be treated with caution, as it can present a severe avalanche risk.

Approaches

From the north

As for Carn Etchachan to Loch Avon, but continue round or across the loch to reach, then follow, the obvious path leading up to Loch Etchachan. Walk along the east shore of the loch, then follow the path by the stream that drains the loch, then contour to below the cliff.

From the south

Approaching from Braemar, drive to the Linn of Dee, then cross the river and go back towards Braemar a short way to the car park. From here go to Derry Lodge and about 200m further turn right, cross a bridge, and take the good path up Glen Derry. Take the left fork in the path at NO 035 990, which leads to the Hutchison Memorial Hut (NO 023 998) then onto the cliff. This fork in the path can be difficult to find in bad weather.

Descents

The cliff can be descended at either end, the northern one being the most obvious.

Conditions

The cliff basically faces east and gets the morning sun, so can it suffer later in the season, especially as it is not a particularly high crag. Early in the season is generally the best time for climbing here, although some of the deeper faults, such as The Corridor, can hold their ice until later in the year.

Forked Gully **120m I**

The gully defining the left edge of the cliff. It is straightforward, and the right fork is more interesting. Can be used as a descent.

Creagan a'Choire Etchachan (overview)

1 Quartzvein Edge III*
2 Bastion Wall IV,4
3 Original Route Direct IV,5
4 The Corridor IV,5**
5 Architrave IV,4*
6 Central Chimney III*
7 Square Cut Gully V,6
8 Winter Route II/III
9 Avalanche Gully VI,6*
10 Carmine Groove IV,5*
11 Red Chimney V,5**
12 Djibangi V,4***

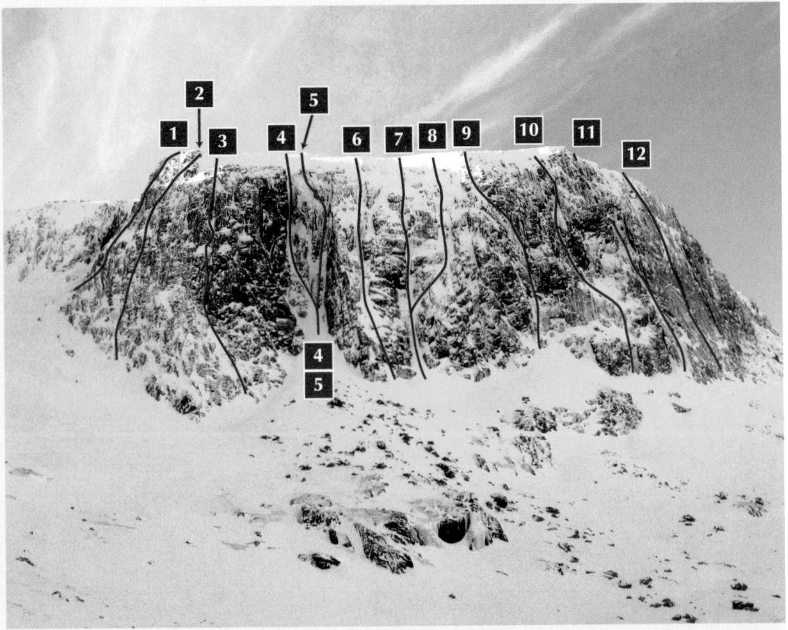

Quartzvein Edge **120m III***

JYL Hay, G Adams, and A Thom, 29 December 1956

Climbs the left edge of The Bastion, overlooking Forked Gully. Start at the foot of Forked Gully, past a huge block. Follow the buttress edge for a pitch, then slabs, which develop into a shelf that leads round a false tower. An open chimney leads to the top.

Bastion Wall **150m IV,4**

J McArtney and D Pyper, 23 February 1963

A good route, although open to much variation – in good conditions it may be Grade III. Start about 60m below and right of the buttress edge. Climb by a choice of line, heading towards long iced grooves and a 30m chimney up near the top of the buttress.

Original Route **140m IV,5**

J Bower and G Boyd, 23 December 1969

Weaves about the Direct route. Start left of the grassy depression leading to the first prominent V-groove. Climb a pitch up to below a steep wall, left of this groove. Avoid this on the left, then work right below a red slab to a large platform. Gain a ramp slanting left and climb this into the large V-groove of the Direct. Follow this to the top.

Original Route Direct **140m V,6****

J Ashbridge and S Richardson, 29 November 1992

Takes a line of grooves just right of the buttress crest. Start to the right of the lowest rocks and go left up an easy depression leading to a deep V-groove, which is best located from directly below. Climb this groove (crux) to a depression. Go out from the right of this, then come back left to gain another large V-groove that leads to easier ground

The Corridor **120m IV,5****

FR Malcolm and A Thom, 20 March 1954

Something of a classic, going up the left corner of the huge open gully. There are usually two main ice pitches – one into and one leaving a cave. The cornice can be large, but is usually easiest on the left.

Architrave **120m IV,4***

A Fyffe and J McArtney, 29 December 1969

A fine companion route to The Corridor, climbing the right corner of the gully. Usually more sustained, but less steep than that route. Climb an ice groove directly

Andy Inglis tackles steep ice on Square Cut Gully (photo: Neal Adams)

to below the chimney continuation. Either go straight up or left across a ramp to join The Corridor.

Central Chimney **120m III***

TW Patey, AO'F Will, G Adams and M Smith, 27 February 1955

Right of The Corridor is Juniper Buttress, which is split into two ribs by the line of this route. An obvious V-cleft gives access to the chimney, which is climbed direct over several ice pitches. Finish via a right-sloping ramp, then the upper snow apron. If a sloping line starting from the foot of Square Cut Gully is used to avoid the initial V-cleft, the route is Grade II.

Square Cut Gully **150m V,6**

M Forbes and M Low, March 1966

The obvious gully right of the twin ribs cut by Central Chimney. The gully is straightforward to the ice pillar at the big overhang. Climb the pillar (or icicle) and continue up the gully. The final slab may also be difficult.

Winter Route **150m II/III**

WD Brooker, JW Morgan and DA Sutherland, 2 January 1949

A good natural line. Start up Square Cut Gully and take the obvious line leading up rightwards. Mixed climbing and an ice pitch lead to the top. The easier grade is applicable in good conditions.

Avalanche Gully **120m VI,6***

D Hawthorn and D Dinwoodie, 17 February 1985

The steep narrow fault going through the lower overhangs has a large overhang at 45m. Climb the icicle direct – this may be slow to form. Above, go leftwards up an icy groove to follow further grooves to the upper part of the buttress and the finish.

Carmine Groove **150m IV,5***

RA Smith and G Stephens, November 1974

A good climb, taking as it main feature the obvious red groove on the upper cliff left of the big overhang. First gain the Meadows, the upper snow field below the overhangs. Start below a rock scar and climb rightwards to the Meadows. Follow the groove from its left corner, mostly on ice, to the top.

Flanking Ribs **150m IV,4**

J McArtney and A Fyffe, 6 January 1967

This first gains the Meadows, the large snow field under the overhangs, then finishes up the rib right of Red Chimney. Start left of Red Gully and climb the rib to

Creagan a'Choire Etchachan (right side)

1 Avalanche Gully VI,6*
2 Carmine Groove IV,5*
3 Flanking Ribs IV,4
4 Red Chimney V,5**
5 Djibangi V,4***
6 Scabbard VI,7**
7 Switchblade VI,7**

Night navigation – it's not uncommon to descend from the Cairngorms plateau in the dark

cross Red Chimney at its easier mid-section. Pull onto the right rib and follow this to the top. Can be an escape from Red Chimney.

Red Chimney 150m V,5**

IA Paterson and SP Hepburn, January 1967

An extremely fine ice climb. Start up twin corners right of the chimney and, higher up, gain the chimney by iced slabs. The chimney is then followed, with another difficult section above the amphitheatre crossed by Flanking Ribs, where a way up and left through ice bulges must be found to gain the final corner. Above this, the climbing eases to the top.

Djibangi **140m V,4*****

J McArtney and WJ Barclay, 31 January 1965

A superb ice climb when formed. It follows the leftmost corner running up the Crimson Slabs. Start directly below the corner and climb iced slabs into the corner itself. Continue up the corner to the top (the overlap may prove to be the crux). Go on up via grooves and iced slabs, trending left to reach straightforward snow that leads to the cornice.

Scabbard **105m VI,7****

C MacLean and A Nisbet, 10 January 1985

The right corner on the Crimson Slabs is Dagger, V,5, but it is slow to come into condition. Scabbard takes cracks in the right rib of this corner. Start in a right-facing corner below the rib. Climb this corner, hopefully on ice but with limited protection, then move left to a stance. Climb the sustained but well-protected cracks in the rib above to a huge spike at the top of the Dagger corner. Move right, descend a short way, and go right to an edge. Climb blocks and cracks to reach the broken ramp-like terrace. Finish up this.

Switchblade **160m VI,7****

J Lyall and A Nisbet, 2 February 1991

A very good technical route which takes the line of turfy cracks that trend right, right of Scabbard. Start up a vegetated line, slanting up left from the bay on the right, and belay just right of Scabbard (20m). Climb the right-facing corner that bounds the right side of Scabbard, then follow a wide crack to slabs. Make a thin traverse right into a turfy left-facing corner and follow it to a turfy bay (40m). Go over an overhang at the top-right corner, climb cracks, then go diagonally left to the terrace just below its top (45m). Climb a thin turfy crack left of the arete (35m). Easy ground leads to the top.

CAIRNGORMS SOUTH

The crux of Shadow Buttress A in the Central and Shadow Buttress Group (The Northern Sector, Lochnagar) (photo: Henning Wackerage)

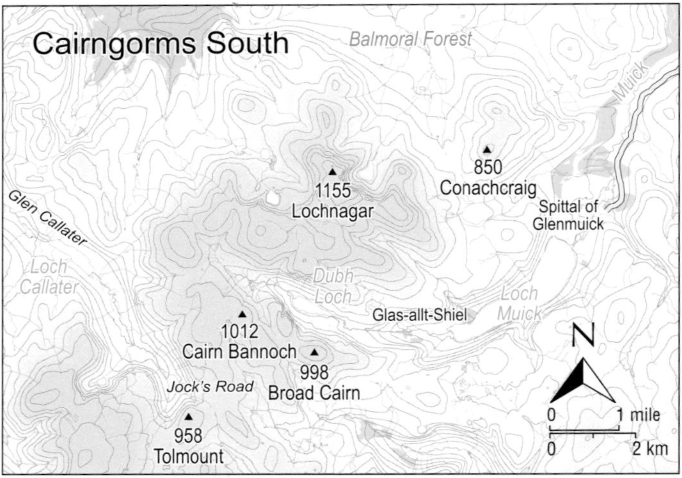

LOCHNAGAR

NO 244 861 *Altitude 1155m*

The North-East Corrie of Lochnagar is one of the finest in Scotland. The cliffs extend in an arc overlooking the loch from which the mountain takes its name, and the corrie consists of a series of well-defined and shapely buttresses separated by major gullies. Classic routes of all grades and types are found here, which combine quality, line, history and mountain scenery. It is one of Scotland's premier winter-climbing areas.

The main corrie is divided naturally into two sections, the **Northern Sector** being the most important, although the **Southern Sector** does provide climbing for those seeking more solitude or a shorter day. The Northern Sector has cliffs that are continuous for about 1km and reach up to 230m in height. These cliffs are generally considered to be four groups of buttresses separated by three important gullies. These are, from left to right – Douglas-Gibson Gully, which is a big, straight gully ascending between high walls; Raeburn's Gully, which slants upwards in the corner of the corrie and cannot be seen from some angles; and The Black Spout, which is an obvious, wide fault.

The huge bay of the Southern Sector contains a number of buttresses that, due to the quicker approach and shorter route lengths, are often a useful option for a short day. These routes can also be a good choice early in the season, as they require little build-up of ice and tend to come into condition readily.

Lochnagar (overview)

1 Central Buttress II*
2 Eagle Ridge VI,6***
3 Parallel Gully A III**
4 Parallel Gully B VI,5***
5 Raeburn's Gully II***
6 Pinnacle Gully 1 III
7 Black Spout I**
8 West Gully IV,4*
9 Gelder Gully II

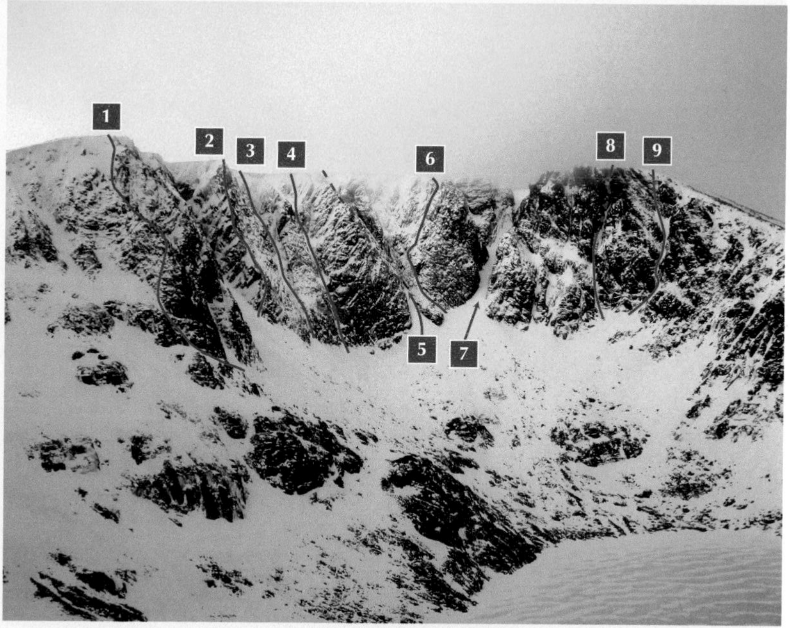

When approaching from the Meikle Pap col, the usually stopping and gearing-up point is the first aid box, which sits on a flat platform below the main snow slope, roughly below Central Buttress. (To reach the Southern Sector routes turn uphill before the first aid box on the normal approach.) In bad visibility, from here it may be necessary to use a compass to locate the bottom of the climbs. The bearings from here to some of the main features are as follows.

- Central Buttress 190°
- Shadow Buttress A 214°
- Parallel Gully A 258°
- Parallel Gully B 260°
- Raeburn's Gully 278°
- Black Spout 290°
- West Gully 314°

Approaches

From Ballater go up Glen Muick to the car park at the Spittal of Glen Muick. The last 5km of this road are across open moor and can be badly affected by drifting snow, and the car park can be crowded at peak periods. Walk through the woods past the visitor centre, then turn right and follow the unsurfaced road across the glen to reach a building by a junction. Take the path by the fence (signposted) and follow this through the woods to reach a track that leads up to the Muick/Gelder col. From this bulldozed track, branch off left on the well-marked and obvious track leading to the summit. Leave this beyond the Foxes' Well (NO 263 856) and go over the col between the Meikle Pap and the Cuidhe Crom, the main mountain, and traverse round to below the cliffs.

Descents

To return to Glen Muick it is usual to follow the cliff edge round and go down the tourist path. In bad weather this may not be straightforward, and map and compass work may be required. It is also possible to go down the Glas Allt to Loch Muick, which is longer but avoids the cornice danger of following the cliff edge. The shoulder above the West Buttress also provides a way down into Glen Gelder, or even back into the corrie. The descent back into the corrie is down the main branch of The Black Spout. The cornice is usually passable on the left, but care is needed on this way down.

Conditions

Because of the variety of routes, there is usually some good climbing to be had in any winter conditions. However, ice routes normally take longer to develop. Avalanche conditions unfortunately can build up much more rapidly, as huge amounts of snow can pour over the edge of the plateau from a variety of wind directions. Cornices can be huge, and spindrift avalanches are common. The decision as to which route to attempt should be made in the light of the conditions, which may be discovered only on close acquaintance. Beware of avalanches coming down main and side gullies that may affect approaches to neighbouring routes, particularly when traversing across from the first aid box.

THE SOUTHERN SECTOR

Perseverance Wall

NO 254 854 *Altitude 950m* *North facing*

This easy angled wall to the left of The Cathedral contains a number of ribs and grooves, which make fine winter routes.

Perseverance Rib **80m III**

C Cartwright and SM Richardson, 7 January 1996

The well-defined rib at the left end of the crag. Climb a shallow groove to the left of a small tower. Continue up the right side of the crest to the top.

Gale Force Groove **70m III***

P Mather and S Muir, 15 December 1999

Takes the slightly right-slanting groove that leads to the apex of the next rib to the right. Climb the groove to a square block roof and then step right to belay (30m). Continue up the groove over bulges and up the crest to the top (40m).

Lunar Eclipse **85m III***

P Mather, S Muir and H Watson, January 2001

The next rib to the right. Start at the base of a short deep gully to the right of a slab. Climb a leftward-leading ramp to the middle of the slab and continue up two short corners to belay on the right of a steep wall (35m). Traverse left below this wall until the upper gully can be accessed and continue to a good belay at a cracked block (40m). Continue up snow to the top.

The Gift **80m II***

SM Richardson, 18 November 2005

The obvious right-trending gully gives a fine route. There is a bulge at about one-third height, and then finish to the right of the final tower.

Lochnagar – Perseverance Wall

1 Perseverance Rib III
2 Gale Force Groove III*
3 Lunar Eclipse III*
4 The Gift II*
5 Temptress III*
6 Windfall III*

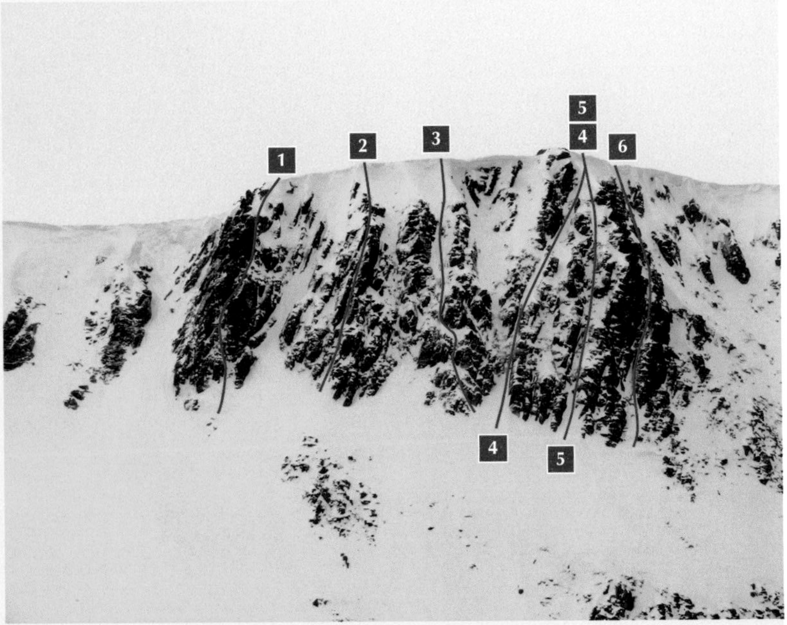

Temptress **80m III***

SM Richardson, 18 November 2005

Good mixed climbing up the obvious groove to the right of The Gift. Climb over three bulges to finish as for The Gift.

Windfall **80m III***

SM Richardson and C Cartwright, 3 January 1999

The gully/groove line up the right-hand side of the buttress. Climb the gully to a stance on the right (30m). Continue to a short snow slope, then climb two short chimneys to a platform (40m). Steep snow leads to the top.

The Cathedral

NO 252 854 *Altitude 950m* *North facing*

The largest and most obvious buttress in the Southern Sector, the Cathedral has an impressive mummy-shaped tower on its left and a trio of grooves right of this. These lead to a prominent left-slanting terrace.

Transept Groove **90m IV,4**

RJ Archbold and GS Strange, January 1983

A good route for a short day. Climb the broken groove immediately left of the mummy-shaped tower, then finish up the leftmost and deepest of the two chimneys at the top-left end of the terrace.

Transept Route **100m V,6***

SM Richardson and R Everett, 22 January 1994

This fine, sustained, turfy mixed route takes the groove on the right of the steep mummy-shaped tower. Climb the groove, with some technical moves surmounting an overhang, to a recess and large block belay (40m). Continue up in the same line to a small snow field. Exit this by the wall on the right to gain a terrace (35m). Finish up the leftmost chimney at the top of the terrace, as for Transept Groove (25m).

Sepulchre **80m V,6***

BF Findlay and GS Strange, 13 December 1987

Takes the central groove starting from a slight bay. Climb a narrow groove going up right to ledges. Above are twin slabby grooves. Gain the right-hand groove from the right and climb this for 6m, then transfer and climb the left-hand groove. Trend left and finish as for the previous routes.

Lochnagar – The Cathedral

1 Transept Groove IV,4
2 Transept Route V,6*
3 Sepulchre V,6*
4 Spellbound VI,7*
5 Judas Priest V,5*
6 Trinity VI,7*
7 Cathedral Chimney III,4*
8 Magic Pillar IV,5**
9 Forsaken Gully II

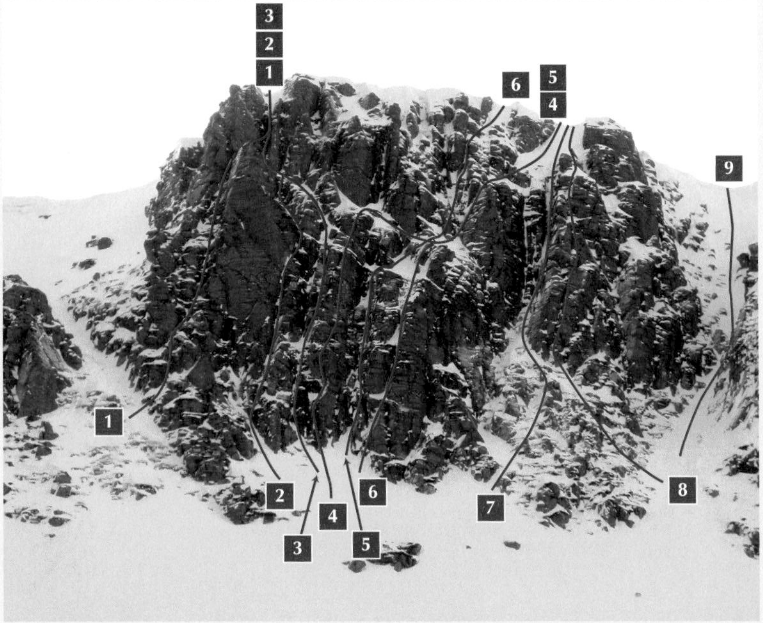

Spellbound 120m VI,7*

C Cartwright and SM Richardson, 15 November 1998

Just right of Sepulchre is a fine tapering arete with a large roof near its base. Start below this and climb a short wall to a niche. Continue up the steep left-slanting corner and pull over the left end of the roof (20m). Continue along the crack line in the arete (40m). Move right along the terrace and through a slot to finish as for Cathedral Chimney (60m).

Judas Priest 100m V,5*

BS Findlay and GS Strange,14 December 1986

The large groove line in the centre of the buttress provides a fine and popular route. Start below the groove, climb a corner on the right, and step back into the main groove. Continue up this to ledges. Trend up and right through a slot to finish in the snow bay of Cathedral Chimney.

Trinity 100m VI,7*

BS Findlay and GS Strange, 27 December 1994

This route follows the stepped corner system to the right of Judas Priest. Climb the stepped corner to easier ground. Continue up, crossing Judas Priest, and climb into an alcove. Climb out of this via the right-hand corner. Easier ground leads to the top.

Cathedral Chimney 60m III,4*

M Freeman and GS Strange, 12 December 1977

This fine route climbs the obvious deep narrow chimney left of the rightmost buttress.

Magic Pillar 80m IV,5**

C Cartwright and SM Richardson, 15 November 1998

This superb mixed route takes the well-defined pillar to the right of Cathedral Chimney. It is easier that its appearance suggests. Start at the base of the pillar. Climb a crack in the crest to a niche (20m). Step right round the roof and continue up the chimney crack to the top of the pillar (40m). Finish easily up Cathedral Chimney (20m).

Forsaken Gully 90m II

E Lawrence and RL Mitchell, 11 March 1950

This is the narrow, generally straightforward gully between The Cathedral the next buttress, Sinister Buttress.

Lochnagar – Central and Shadow Buttresses

1 Central Buttress Direct IV,6*
2 Centrist V,5*
3 Shallow Gully IV,4
4 Shadow Rib V,5*
5 Shadowlands VI,7**
6 Shadow Buttress A IV,5**
7 Polyphemus Gully V,5***
8 Shadow Buttress B, Bell's Route V,6**
9 Penumbra V,5*
10 Douglas-Gibson Gully V,4**
10A Central fork VI,5
10B Right fork V,5

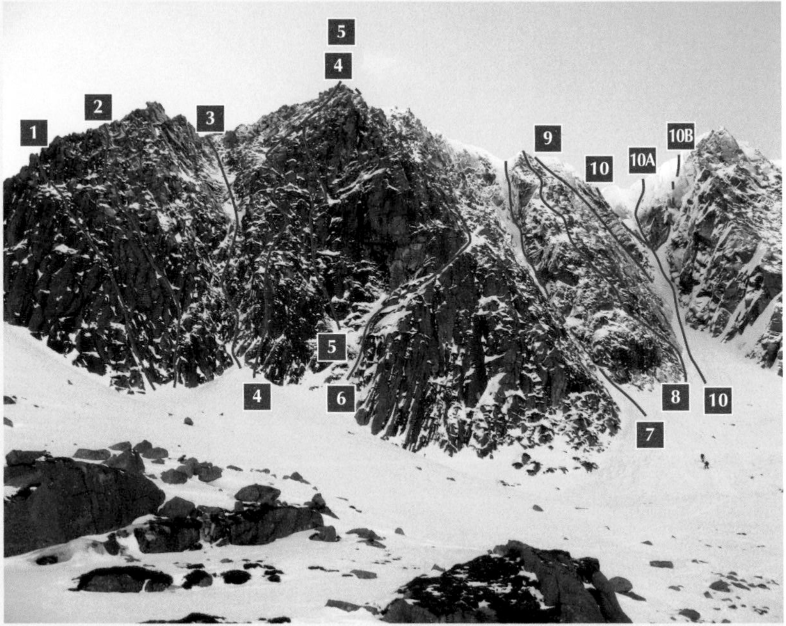

THE NORTHERN SECTOR

Central and Shadow Buttress Group

NO 248 856 Altitude 900m North to north-east facing

This consists of three buttresses on the left of the northern sector of the corrie. First is Central Buttress, with broken ground on its left and the poorly defined Shallow Gully on its right. Next comes Shadow Buttress A, with its great overhangs, and then Shadow Buttress B. Between Shadow Buttress A and B is Shadow Couloir, from which rises Shadow Chimney, Giant's Head Chimney and Polyphemus Gully, which separates the two buttresses. Right of Shadow B is the great gash of Douglas-Gibson Gully, defining the right side of the group.

Central Buttress 300m II*

SR Tewnion and J Tewnion, January 1948

The leftmost buttress gives a good introduction to this type of climbing. Start up an introductory left-trending gully below a very steep right wall at the foot of the buttress proper. At its top, traverse right above it as soon as possible to gain the crest, which is followed to a level section with two pinnacles. Above this easier ground leads to the top.

Mantichore 60m VII,7*

W Moir and N Ritchie, 7 Feb1998

A fine sustained mixed route. Start just within the initial gully of Central Buttress, below a steep rippled slab. Climb an easy ramp to gain a small groove in the slab. Continue up to the top of the slab, then step down to a belay ledge (25m). Move up and right to climb a tapering slab into a groove. Climb this, then step left and continue to below a square roof. Continue up and left to easy ground (25m). Finish up or down Central Buttress.

Central Buttress Direct 90m IV,6*

M Geddes and ND Keir, 23 March 1975 (3PA); A Nisbet and D Wright, December 1979 (FFA)

To the right of the initial gully of Central Buttress is a steep wall containing several harder routes. Above and to the right of this wall, a line of grooves leads up to join Central Buttress on the crest.

Vivian Scott on the first technical pitch of Mantichore (photo: Vivian Scott collection)

Centrist 140m V,5*

M Freeman and N Keir, 3 February 1974

Climbs the right side of Central Buttress to gain that route at the pinnacles. This can then be followed to the top, or a descent to the left taken back to the corrie. Start just right of the lowest rocks and about 20m left of Shallow Gully. Climb an open groove slightly right and up into a big groove that has overhangs at its top. Turn the overhang on the left (crux), then curve left up ramps until an easier groove leads right to the crest, just before the pinnacles.

Shallow Gully 300m IV,4

DL Macrae and FG Henderson, 8 February 1959

The depression between Central Buttress and Shadow Buttress A. It is graded assuming the lower section is iced up, and this can take a while to occur. Start in the gully up from the foot of Central Buttress and climb it direct, with the lower 60m being the crux. Rock protection can be difficult to find. Above, either continue up the fault or slant left to gain to the crest of Central Buttress.

Shadow Rib 300m V,5*

BS Findlay and GS Strange, 31 January 1990

The slabby rib immediately right of Shallow Gully and left of the big overhangs of Shadow Buttress A. Start at the foot of the rib and climb twin left-facing grooves overlooking Shallow Gully (crux). Continue up the crest to below a steep wall. Traverse right below a steep wall to a flake crack, which leads awkwardly to a ledge going back left. Where the ledge ends, make an exposed step round a corner, then go left and up to gain and follow an easy gully leading to a small col on the crest. Finish up the crest to the plateau, as for Shadow Buttress A.

The original start, which makes the climb a grade easier, trends up and left from the introductory gully of Shadow Buttress A to gain the line after the crux.

Shadowlands 250m VI,7**

AD Robertson and SM Richardson, 19 March 1995

A superb and popular mixed route. Start at a cave up and left of the introductory gully of Shadow Buttress A. Climb up and left to a good stance (30m). Trend right over short steep walls until an awkward step down leads to the base of an imposing left-trending fault that cuts through the headwall (25m). Gain this fault from the right, and climb it for 15m until it is possible to gain an overhung niche on the right. Pull over this to reach another fine belay stance (20m). A tricky step left regains the fault, which is followed to its end (25m). Move up and right to the crest to join and follow the top section of Shadow Buttress A to the top (150m).

Lochnagar – Shadow Buttresses

1 Shadow Buttress A IV,5**
2 Shadow Chimney IV,4
3 Giant's Head Chimney Direct V,5*
4 Giant's Head Chimney IV,4*
5 Shadow Buttress B, Bell's Route V,6**
SC Shadow Couloir
PG Polyphemus Gully
DGG Douglas-Gibson Gully

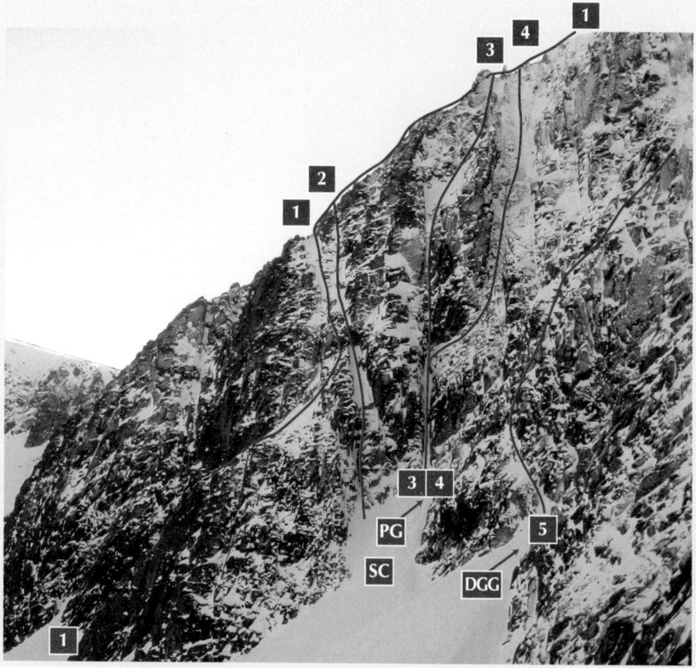

Shadow Buttress A — 300m IV,5**

WD Brooker and JW Morgan, 27 December 1949

A great mountaineering route, but unfortunately made a bit unbalanced by a recent rock fall. Start in the bay below large overhangs near the foot of Shallow Gully. Climb the gully to reach the prominent Spiral Terrace, which is followed to its upper right end. Climb a vague narrow rib overlooking Shadow Chimney to its top (crux). This can be made a more amenable technical grade with a point of aid. Alternatively, climb the narrow Shadow Chimney on the right to bypass this section. Above, trend left and climb a shallow gully to regain the crest. Follow this, passing the small tower by a descent on the right, and continue to the plateau.

Shadow Chimney — 225m IV,4

F R Malcolm and DJ Ritchie, 22 November 1952

This is the prominent chimney on the left side of Shadow Couloir and left of Giant's Head Chimney. The chimney is followed throughout to finish up Shadow Buttress A.

Moon Shadow — 225m V,5*

SM Richardson and J Ashbridge, 21 November 1992

This fine turfy route takes the well-defined buttress between Shadow Chimney and Giant's Head Chimney. Start as for Giant's Head Chimney and climb diagonally up and left to enter a steep right-facing corner. Climb this and step left to belay in Shadow Chimney (40m). Climb a wall on the right to gain a hidden ramp, which cuts back right to the crest. Pull over a small roof to reach a ledge (25m). Continue easily to a wall cut by parallel cracks. Climb the right side of this to easier ground and a ledge (40m). Climb a short corner above to gain a right-trending weakness (40m). Continue more easily to gain Shadow Buttress A and then the top (80m).

Giant's Head Chimney Direct — 200m V,5*

D Dinwoodie and ND Keir, 12 February 1972

The right-hand of the faults on the flank of Shadow Buttress A, which is hidden from below. Climb the lower narrow chimney to a large overhang and move right to belay. Traverse left across the overhang (crux) and gain the shallow upper chimney. Follow this to a snow bowl, from which the crest on the right leads to Shadow Buttress A, then the top.

Giant's Head Chimney — 220m IV,4*

WD Brooker and JW Morgan, 29 January 1950

Another fine route. Climb the lower chimney for about 60m to the overhang. Go right on a terrace into a prominent trough, which may contain much ice. Climb the trough to easier ground leading to the plateau. Where the trough eases, more difficult climbing may be found by following the 'Feathered Arete' on the right.

Polyphemus Gully — 200m V,5***

K Grassick and HSM Bates, 24 January 1953

Another of the classic Lochnagar gullies. It lies between Shadow Buttresses A and B and is not obvious from most angles. In good conditions it can be easy for the grade. The gully is reached by traversing steep snow from the base of Giant's Head Chimney. The route contains two big pitches separated by about 60m of steep snow. The initial pitch is often the crux. Easier climbing leads to a steepening above a cave. This can be climbed direct, or on the left or the right, depending on the build-up. Continue up to the cornice, which is usually passed on the right.

Shadow Buttress B, Bell's Route — 200m V,6**

TW Patey and AO'F Will, 23 February 1955

A very fine winter buttress route. Start just inside Douglas-Gibson Gully at a shelf that leads left to the centre of the buttress. Climb a crack to reach two teeth below a steep wall. From the left tooth gain the shaky flake handrail, after which a groove leads to the top of the steep section. Finish up the crest, where the cornice can be difficult.

Shadow Buttress B, Original Route — 200m V,6*

J Bolton and C Butterworth, 5 March 1972

A good route of a more consistent standard up this shapely buttress. Start just inside Douglas-Gibson Gully at an obvious break about 10m above the start of Bell's Route. Climb up the fault by shallow corners, grooves and ledges, trending up to reach the crest above the lower steep section. Follow the crest to the top.

Penumbra — 110m V,5*

C Butterworth and P Arnold, 18 March 1972

An interesting climb up the line of the left-slanting corners high on Shadow Buttress B. Start at the narrows in Douglas-Gibson Gully and follow the obvious corners and slabs running to the top of the buttress.

Douglas-Gibson Gully — 200m V,4**

TW Patey and GB Leslie, 28 December 1950

The obvious large gully with imposing walls is a climb with a wealth of history to its name. The gully is climbed direct, with a line on the left of the headwall being taken. The cornice can be immense. There are also other forks, as follows.

Right fork **V,5**

The Eagle Ridge side of the headwall.

Central fork **VI,5**

Occasionally an icicle down the headwall leads to an icy groove. Turn the bulge on the right to finish by a hidden right-trending line.

Far left fork **V,5**

Traverse left and up into the gully with a huge chokestone.

Eagle Ridge and the Parallel Buttress Group

NO 247 857 *Altitude 900m* *North-east facing*

This forms the main back wall of the corrie and lies between the straight-cut Douglas-Gibson Gully and Raeburn's Gully, which slants up leftwards behind Tough-Brown Ridge and is hidden from most viewpoints. On the left, overlooking Douglas-Gibson Gully, is the narrow crest of Eagle Ridge, then Parallel Gullies A and B bracketing Parallel Buttress. Huge rock falls in 1995 and then again in 2000 altered the area between Parallel Gully B, which lost its narrow lower chimney, and just left of Trail of Tears. Between this and Raeburn's Gully is the huge Tough-Brown Buttress, with its steep, compact lower wall.

Eagle Ridge 250m VI,6***

TW Patey, JM Taylor and WD Brooker, 25 January 1953

The narrow soaring crest whose left wall plunges into Douglas-Gibson Gully is often called the Queen of Lochnagar's winter climbs, and is one of Scotland's great winter routes. In lean conditions or under powder it can be very hard and should not be underestimated; conversely, in good conditions it can be considerably easier. Start just inside Douglas-Gibson Gully and climb the first obvious groove. Continue in the same groove line, which is almost a chimney in places. A pitch of easier ground then leads to one of several groove lines that lead back left onto the crest at the base of the first tower. This is an extremely well-marked but sustained pitch, climbed via a recess on the right then into a sentry box near the top. This is usually considered to be the winter crux. Go along the narrow crest of the Whaleback until a ledge leads right to a stance in a corner with a slabby left wall. Climb this to the knife-edge crest and climb the short vertical wall via the crack on the left, which can be very hard but is well protected (summer crux). Continue along the short ridge, then go up to a square-cut overhang, and traverse right to gain a corner system slanting up and right to finish.

Lochnagar – Eagle Ridge to the Amphitheatre

1 Douglas-Gibson Gully V,4**
1A Central Fork VI,5
1B Right Fork V,5
2 Eagle Ridge VI,6***
3 Eagle Buttress IV,3
4 Tough-Brown Traverse IV,3**
5 Parallel Gully A III**
6 Parallel Buttress VI,6***
7 Parallel Gully B VI,5***
8 Trail of Tears VII,8***
9 Mort IX,9***
10 Tough-Brown Ridge Direct V,6*
11 Scarface V,4*
12 Amphitheatre Route III
13 Pinnacle Gully 1 III

RG Raeburn's Gully

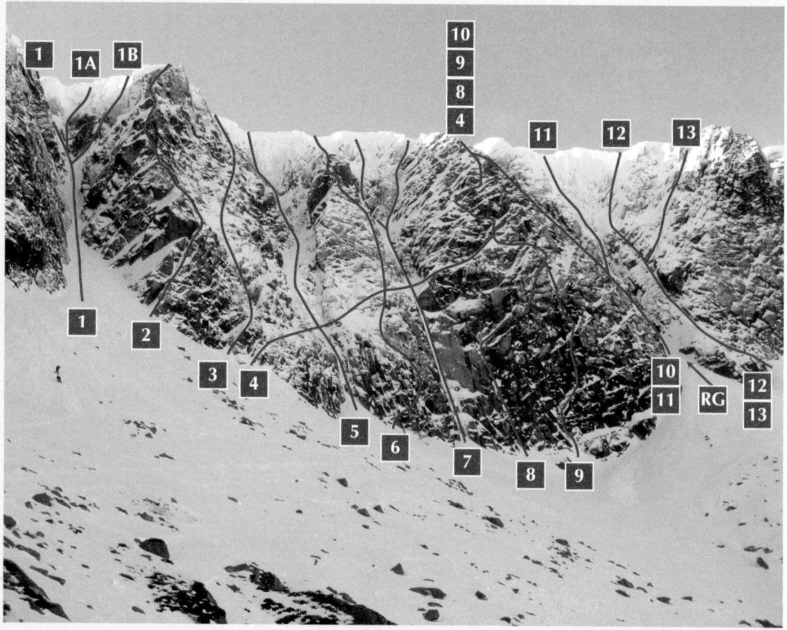

Eagle Buttress **250m IV,3**

WD Brooker and JM Taylor, 31 March 1956

Lies between Eagle Ridge and Parallel Buttress. Start midway between these routes and climb fairly easily to the head of a snow scoop after about 120m. Then trend right to below the steep upper wall, where a ledge goes right to below three parallel grooves overlooking Parallel Gully A. Climb the central groove (crux), then follow the edge close to Parallel A to the top.

Eagle Groove **IV,5**

A variation finish. From the snow scoop climb the obvious groove trending left to finish up Eagle Ridge.

Tough-Brown Traverse **300m IV,3****

TW Patey and DA Aitken, 20 January 1952

A classic mountaineering route crossing this impressive face. It takes the diagonal line of weakness cutting the face above the lower overlapping slabs of Tough-Brown Buttress. Start left of Parallel Gully A and go diagonally right to cross it above its initial ice pitch. Cross Parallel Buttress by the obvious line to arrive in Parallel Gully B in the bowl above the lower fault. From the right side of the bowl climb a short chimney onto the Great Terrace. Follow this and, before it ends, go up then right on a ramp, then left on a ledge, then zig-zag obviously to the crest leading to the top. Finding the correct point at which to leave the Great Terrace can be a problem, especially in poor visibility.

Going up from the far end of the Terrace gives a pitch and a half of Grade IV climbing.

Parallel Gully A **270m III****

GW Ross and R Still, 28 March 1948

A good climb, although it can vary between having several ice pitches to banking out. Start up the initial pitch, which may be full of ice and is often the crux, although it can be avoided on the left. Continue up the gully, which may contain other ice pitches. At the junction take the left fork to the top. The right fork, which is much steeper, can be climbed at IV,4.

Parallel Buttress **280m VI,6*****

TW Patey, J Smith and WD Brooker, 4 March 1956

Another superb climb up the narrow elegant buttress that tapers to a tower near the top. Start up a wide groove right of Parallel Gully A, then traverse right into a defined chimney. Climb this to a ledge on the right and go up corners on the right to a flake, then back left to easier ground above the steep base of the buttress. Work upwards until forced to trend right to the buttress edge. Continue very close to

Steve Fortune on the lower section of Parallel Gully B (photo: Chad Harrison)

the gully by a shelf and then grooves to the tower. Climb this by a shallow groove (crux), then a shelf, until the crest behind the tower is regained. Continue more easily to the plateau via a narrow ridge.

Parallel Gully B — 280m VI,5***

JR Marshall and G Tiso, 22 February 1958

This was a magnificent climb up the fault that started as a narrow chimney before opening out in its upper section. Unfortunately, large rock falls in 1995 and 2000 removed the right-hand side of the lower chimney, leaving only a smooth right-facing corner. Ice sometimes forms all the way down this corner. The difficulty and seriousness of the route very much depend on the build-up of this ice, and at the time of writing the route had seen only a handful of ascents in its altered state. However, conditions should be easily assessable from the ground. Climb the pleasant bulging wall to a belay below the corner (25m). Follow the corner, and at the top either continue directly up steep ice or step right onto an airy snow ramp to return back left higher up (55m). The upper gully is followed until blocked by a bulge. This can be climbed on the left or bypassed by a groove on the right. Either way leads to the end of the difficulties, although the cornice can be huge.

If there is insufficient ice in the lower corner, the upper gully can still be accessed from the Tough-Brown Traverse and provides a worthwhile Grade IV,5.

Trail of Tears — 130m VII,8***

D Dinwoodie and A Nisbet, 7 March 1986

A magnificent hard route using various parts of several summer lines. Start below the right-facing corner right of the rock-fall scar and climb this grassy corner to a ledge on the left (30m). Continue straight up the corner, over a bulge, and up to some huge flakes (possible belay). Continue up the groove to a ledge, move right, then up a ramp to a good stance (30m). Climb the big ramp, going right to a grassy niche (10m). Climb the ramp to a break, descend right to a lower ramp, and make hard moves round the corner then up to the continuation of the main ramp. Climb cracks in the ramp to its top, then go up round a block (40m). Flakes now lead up and left to the Tough-Brown Traverse (20m), which can used to finish up or down.

Mort — 130m IX,9***

B Davison, A Nisbet and D McGimpsey, 15 January 2000

Another magnificent and very difficult winter route. After numerous attempts spread over 15 years, Davison took advantage of usually icy conditions to make the first ascent. At the time of writing it remains unrepeated, despite various attempts by some strong teams. Start below the obvious groove to the right of Trail of Tears, climb this, and move right along a ledge (35m). Climb up, passing to the right of a downward-pointing tooth, and pull through the obvious roof at twin cracks. To the left is a well-defined rib. Climb to the top of this rib – either on the left, if sufficiently iced, or on the right. Continue to a ramp, and move 5m along this to belay (35m). Traverse left to the continuation groove, and continue over a bulge to a bay and block belay (40m). Follow Trail of Tears left to join the Tough-Brown Traverse (20m), and either continue up this to the top or descend it back to the ground.

Tough Guy — 120m VII,7**

A Nisbet and B Davison, 18 December 1984

Another fine and difficult mixed route, based on the right-hand intermittent crack line located at the right side of the face before it bends round to the Tough-Brown Ridge Direct. Start from a shelf that is usually gained by traversing leftwards from the base of Tough-Brown Ridge Direct. Climb up and left to gain and follow a crack, which passes a roof, and continue to a large block belay (30m). Climb a few moves up a corner behind the block, then traverse left round a rib, under a rock-fall scar, and climb up to gain a long ledge. Belay at the right end of this (30m). Move up and left to gain and climb a thin left-slanting crack to reach a ledge (it is possible to escape out rightwards along this). Continue diagonally left past some large flakes and cracked blocks to a ledge (35m). Continue up to gain and finish via the crest of the Tough-Brown Ridge Direct (25m).

Tough-Brown Ridge Direct — 250m V,6*

M Rennie and ND Keir, 23 December 1969

This route takes a line on the extreme right of the Tough-Brown Face, then follows the crest above. Start just inside Raeburn's Gully and climb the groove line slightly left, with a difficult section exiting a short deep groove to gain easier ground. Slant right under a steep wall to a little arete above the gully. Either climb the groove above the arete or descend right beyond the arete and climb the wall. These both lead to easier ground and a finish either up grooves left of the more prominent groove of Backdoor Route or by making a traverse right to finish up Backdoor Route.

Backdoor Route — 220m IV,4*

TW Patey, AO'F Will, G McLeod and A Thom, 20 March 1954

The big, obvious left-facing corner right of the crest of Tough-Brown Ridge Direct. Start before the bend in Raeburn's Gully. Climb the big corner for about 10m, then traverse left, then slant back right to its top. Alternatively, climb the corner direct (harder). Both alternatives can be poorly protected. Follow the groove above to reach the crest a pitch below the top.

Raeburn's Gully — 200m II***

GR Symers, AW Clark and WA Ewan, 27 December 1932

The large gully that slants up leftwards. It gives a good climb, particularly when not banked out, but then it is harder. This climb is noted for its avalanche danger, particularly from the large number of cornices which overlook it. The gully is climbed direct, and the crux is normally an ice pitch at the jammed boulder above the cave.

The Gutter 80m III

TW Patey and AO'F Will, 23 January 1955

A variation finish to Raeburn's Gully, taking the fault in the right wall about 80m from the top of that climb.

Black Spout Pinnacle

NO 246 858 Altitude 900m North-east facing

This group, lying between Raeburn's Gully and the massive and unmistakable Black Spout, is dominated by the superb Black Spout Pinnacle. This is isolated by its attendant gullies and connected to the plateau by a narrow ridge and col. To the left of the Pinnacle, the face overlooking Raeburn's Gully is more broken and faulted; the right side, however, plunges steeply into The Black Spout, whose left-hand branch curves up behind it. Between the two branches of The Black Spout is The Stack. For routes that finish on the top of the Black Spout Pinnacle it may be necessary to abseil down to the col from a large spike to gain the ridge, narrow and exposed in places, running up to the plateau.

Scarface 170m V,4*

D Stuart and GS Strange, 12 February 1972

Climbs directly into the Amphitheatre, a large bowl overlooking Raeburn's Gully on the right. At times the lower section can be very icy. Start just above the bend in Raeburn's Gully. Climb ice as directly as possible into the Amphitheatre, then go up its left edge to finish up the leftmost of three faults, an icy groove.

Amphitheatre Route 200m III

TW Patey, GH Leslie and S Long, 10 March 1957

Lies up the large depression left of Pinnacle Gully 1, overlooking Raeburn's Gully. Climb Pinnacle Gully 1 to above the cave and continue up a small gully, then a chimney, to enter the Amphitheatre. Finish by the right-hand of three faults above, a narrow gully. The cornice here can be large.

Pinnacle Gully 1 200m III

TW Patey and C Morrison, 27 January 1951

This runs up to the col behind the Black Spout Pinnacle. Start at the Mound, a subsidiary buttress at the bottom-left corner of the Black Spout Pinnacle. Climb from

Lochnagar – Black Spout Pinnacle and West Buttress

1 Pinnacle Gully 1 III
2 Grovel Wall V,5
3 Pinnacle Face VI,7**
4 Route 1 V,6**
5 The Link Direct VIII,7***
6 Black Spout Left Branch I***
7 The White Spout IV,4
8 The Black Spout I**
9 Black Spout Buttress III,5*
10 Gargoyle Chimney IV,4*
11 Bells Pillar V,5*
12 Prince of Darkness VI,7**
13 West Gully IV,4*
14 Gelder Gully II

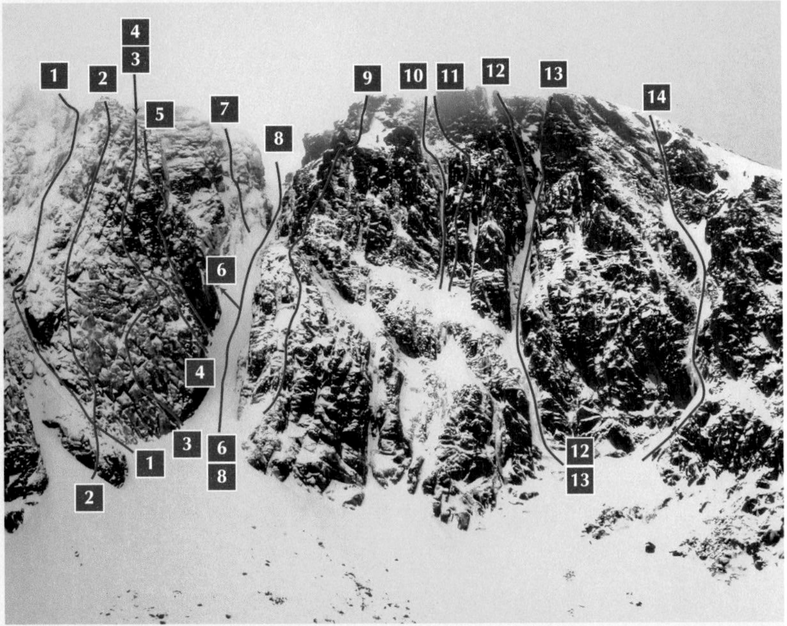

the lowest rocks to the top of the Mound, then go left and follow a chimney slanting left, then follow broken ground. Traverse right across a slab above a cave, go up a short chimney, then go right to easier ground leading to the col. A pleasant ridge leads to the plateau. To gain the summit of the Pinnacle go right just before the col, then by slabs to its top.

Grovel Wall — 200m V,5

M Freeman and A Nisbet, 15 February 1977

Takes a line from the Mound to the summit of the Pinnacle – a big build-up may be required. This may require a degree of route finding in the lower section, but above it takes more obvious grooves parallel to the left edge of the Pinnacle. Start in Raeburn's Gully, and from the left side of the Mound go diagonally right for a pitch, working up slabs, shelves and ledges running right below the obvious steep wall. Turn this on the right, and follow a line of grooves and shallow chimneys parallel to Pinnacle Gully 1 to the top of the Pinnacle.

Pinnacle Face — 100m VI,7**

KA Grassick, J Light and AG Nicol, 16 January 1966

A very fine climb, often on thinly iced slabs; generally, the more ice, the easier it becomes. Start about 10m up from the lowest rock in The Black Spout and climb a prominent V-groove for about 10m, then go left into another groove and continue via a short chimney and cracks (35m). Go up into a corner and go right onto the slab, then climb up and left by a slabby fault to a stance (25m) – this needs some ice or it is very hard. Continue up vegetated corners to a steep wall, then go right past this wall to a groove leading into Route 1, which is followed to the top. In very good conditions a more direct line can be taken to the top of the Pinnacle.

Route 1 — 200m V,6**

J Smith and WD Brooker, 11 March 1956

An excellent climb on the right side of the Pinnacle. It first gains the Springboard, a large platform about 40m up, then moves onto the front face, where route finding can be tricky. Start in The Black Spout beyond a vertical groove in a smooth wall. Climb the obvious slabby ramp past an overlap, and shortly above it traverse left and gain the Springboard by a short wall. Go up ledges above, then traverse left into the left-hand of three faults. Climb this out onto the front face, then work back right, starting by a large flake, to gain the crest and follow this to the top.

The Link Direct — 185m VIII,7***

C Cartwright and SM Richardson, 1 February 1998

An outstanding mixed route – sustained but never desperate. Start in a snow bay just right of Route 1, below a steep vegetated groove. Climb steep parallel cracks and continue up and left over steep slabs to reach a stance on the rib (30m). Step left into the groove and climb it to below a prominent triangular overhang. Move up and right round a huge block to a recess (25m). Pull over the overhang to gain a vegetated groove. Continue up this to a good stance on the left (25m). Continue up the groove for another 5m to join Route 2. Step down and right (reversing the crux of Route 2), and move up to the groove running through the headwall (15m). Climb the groove to a good stance (20m). Pull over the overhang above (crux) (10m). Move up to join Route 1, which is followed to the summit of the Pinnacle (60m).

Route 2 — 120m VI,6*

JR Marshall and J Stenhouse, 28 February 1962

A serious route in a very exposed position. Start above the fork in The Black Spout at the bottom-left end of a broad sloping shelf. Climb the chimney crack, which slants left to end in a short ridge. Descend leftwards for 5m, then traverse a long way left, hard and sustained, into a big groove. Climb this to a large ledge, then on to the summit of the Pinnacle.

The Ice Ox — 100m IV,5*

G Livingstone and A Matthewson, 24 December 1984

The big corner starting from the fork in The Black Spout is the line of the climb. It can be good early in the season.

Twin Chimneys Route — 100m IV,5

TW Patey, WD Brooker and CM Dixon, April 1961

Start as for The Ice Ox, but climb the obvious chimney on the right to a rib, which is followed to the top of the Pinnacle.

Pinnacle Gully 2 — 90m II

AW Clark and WA Ewan, 28 December 1932

A good little route which starts high up The Black Spout Left Branch and ends at the col behind the Pinnacle. Climb the gully direct – the blocked through-route behind the chokestone is climbed on the outside and is often the crux, awkward in lean conditions. Above this continue on the right to the col. To gain the Pinnacle from the col descend a little way on the other side, then climb a crack going right, go round a corner and climb slabs to the top. An abseil return may be required.

The Black Spout Left Branch — 250m I***

The left-hand branch is steeper and more interesting than the normal route. The scenery is magnificent.

Crumbling Cranny 60m II

Miss Inglis Clark, Mrs Hunter and H Alexander, 21 December 1913

This is the wide chimney in the right wall of The Black Spout Left Branch. It can have a huge cornice, which can require tunnelling.

Sour Grapes 50m V,7*

SM Richardson and RG Webb, 18 December 1994

A short, fine little route taking the chimney and hanging corner on the right wall of Crumbling Cranny. Climb the chimney to a good ledge with perched blocks (25m). Step left and climb the corner over a bulge (crux) to the top (25m).

The Stack 150m V,6*

JM Taylor, GB Leslie and TL Fallowfield, 20 November 1952

This sustained route lies on the buttress between the two branches of The Black Spout and can be very icy. Start in the left-hand branch and climb the ice fall to a platform. Go to a chimney with jammed blocks, which is climbed for a short way until a descending traverse left leads to a platform. Return right via two short chimneys to the main chimney, which is climbed to a bollard (it is sometimes possible to avoid this detour). Step off the bollard onto a shelf on the right, then go up a wall to a ledge. Move left then up a slab to broken ground. A terrace goes left below the final wall, then a short step leads to the top.

The White Spout 70m IV,4

M Freeman and ND Keir, 2 February 1974

This is an ice fall that can develop on the right wall of The Stack near the top of The Black Spout. Climb it rightwards, then by the easiest line at the top.

The Black Spout 250m I**

JH Gibson and W Douglas, 12 March 1893

The huge, easy angled corridor is straightforward. The cornice is also usually avoidable on the right.

West Buttress Group

NO 247 859 *Altitude 900m* *East facing*

This collection of buttresses and gullies lies at right angles to the rest of the cliff. On the left it is terminated by The Black Spout, and the right-hand side gradually merges into broken ground. It is generally more broken than the other groups, but West Gully, with its lower ice fall, is well defined and prominent. Conditions here may not be as reliable as on the other groups, particularly later in the season, when these rocks are more affected by the sun.

Black Spout Buttress **250m III,5***

J Tewnion, C Hutcheon, DA Sutherland and K Winram, 9 January 1949

A fine climb following the crest of the buttress immediately right of The Black Spout. Start about 10m right of The Black Spout and climb the chimney fault, which may contain ice. Above, continue more easily to the step. Climb a ridge and a 4m chimney. Easier ground leads to a short wall (crux), which is started in the middle and finished by a corner on the right. Above this, another wall is turned by a right traverse into a gully. Return left to the crest as soon as possible.

Gargoyle Chimney **120m IV,4***

JM Taylor and WD Brooker, 20 January 1952

A good winter line up the obvious fault in the centre of the upper face. The Midway Terrace at the foot of the route is gained by one of the three faults right of Black Spout Buttress, the centre one being the easiest. The chimney itself is climbed direct, and the lower section can contain much ice.

Bells Pillar **120m V,5***

GS Strange and BS Findlay, 25 October 1992

The well-defined rib to the right of Gargoyle Chimney. Start just to the right of this, and climb a left-facing corner until it is possible to pull onto the crest. Climb the crest until this is blocked by a smooth wall. Skirt left and finish up a fault just left of Gargoyle Chimney.

Prince of Darkness **70m VI,7****

SM Richardson and C Cartwright, 20 December 1998

A fine, steep and sustained mixed route that climbs the imposing tower rising from above the upper section of West Gully. Start by climbing West Gully for 180m to the foot of this tower. Climb up a turf ramp and move left to a ledge. Move back right to a niche, and then climb straight up to a second niche. Step right around the arete to reach a hanging groove and follow this to a good belay stance (25m). Climb the prominent right-facing corner above to another good stance (25m). Climb the steep cracks above to the top of the tower (20m).

West Gully **250m IV,4***

A Fyffe and MDY Mowat (direct), 4 April 1966

The obvious gully on the right of the cliff. It starts with a fine ice fall, which is climbed direct and forms the crux. Above, the gully is impressive but straightforward. The central branch at the top gives the best finish, but the left branch is easier.

Gelder Gully **250m II**

MCS Philip, J Henderson and A Grattidge, 25 January 1953
The shallow gully to the right of West Gully. Trend rightwards up a snow ramp to gain the gully, which is followed (via a possible ice pitch) to a large snow bay. Here the gully forks. The right branch quickly leads to easy ground, while the left continues with more interest to the top.

CREAG AN DUBH LOCH

NO 235 825 *Altitude 730m* *North-east to east facing*
Lying on the flank of Broad Cairn, overlooking the Dubh Loch, is the biggest cliff in the Cairngorms. It stretches as a relatively straight face for 1km and gives routes up to 300m in length. In the centre of the cliff is the enormous Central Gully; the only other easy faults, South-East and North-West Gullies, lie at the extreme left and right ends of the cliff respectively. Right of South-East Gully, at the top of the cliff, is Broad Terrace Wall. This vertical and overhanging wall lies above the inappropriately named Broad Terrace, which runs out left from the great scoop of the Hanging Garden, which is separated from the Central Slabs by the left-facing fault of the Labyrinth.

The Central Slabs themselves are huge and unmistakable. There is a terrace running diagonally right below the steeper Upper Tier, which can be used as an escape onto Central Gully Buttress. On the right, the Central Slabs become more broken and end at Central Gully. Right of Central Gully, the Central Gully Wall looms over the gully, the massive overlapping tile-like formation giving one of the most impressive rock walls in the country. This wall then swings round to form a slightly less intimidating frontal face, which is defined on its right by False Gully. This shallow fault starts an open grassy ramp, and has another steep and massive right wall, the False Gully Wall. Right of this, the ground is again more hospitable before North-West Gully is reached and the cliff becomes much more broken.

Approaches

The normal approach is from Ballater, where the minor road up Glen Muick is followed for 15km to the same car park as for Lochnagar at the Spittal of Glen Muick. The last 5km are across open moor and can be difficult with drifting snow. The car park can be very busy at peak holiday times. Walk along the unsurfaced road on the north-west shore of Loch Muick to the head of the loch, and continue up the path on the north side of the stream to the Dubh Loch. Cross to the south side of the glen either at the head or the outlet of the loch, depending on the part of the cliff to be visited. Cycling along the side of Loch Muick is a good option if there is no snow on the track.

Descents

Central Gully gives a convenient way down, the cornice usually being avoidable on the right looking down. Either end of the cliff can also be descended – the north-west end being the better alternative, with the outcrops being more easily outflanked.

Conditions

As the base of the cliff is fairly low at just over 700m, Creag an Dubh Loch is not as reliable a winter venue as its neighbour Lochnagar. However, when in good condition it offers superb icy mixed climbing, with some of the most sought-after routes in this guidebook being found here. Good conditions can be difficult to predict, with cold weather being required for the ice to form, but if it is too cold the springs can freeze at source. Unfortunately it can strip rapidly in a thaw, although the Hanging Garden area can hold ice for longer periods and later in the season. Sometimes the routes on Eagles Rocks or Broad Cairn Bluffs can provide a good alternative, should conditions on Creag an Dubh Loch not be as good as expected.

South-East Buttress 200m II

F Patterson and A Alexander, March 1948

The buttress on the left of the cliff. The route follows the crest overlooking South-East Gully. After a slab-corner pitch on the gully side of the buttress, the climbing is straightforward.

Henning Wackerage on the crux pitch of Labyrinth Direct, Creag an Dubh Loch (photo: Henning Wackerage)

Creag an Dubh Loch (left side)

1 South-East Buttress II
2 South-East Gully I/II**
3 The Snow Desert V,4
4 The Last Oasis VI,6***
5 Bower Buttress V,5*
6 The Aqueduct V,4
7 Hanging Garden Route Left Fork V,4**
8 Hanging Garden Route Right Fork V,4**
9 Labyrinth Left-hand V,5*
10 Labyrinth Direct VII,6***
11 Labyrinth Edge IV,5*
12 The White Elephant VII,6**
13 Theseus Grooves III
14 The Golden Thread IV,4
15 Centaur III
16 Central Gully I**
17 Sabre Cut IV,5
18 Vertigo Wall VII,7***

HG Hanging Garden

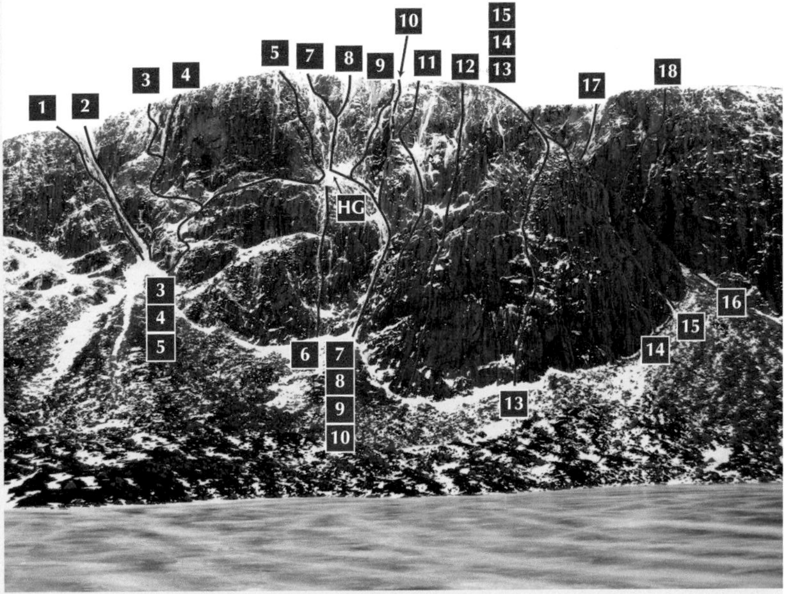

South-East Gully 200m I/II**

WA Russell, M Smith and W Stephen, 26 January 1947

The obvious gully that slants up to the left. The chokestone may give an interesting pitch early in the season, but bank out later on.

The following routes (with the exception of The Aqueduct, which is on the lower tier) are usually approached by either zig-zagging up from the start of South-East Gully onto Broad Terrace, or by climbing the lower section of Labyrinth Direct and breaking left to gain the Hanging Garden. The route lengths given include these approaches.

The Snow Desert 300m V,4

RA Smith and D Wright, February 1977

An exposed route overlooking South-East Gully. Gain and then traverse left from Broad Terrace to the foot of the left-hand of two faults that contain an ice fall, The Last Oasis. Climb a pitch up The Last Oasis and go left over a ramp to gain a hanging snow field. At the left end of this is a broken chimney, which is climbed to a left exit. Make a difficult horizontal traverse to easier ground and the top.

The Last Oasis 300m VI,6***

A Nisbet and N Spinks 30 March 1980

The left-hand of twin faults above South-East Gully; the right-hand fault is the right-facing corner of Sword of Damocles (VIII,8). It can form an impressive ice fall with

Ross Hewitt enjoying good conditions on Hanging Garden Route (photo: Henning Wackerage)

a very steep finish, which is unfortunately susceptible to the morning sun. The finish may be turned on the left by the summer line (one nut and one peg for aid on the first ascent).

Bower Buttress **300m V,5***

J Bower and GR Simpson, March 1970

A fine route that takes the edge between the vertical Broad Terrace Wall and the left margin of the Hanging Garden. In good conditions it can be all on ice; otherwise it can give a fine mixed route. Start near the foot of South-East Gully and climb the zig-zag line of ramps up to the Broad Terrace. Go right below the vertical wall to where it turns into the Hanging Garden. Alternatively, this point can be gained by climbing Labyrinth and traversing left across the Hanging Garden. Climb grooves in the crest slanting left to the Gallery, a large ledge. Cracks trending slightly right lead to a shallow gully, which leads to snow slopes and the cornice, which is taken on the left.

The Aqueduct **120m V,4**

RA Smith and J Moreland, 26 January 1975

In good conditions a fine ice fall forms out of the left-hand side of the Hanging Garden. This gives a fine but serious direct route to the Hanging Garden.

Yeti **300m V,4****

RA Smith and J Moreland, 26 January 1975

This takes the line of the slabby ramps between Bower Buttress and Hanging Garden Route. These can become sheathed in ice and give an exposed, sustained and serious climb. Gain the Hanging Garden by the first part of Labyrinth Direct. There may be two branches to the lower ice fall, either of which can be climbed.

Hanging Garden Route **300m V,4****

Another excellent ice route, which has two forks. Climb the lower section of Labyrinth Direct for about 150m and go left to gain the Hanging Garden. Follow the gully above to below a steep triangular buttress that separates the two forks.

Left Fork

A Nisbet and A Robertson, 6 January 1977

The classic line that goes up the groove until a wall forces a traverse left across an exposed iced slab to gain snow and a cornice, which is climbed on the left.

Right Fork

D Dinwoodie and G Strange, 9 December 1972

From the pedestal move down and right to gain a stepped icy fault that leads right to a cornice. This can be difficult and is taken on the right.

Steve Holmes approaching the crux pitch of Labyrinth Direct (photo: Henning Wackerage)

Labyrinth Left-Hand **300m V,5***

D Dinwoodie and A Williams, March 1979

The Labyrinth is the huge fault defining the left edge of the Central Slabs. Climb the lower fault up and left into the Hanging Garden. Near the right margin, left of Labyrinth Direct, is an ice fall leading up to a big roofed slab, also ice covered. Climb this ice up and right into the top section of the main fault.

Labyrinth Direct **300m VII,6*****

AJ Bolton and P Arnold, 11 March 1972

A superb but poorly protected ice route following the fault direct. This is one of the most sought-after ice routes in the Cairngorms. After an initial ice pitch easier snow leads to the upper section. Climb the main fault into a steep groove and so to the cul-de-sac (40m). There is a good belay on the right if the rock is visible. Ten metres of very steep and perhaps thin ice leads to a steep groove, which continues for another 30m to easier ground (40m). Continue up easier ground to the top (40m).

Labyrinth Edge **300m IV,5***

WD Brooker and D Duncan, 10 February 1959

This takes the left edge of the Central Slabs, overlooking the fault line of the Labyrinth; difficulty increases with height. Start at the foot of the Labyrinth and go right onto the edge, which is climbed to a bay. Then follow grooves to a smooth area, the Sea of Slabs. Climb cracks on the left edge to a ledge on the left, turn the Lower Tower above this on the right and go up to below the Fang, a rock tooth. Turn this on the left to below the Upper Tower. Traverse to a chimney on its right, go up this, then out right to easier ground and the top.

Mammoth 360m IV,4

J Bower, J Furnell, N Blenkinsop and I Rae, 31 January 1970

A huge route that goes diagonally right across the Central Slabs. Start at the foot of the Labyrinth and work up and right into the gully on the left-centre side of the slabs, the Dinosaur Gully. Climb this gully, taking the right fork, and then continue up and right across shelves. Finish up the fault on the right side of the steep upper rocks, or continue trending right to finish up Central Gully Buttress.

The White Elephant 320m VII,6**

R Anderson and R Milne, 12 January 1980

Can give a magnificent climb on ice that oozes from the big left-face curving groove about 60m right of the top section of Labyrinth Edge and runs down the left side of the slabs. Unfortunately the bottom section is slow to form. Climb ice up to and over the overlap and enter the gully system in the slabs, the Dinosaur Gully. Climb the right branch of this Y-shaped gully, or if conditions allow go direct, to reach the terrace running below the steeper upper rocks. Climb ice up a corner and into the big groove, which is followed to the plateau.

Theseus Grooves 300m III

JT Campbell, BS Findlay, GR Simpson and GS Strange, 12 January 1969

The line of grooves on the right side of the main slabs. Start directly below the grooves at a shallow corner, possibly iced or even banked out. Climb this corner to enter the main groove system, which is climbed to a snow field. From the top of the snow field trend left up a depression until a line leads back right onto the crest of Central Gully Buttress, which is followed to the top. In lean conditions IV,4 may be a more appropriate grade.

The Golden Thread 300m IV,4

S Richardson and J Ashbridge, 16 November 1991

Start 5m right of a prominent rock pedestal at a vegetated groove and climb this to a stance (45m). Climb the steep right-facing corner and move left at its top (30m). Climb the groove system on the left to reach a terrace and move left, passing below a chimney, to reach the left edge of the upper buttress (50m). Climb a short steep gully in the wall on the right of the top of Centaur to reach easy ground and finish up Central Gully Buttress.

Centaur — 300m III

A Fyffe and D Whitcombe, 14 March 1970

Takes a line of chimneys and ledges that lie to the left of, and parallel to, the crest of Central Gully Buttress before joining that route above the steeper lower section. Start in a bay about 30m from the corner of the buttress. Climb either of two wide grooves and go up to the top of the fault. (The ice fall above gives a IV,5 finish.) Go diagonally left, passing below a deep chimney, until a wide corner can be climbed and the buttress crest gained by going right.

Central Gully Buttress — 300m II

TW Patey, March 1955

The ridge bordering the left side of Central Gully. Start either by an open chimney fault on the left of the crest or by a slab just inside Central Gully. Above the initial steep section the climbing is straightforward.

Central Gully — 300m I**

Miss McHardy and Miss Stewart, February 1933

An easy but spectacular way up the cliff underneath the magnificent Central Gully Wall. The lower blocks often show through, and the cornice can be avoided on the left. A good descent route.

Four Corners Route — 70m V,7*

A Cunningham and A Nisbet, 21 February 1987

A pleasant mixed route that comes into condition readily. It starts in a corner just right of a corner containing some blocks. This is about 35m left of Sabre Cut. Climb the corner until it is possible to step left into another corner to step left again to belay beside a small pinnacle (20m). Descend left to below another corner (10m). Climb the corner with a deviation out right above a platform (20m). A crack on the left leads to corner number four, which is climbed direct to the top (20m).

Sabre Cut — 80m IV,5

TW Patey, FR Malcolm and A Thom, 13 February 1957

The large fault that cuts Central Gully Wall near its top usually fills with ice. Climb the main groove line, which is steep. The cornice may be large and difficult.

Vertigo Wall — 160m VII,7***

A Nisbet and A Robertson, 3/4 December 1977

A Cunningham and A Nisbet (FFA), November 1985

An extremely fine mixed route that takes the huge open corner below Sabre Cut. Early in the season it often holds ice in quantity, but later on the headwall is often

Creag an Dubh Loch (right side)

1 Central Gully II
2 Sabre Cut IV,5
3 Vertigo Wall VII,7***
4 Mousetrap VII,8**
5 False Gully VI,7
6 North-West Buttress III

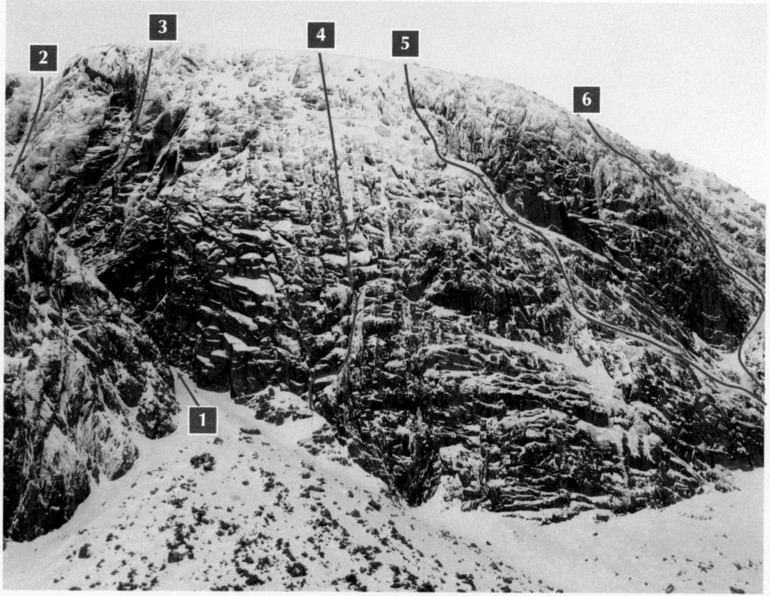

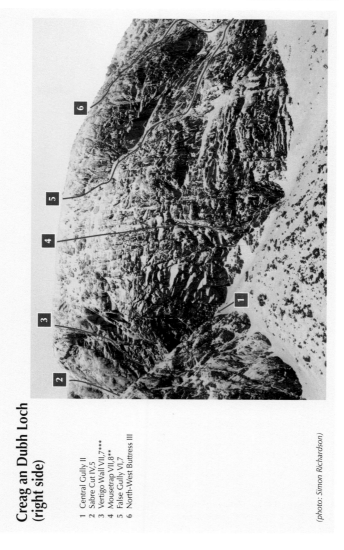

(photo: Simon Richardson)

Andrew Melvin on pitch 3 of Vertigo Wall (photo: Henning Wackerage)

stripped by the morning sun. Start up Central Gully from the main line of the fault. Traverse right on a grass shelf and climb the corner to a platform (30m). Gain a large block, then go right, then left, to reach slabs leading right to the main corner (35m). Climb the chimney, ice required, to a steeper section and go right for about 10m, then back left into the corner (30m). Climb the slab to the headwall, then traverse right along a creaking flake to shallow corner (it is best not to belay directly below this flake). Climb the shallow corner, then traverse right and go up to a belay (25m). Continue to the top (40m).

More Vertigo Finish **65m VII,8****

A Melvin, R Miller and H Wackerage, 12 March 2011

A fine alternative finish to Vertigo Wall which climbs through some unlikely looking terrain at a reasonable grade. Climb the first three pitches of the normal route. Climb thin ice up and left to get established on a small ledge. Traverse leftwards to the prominent icicles and continue up steeply to a belay (20m). Follow easy turfy ramps up and left to belay below a left-leaning off-width crack (15m). Climb the crack with difficulty and continue to a sharp spike. Step up from the spike and boldly climb the slab on thin hooks and continue to the top (30m).

Mousetrap **180m VII,8****

M Hamilton, K Spence and A Taylor, 19 January 1980

A big route that takes the grassy recess and cracks just where the Central Gully Wall changes angle. Start at the top of the mound, where the face bends. Make a short right traverse, climb a corner to a ledge on the right (as for the summer route Predator, technical crux), and traverse right round a shelf under twin cracks. Continue right, then climb into the grassy recess of Mousetrap. From the top of the recess pull out on the left to gain a crack system, which is followed to the top. This is sustained and thin, but being iced up will help.

False Gully **200m VI,7**

Original finish: K Grassick, W James and JM Taylor, 19 December 1964
Direct finish: S Richardson and J Ashbridge, 4 March 1995

An unusual route with the crux right at the top. It takes the diagonal fault on the front face running below the smooth and steep False Gully Wall. Start up the initial fault, which is indefinite but uncomplicated, to a ledge below steeper rocks. Go along the ledge to near where it fades out, then up to a steep chimney. Climb this and exit left (25m). Go left to a left-facing corner and climb its left wall to easier ground (35m). The original route used tension to gain the chimney's left arete at V,5.

North-West Buttress **250m III**

W Church and G Strange, 26 February 1995

The central line up the buttress starting at the break on the left side of the lower tier, up and right from the shelf leading onto False Gully. Go up and left in a shallow groove, then go right to a terrace. Cross this, and climb up right to follow snow then grooves and chimneys. Move left to finish.

North-West Gully Arete **200m II**

D Pyper and S Wilkinson, March 1967

The ridge on the left of North-West Gully. Start near the foot of North-West Gully and climb a trough to gain the crest. This is then followed to the top.

North-West Gully **200m II/III***

TW Patey, WD Brooker, JM Taylor and JW Morgan, 29 December 1952

A good climb up the obvious gully on the right of the cliff. It may contain an ice pitch at the bottom and the top.

Blizzard Nightmare **50m V,5**

C Jamieson, G Livingston, C Ord, G Strange and E Todd, 6 February 1985

This is the ice fall that forms on the left side of the broken North-West Gully Buttress, which lies on the right of North-West Gully.

EAGLES ROCKS

NO 235 835 Altitude 770m South facing

This is the band of broken cliffs that lies high up on the opposite side of the glen from Creag an Dubh Loch. It consists of several slabby buttresses that are south facing and something of a contrast to the shaded faces across the way. There is a conspicuous waterfall near the edge of the rocks, and towards the right side is the large Diagonal Gully, which slopes left to right.

Approach

As for Creag an Dubh Loch, but stay on the north side of the Dubh Loch and ascend to the appropriate place.

Descent

Descend either well to the west of the waterfall or by Diagonal Gully.

Conditions

These cliffs may hold ice in quantity in cold weather, even if there is little snow. However, later in the season much of the lower slabs may bank out, and it is very susceptible to thaw and bright sunlight.

Eagles Rocks

1 The Waterfall II*
2 Spectrum III**
3 Lethargy II/III*
4 Indolence III*
5 Nomad's Crack V,5*
6 Sliver III*
7 Gibber IV,3*
8 Shiver III

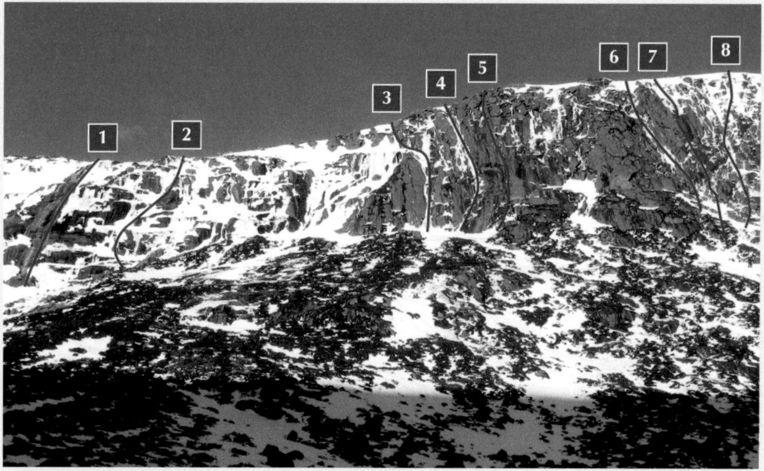

The Waterfall 150m II*

ND Keir and J Taylor, 2 January 1974

Climb ice on the left of the main fall. Escapes to the left are possible.

Spectrum 110m III**

D Dinwoodie and J Mothersele, 1 December 1971

Follows the obvious corners and grooves right of The Waterfall. Climb the ice leading into the V-groove near the top, which gives a fine finish. Can give a sustained climb on water-ice.

Mid-West Buttress

This is the highest and most continuous buttress to the right of the waterfall, although the lower slabs may blank out completely.

Lethargy 120m II/III*

J Bower and GR Simpson

The obvious corner on the left of the buttress usually forms a continuous line of ice. Climb the corner and go left above it. The obvious direct finish up the steep ice fall above the corner is IV,5.

Indolence 140m III*

A Nisbet and A Robertson, 12 December 1976

The next ice fall right of Lethargy, which has its best and steepest ice high on the buttress.

Nomad's Crack 150m V,5*

A Nisbet and A Robertson, 26 December 1976

The next and best-defined groove right of Indolence can give a good route up a narrow ribbon of ice that forms in grooves. The lower slabs can bank out.

Mid-East Buttress

This triangular mass is characterised by a big inverted L-shaped corner, the line of Gibber. It lies on the left of the obvious Diagonal Gully.

Ross Hewitt finding good ice on Funeral Fall, Broad Cairn Bluffs (photo: Henning Wackerage)

Sliver — 150m III*

RJ Archbold and GS Strange, 15 December 1974

This takes the fairly continuous line of water-ice that runs up the right side of the broken ground between Mid-West and Mid-East Buttresses.

Gibber — 130m IV,3*

A Nisbet and N Spinks, 2 February 1977

The big inverted L-shaped corner gives the line of this climb. The amount of ice is variable, and it may be poorly protected if the crack in the corner is not accessible.

Shiver — 150m III

RJ Archbold and GS Strange, 31 January 1976

This is the ice fall on the right side of the slabs. A choice of lines may be possible.

Broad Cairn Bluffs

NO 248 818 Altitude 700m North facing

This is the cliff on the left about 1km before the Dubh Loch. The main face is the left wall of an open gully. It may provide an alternative for a short day or when the going is extremely heavy.

Funeral Fall — 50m IV,4**

M Freeman and ND Keir, 3 March 1974

The prominent ice fall gives a good climb.

The other routes here are **Coffin Chimney**, III, the narrow chimney; **Rake's Rib**, III, on its right; and **Yoo-Hoo Buttress**, III, the front of the buttress facing the glen.

Glen Clova

Glen Clova lies to the south-east of the main Southern Cairngorms mass of Lochnagar and Creag an Dubh Loch, and is different in many ways from the rest of the guide. The rock is not granite, it is generally lower and more vegetated, and the area is easily accessible only from the south and east. However, it can be more sheltered from bad weather from the north and west, and there are a number of fine climbs, particularly in the lower grades. The two main winter-climbing areas are the **Winter Corrie** of Driesh and **Corrie Fee**.

Glen Clova – Winter Corrie

- 1 Central Gully II
- 1A Left-hand Branch II/III
- 2 Easy Gully I
- 3 Backdoor Chimney II/III
- 4 Backdoor Gully II*
- 4A Right-hand Finish II*
- 4B Direct Finish IV,4
- 5 Diamond Slab IV,4
- 6 Diagonal Gully III**
- 7 Pinnacle Gully II
- 8 Wiggle III
- 9 The Shute I

(photo: Greg Strange)

Winter Corrie

NO 277 745 *Altitude 650m* *North-east facing*

The Winter Corrie of Driesh is the obvious corrie overlooking the road-head and lies to the south of The Scorrie, a distinctive cone-shaped buttress. The rocks are very broken, but do offer some interesting routes. The Waterfall is on the left of the main rocks. The Main Buttress is the highest section of cliff and is characterised by The Basin, a big snow patch in its centre.

Access

From the car park at Braedownie follow the track into the Glen Doll forest and after 500m cross the bridge over the White Burn and head back out of the forest. Continue south-east by the fields to the burn draining the corrie, then go directly into the corrie. Alternatively, go diagonally under the steeper rocks of The Scorrie to gain the corrie, with some big boulders and awkward ground.

Descents

Easy Gully is the simplest descent in good conditions. Alternatively, contour round the corrie edge and go down the northerly slopes of The Scorrie to the path in Glen Doll.

Conditions

Several of the climbs are water courses and come into condition quite quickly in cold weather.

The Waterfall 70m II/III*

The ice fall high on the left side of the face gives the line of this climb. The easiest line is the inset corner on the left of the main stream, but if fully frozen it is better to start up the V-groove on the right and climb this to the main fall.

Central Gully 120m II

In the centre of the corrie is an obvious deep gully. There is a left branch, which is Grade II/III.

Easy Gully 120m I

This is the straight, straightforward and obvious gully in the centre of the corrie.

Backdoor Chimney 200m II/III

Where Backdoor Gully bends right, climb the deep chimney.

Backdoor Gully 200m II*

The deep gully that cuts up behind the Main Buttress to reach The Basin. There, either move left as soon as possible to easier ground, or go to the top right of The Basin and finish up a gully on the right.

Solo climber on Diagonal Gully, Winter Corrie
(photo: Greg Strange)

Direct Finish **80m IV,4**

From the top-left corner of The Basin climb ice to below a deep crack. Go right then back left to climb the wall right of this crack. Go up and slightly right to finish.

Diamond Slab 70m IV,4

GR Simpson and party, 1980

Left of Diagonal Gully are a chimney and steep slab that give a good climb and can be combined with the Direct Finish to Backdoor Gully.

Diagonal Gully 200m III**

In the middle of the Main Buttress a 30m ice fall descends from a right-slanting chimney. Climb the ice and chimney into The Basin and go to its top-right corner. Climb the ice fall above until forced right to a block belay. Easier ground leads to the top.

Wild Cat Wall 220m V,6*

C Cartwright and S Richardson, 27 November 2005

A direct mixed line up the centre of the cliff, starting 40m right of Diagonal Gully below a hidden left-slanting chimney ramp. Climb the gully over a chokestone to The Basin, then continue to the foot of the inverted triangle-shaped headwall (80m). Gain the headwall steeply from the left, then climb easier ground to the foot of the vertical wall and a belay below an obvious off-width crack. (40m). Climb the crack and continue up the steep continuation crack to a good ledge below and right of a large sloping roof (20m). Continue up the right of twin corners above and exit onto a left-trending ramp that leads to a long horizontal ledge (40m). Move right along the dwindling ledge to a break that leads to the top (20m).

Pinnacle Gully 120m II

This is deep gully right of Diagonal Gully that leads to The Basin. From the top of the snows here finish up rightwards.

Wiggle 220m III

Right of Pinnacle Gully climb some heathery grooves, then go left and up to steep wall. Climb the narrow chimney on the left to easier ground and finish up a broad ridge.

The Shute 120m I

The wide snow gully on the right of the cliff.

Brian Findlay on the first pitch of Diagonal Gully, Winter Corrie

Corrie Fee

NO 250 750 *Altitude 550m* *North-east facing*

This is the biggest and best winter-climbing area in Glen Clova. The corrie has two walls that meet at the Fee Burn. The South Wall is the more important and stretches south-east from the burn towards the Shank of Drumfollow. There are five gullies that split the crag, and from left to right they are A, B, Look C, D and E. Look C is much less defined than the others and runs up the left side of Central Buttress, the steepest and largest mass of rock.

Access

From the car park at Braedownie follow the track into the Glen Doll forest and cross the White Water by the bridge at NO 267 758. Continue west along the track and continuation path to a stile at the edge of the forest and the start of the corrie.

Descents

A and D Gullies can be used for descent. Alternatively, follow the fence from the top of B Gully Chimney round to the Shank of Drumfollow and descend that to gain the Kilbo path and the Glen Doll forest.

Glen Clova – Corrie Fee

1 A Gully I
2 B Gully Chimney III,4**
3 B Gully Buttress III
4 B Gully II*
5 Look C Gully IV,4***
6 Wet Knees IV,4*
7 D Gully I
8 The Pyramid IV,5

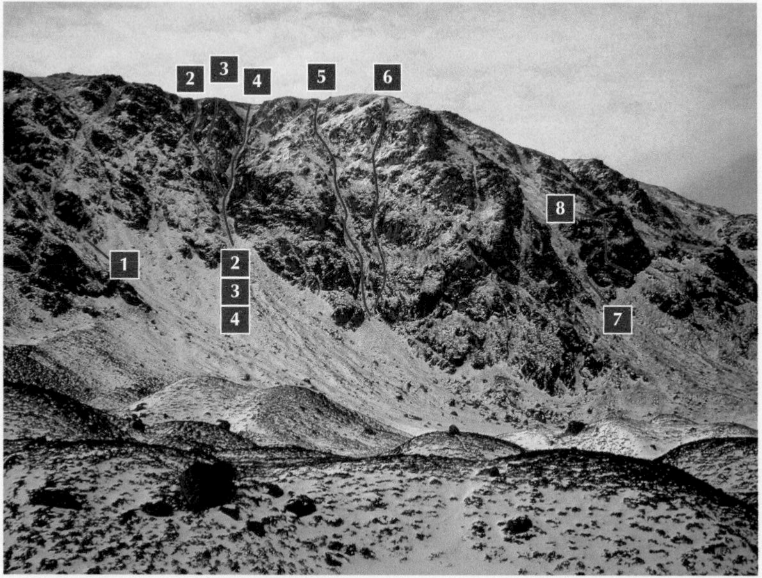

(photo: Greg Strange)

A Gully — 200m I

The gully in the left corner of the corrie is straightforward.

A-B Integrate — 200m II

Right of A Gully is a 100m easy angled corner that can be icy early in the season. Finish up easier ground to the top.

B Gully Chimney — 150m III,4**

D Crabb and D Lang, 29 December 1962

B Gully is well defined, and after about 60m this route breaks out left. It can be icy, although some pitches can bank out.

B Gully Buttress — 150m III

The buttress between B Gully Chimney and B Gully is climbed direct.

Pete Trudgill on some continental-style ice on the crux pitch of Look C Gully (photo: Henning Wackerage)

B Gully 200m II*

H Raeburn, W Galbraith and WA Reid, May 1915

This well-defined gully may have at least one ice pitch, although it can be avoided on the right. The left branch, the obvious deep chimney containing several chokestones, is the best finish.

Look C Gully 200m IV,4***

CL Donaldson and JR Marshall, 15 February 1953

This takes the shallow fault in the left of Central Buttress and gives the best route in the area, although it does require a good freeze to come into condition. Climb up stepped ice to above a short chimney. Take the left-hand gully line into a basin, then climb the rib on the right to below the main ice fall. Climb the ice direct, then continue up short pitches to where the gully forks. Above it is easier, so a good finish is to go up the left fork until a descent down a short gully leads into B Gully, where B Gully Chimney provides a more appropriate continuation.

Wet Knees 200m IV,4*

ND Keir and A Lawson, 30 January 1972

Takes a line of discontinuous chimneys immediately right of Look C Gully. Start up an ice smear at the foot of Look C. The last chimney is the best pitch.

D Gully 200m I

This gully lies on the right side of Central Buttress and is straightforward.

Diamond Buttress 60m V,7

S Stewart and BA Strachan, November 1985

Right of D Gully are two rock pyramids; this is the upper and left one. Start in a recess on the right and climb a flake crack and a slab to a rib. Above, a groove is followed to the top.

The Pyramid 60m IV,5

A Paul, G Reilly, I Reilly and W Taylor, November 1985

The right and lower of the pyramids is climbed by a line close to the crest. Escapable between pitches.

E Gully I

This is the short open gully high up at the right end of the face.

CREAG MEAGAIDH

Climbers on The Pumpkin, in the Inner Corrie (photo: Paul Cummingham)

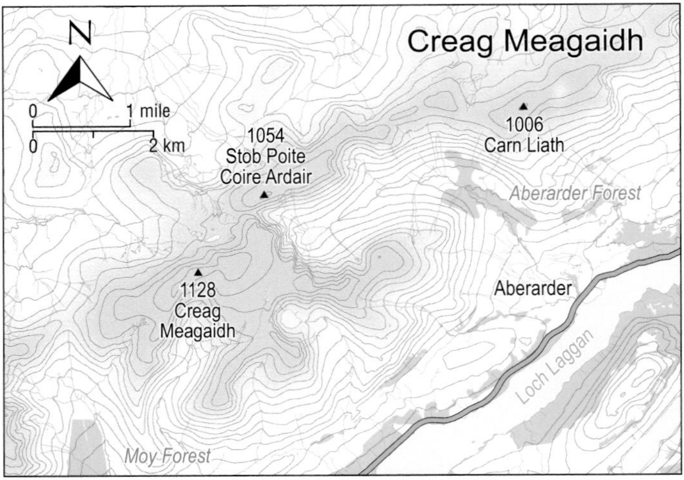

CREAG MEAGAIDH

NN 418 875

Creag Meagaidh lies north of Loch Laggan in the Moy Forest and is currently owned by Scottish Natural Heritage (SNH). It is noted for its native birch woods, which SNH are trying to regenerate. Creag Meagaidh is situated roughly halfway between the west coast and the Cairngorms. The conditions found here tend to lie between what are found in those areas. There is generally more ice here than in the Cairngorms, but it is less affected by thaw than the mountains nearer the sea. The main corrie, Coire Ardair, is about 1km east of the summit and is backed by an extensive plateau. The rock is mica shist, which is generally fairly shattered and has a horizontal strata that dips back into the hillside. These factors, combined with the large amounts of vegetation present on the rock, mean that snow and ice accumulate to considerable depths in places. This can produce very fine winter routes with some superb ice lines. It also, unfortunately, means there is often a significant avalanche hazard.

The main cliff of Coire Ardair is about 3km long and nearly 500m in height. The bulk of the cliff, as clearly seen from the lochan in the corrie bottom, is divided into three main buttresses split by two very large gullies. High up on the left is **Bellevue Buttress**, which is separated from the impressive **Pinnacle Buttress** by the left-slanting Raeburn's Gully. Right of Pinnacle Buttress is the left-trending highway of Easy Gully, above which rises the **Post Face**, split by the four distinctive gullies or posts. At right angles to the Post Face, and hidden from the lochan, is the more broken **Inner Corrie**, which stretches to the Window (NN 426 886), the prominent col to the north.

Because of the nature of the rock, the cliffs here are cut by some prominent and distinctive ledge systems. These lend themselves to traverse lines and give what is probably the finest horizontal excursion in Scottish winter climbing, the Crab Crawl. This is described as its four constituent parts, but it also means that pitches can be interchanged on other routes as well.

Access

The approach starts from the A86, Newtonmore to Spean Bridge road. It is therefore readily accessible from both Aviemore and Fort William. Start from the car park NN 483 872 at the track to Aberarder farm, which is well signed. Take the track to the farm and pass to the east of the buildings, where the SAIS avalanche forecast is posted. Follow the very good path on the north-east of the Allt Coire Ardair, which takes a high line parallel to the burn. This takes a big curve round into the corrie to eventually descend to the corrie floor then on to the lochan. When there is heavy snow it may be best to keep high up on the right side of the glen until the approach into the corrie is obvious. Depending on snow conditions, the approach can be long and arduous.

Descents

The summit plateau is flat and featureless, and care must be taken when navigating to the descent routes. Raeburn's Gully and Easy Gully give quick descents for competent parties in suitable conditions. From climbs on Bellevue and Pinnacle Buttresses, the ridge of Sron a'Choire leads back down to Aberarder farm. From climbs on the Post Face and the Inner Corrie, a descent by the Window to the corrie floor and the lochan is probably the easiest.

Conditions

This corrie holds plenty of snow and ice and is usually in condition at some time during the winter. It gets the snow from the west, but avoids the worst thaws from that direction. In general the gully lines are better than the buttress routes here, and as many of the routes are ice climbs they tend to be better slightly later in the season, when they have had a chance to build up. Some of the deeper and thicker ice routes can withstand a reasonable thaw. The rock varies from quite compact to shattered, and so a variety of nuts and pegs is useful. Ice screws are essential on many of the ice routes, with drive-in Spectre/Bulldog ice-hooks being useful in frozen turf and icy cracks. Longer ropes can be very useful on some of the harder climbs here. There are some large snow fields that may require snow anchors, even on harder routes. The large cornices and open slopes on and above many of the climbs constitute a very real avalanche hazard.

Girdle Traverse

Crab Crawl **2400m IV,4*****

TW Patey, 23 March 1969

This huge horizontal excursion is an aptly named and natural line. It is best from left to right, and consists of The Scene, Appolyon Ledge, Post Horn Gallop and The Last Lap. For further detail refer to these routes, which link in a logical manner.

Bellevue Buttress

NN 436 875 *Altitude 900m* *North-east facing*

This is the buttress at the left or east end of Coire Ardair. On its right is the huge Pinnacle Buttress, and between the two is tapering Raeburn's Gully Buttress.

The Scene **450m II***

D Gray and A MacKeith, 15 January 1966

The first part of the girdle traverse. Follow the obvious horizontal ledge from left to right across the buttress into Raeburn's Gully. Spectacular and exposed in places.

Naevueata **120m IV,4***

A MacKeith, G Anderson and J Heron, 19 February 1966

This takes a line up the left side of the buttress. Start just to the left of The Scene. Climb snow, then an ice pitch, to the next snow field. Climb the right-hand of the two ice pitches above and continue on steep snow to the cornice and the top.

Eastern Corner **300m III****

CGM Slessor and K Bryan, 28 January 1961

At the right side of Bellevue Buttress, where it abuts the smaller Raeburn's Gully Buttress, is an obvious open corner. The corner is followed throughout, with the lower section providing the more technical pitches, and it can be more or less continuous ice, when it will be harder. The upper section is straightforward snow climbing.

Raeburn's Gully Buttress

NN 435 876 *Altitude 850m* *North-east facing*

This is the long narrow buttress with a steep left wall lying between Eastern Corner and Raeburn's Gully. It contains a number of good mixed routes, and can be a useful alternative early in the season or when the big ice routes are not in condition.

Creag Meagaidh – Bellevue and Pinnacle Buttresses

1 Eastern Corner III**
2 Barry White IV,6 *
3 Do What Thou Wilt IV,4*
4 Raeburn's Gully I*
5 Ritchie's Gully IV,4**
6 Smith's Gully VI,5***
7 The Fly Direct VII,6***
8 The Midge VI,5*
9 The White Spider IV,4
10 Pinnacle Buttress Direct VI,5**
11 1959 Face Route V,4**
12 Easy Gully I
13 Missed the Post V,5*
14 The Last Post V,5***
15 South Post Direct V,4**

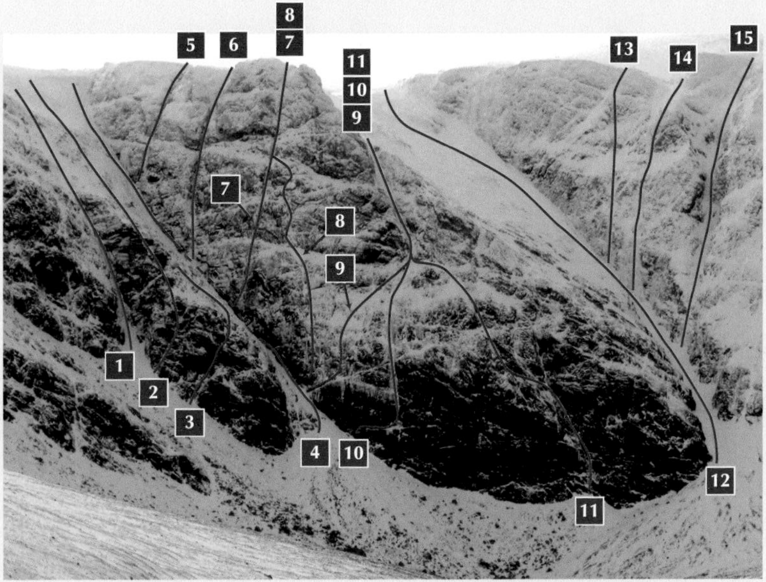

Barry White — 350m IV,6*

A Clarke, A Perkins, I Taylor and P Thorburn, January 1999

A fine, reasonably well-protected mixed route. Start just to the right of Eastern Corner, where a curving fault runs rightwards. Climb this to a ledge below a crack, which is followed to easier ground below a chimney. Climb this and continue more easily along the crest of the buttress.

Do What Thou Wilt — 400m IV,4*

A Powell and S Grayson, 12 February 1994

Start in a snow bay by a small tower. Climb this snowy groove, trending rightwards, then take an obvious yet unlikely looking ramp through a roof. Move right and climb a short wall to easier ground.

Raeburn's Gully — 350m I*

H Raeburn, C Walker and H Walker, 31 October 1903

The leftmost of the two large left-trending gullies is climbed direct below the spectacular wall of Pinnacle Buttress. There may be the occasional ice pitch or awkward cornice exit.

Pinnacle Buttress

NN 434 877 — Altitude 850m — East facing

This is the steep and impressive buttress lying between Raeburn's and Easy Gully. There is a very steep wall rising above Raeburn's Gully, which is cut by three parallel faults – the lines of Ritchie's Gully, Smith's Gully and The Fly. Pinnacle Buttress is also traversed by three horizontal lines – the central of which is Appolyon Ledge, and the lower is Vanishing Ledge. The lower section of the front face has an extremely steep initial wall, with some lines of weakness on its right side. Higher up, this section tapers inwards and forms the left side of Easy Gully.

Appolyon Ledge — 500m II*

D Gray and A MacKeith, 16 January 1966

The second part of the girdle takes the middle of the three faults cutting Pinnacle Buttress. Start in Raeburn's Gully about 90m from the top and cross the face by the middle of the three ledges. It is extremely exposed and spectacular, and leads to easy ground and into Easy Gully.

Helen Rennard finding some good ice on the crux pitch of Smith's Gully (photo: Henning Wackerage)

Ritchie's Gully **160m IV,4****

GN Hunter and N Quinn, March 1969

The leftmost of the three parallel faults above Raeburn's Gully. Climb the initial ice fall, turning an overhang on the right, and continue up to Appolyon Ledge. Climb the gully above, with several ice pitches. The cornice may be difficult.

Smith's Gully **180m VI,5*****

JR Marshall and G Tiso, 8 February 1959

The steep gully cutting straight up Pinnacle Buttress from Raeburn's Gully gives a magnificent, sustained and serious ice route, one of the finest in the country. Unfortunately it takes a while to come into good condition. Climb the gully to belay on the left above a snow bay (35m). An icy bulge leads to a belay in another snow bay (20m). Continue the still steep gully to where Appolyon Ledge cuts across the face (45m). Climb the steep ice above (crux) to reach easier ground (45m). Easier snowy ground above leads to the top (35m).

The Fly Direct **240m VII,6*****

M Fowler and A Saunders, 19 February 1983

The right-hand fault is a narrow gully – serious, sustained and superb when in condition, which unfortunately is not all that often. Start about 10m left of the gully and climb mixed ground up and right to reach the gully proper. Alternatively, start in a niche about 10m right of the gully, climb a groove, then traverse left below a roof to the foot of the gully line. Climb the wide crack in the bulge into the gully and continue up the depression. Ascend a steep ice fall, then continue more easily to Appolyon Ledge. Go up the open chimney and exit right below the big roof, then diagonally right to an icicle. Climb this and the ice fall above to eventually gain an easy snow groove leading to the top.

The Midge **400m VI,5***

G Harper and A Nisbet, 19 February 1983

Another huge route up the wall right of The Fly. Ice is needed in the initial section and in The Fly ice fall. Start near the foot of Raeburn's Gully where a fault, Raeburn's Ledge, slopes up to the right. Climb a steep icy corner for two pitches to the left end of a large snow patch. Go up a short groove, then left, and climb iced slabs on the right of a big right-facing corner to Vanishing Ledge. Go left to belay below a second right-facing corner. Climb this corner, which leans right at the start with an exit left at the top. Continue up to belay below a roof. Turn this on the right, go left a short way and trend right to Appolyon Ledge. Traverse for about 30m left to join and finish up the top three pitches of The Fly Direct.

The White Spider — 300m IV,4

AL Wielochowski and JP Nash, 16 February 1976

A fine route. Start as for The Midge, and traverse 30m rightwards along Raeburn's Ledge to a corner. Climb this to a snow field (40m). Continue straight up (40m), and then climb a 20m ice pitch on the left to another snow field. Traverse right for 60 metres, and climb another 20m ice pitch onto a ledge. Finish up the final gully of 1959 Face Route.

A direct start, **White Knuckle Ride** (VI,6), heads up diagonally rightwards to climb a thin ice pillar, and then moves back left to the end of the initial traverse on the original route (60m).

Nordwander — 300m IV,4*

D Dinwoodie, B Lawrie, M Freeman and D Stuart, 11 March 1972

From the foot of Raeburn's Gully, this route goes diagonally right to finish in the prominent gully on the right of the upper section of the face. This top gully is common with 1959 Face Route. Start just up from the foot of Raeburn's Gully, where Raeburn's Ledge slants up right. Traverse this for a pitch, then break through iced slabby walls above to reach easier grooves leading to the central snow ledges. Go up and right to gain the prominent gully, and finish as for 1959 Face Route.

Pinnacle Buttress Direct — 320m VI,5**

J Sylvester and K Howett, 22 March 1984

In very icy conditions an ice fall can form all the way down the buttress from the exit gully of 1959 Face Route to reach the left toe of the buttress at the foot of Raeburn's Gully. This ice is reached by traversing a ledge starting about 45m up the gully (45m). Climb the icicle and continue up very steep ice to a short icy slab (40m). Climb the steepening slab on the left to reach a vague vertical groove leading to a thread belay (45m). Climb ice smears to join Nordwander and finish as for 1959 Face Route.

1959 Face Route — 450m V,4**

JR Marshall, J Stenhouse and D Haston, 9 February 1959

A fine mixed climb that takes a left-slanting line across the lower face to reach the central snow fields, above which the deep prominent gully right of the summit tower is followed. Start in a small bay just right of the lowest rocks and about 80m right of Raeburn's Gully. Climb the left-trending depression for 60m, then go left into a shallow gully, which develops into ice chimneys. A pitch below the ice chimneys, traverse left for 60m to gain a slanting chimney with a prominent chokestone. Climb this for two pitches to the central snow fields. Above, enter the obvious gully, turning its barrier ice fall on the right, and follow this to the top.

Creag Meagaidh – The Post Face

1 Easy Gully I
2 Missed the Post V,5*
3 The Last Post V,5***
4 South Post Direct V,4**
5 Centre Post III**
5A Centre Post Direct V,5**
6 North Post V,5**
7 Postman Pat VII,7**
8 Staghorn Gully III***
9 South Pipe IV,4**

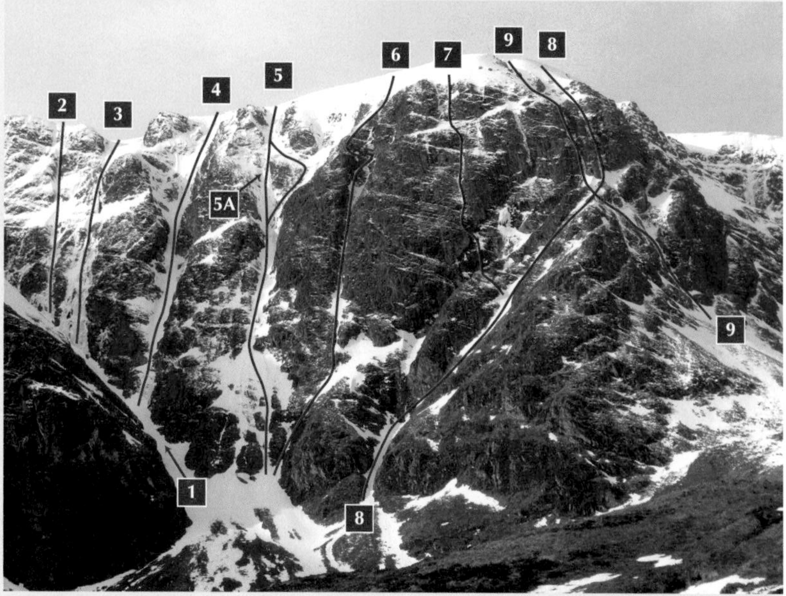

The Post Face

NN 432 879 *Altitude 900m* *East facing*

This is the face rising above the wide left-trending Easy Gully and extending right to Staghorn Gully, where the cliff bends round into the Inner Corrie. It is characterised by the four large parallel faults of the Post Climbs. These are separated by large buttresses, the Pillars, which give climbs of IV,4 standard. To the right of North Post, the rightmost fault, is Great Buttress, whose lower section is cut by two shelves that slant up to the right to two smaller parallel gullies, known as the Pipes.

Easy Gully 450m I

W Tough, W Douglas and H Raeburn, April 1896

The obvious, wide left-sloping gully. It is narrow at first, widening out at about half-height into open snow fields. The easiest line moves left in the upper section. If used in descent, keep well out from the Post Face initially, then cut back underneath it in the lower section.

Missed the Post 220m V,5*

P Brownsort and P Smith, 9 February 1985

The narrow line left of, and parallel to, The Last Post. Start at the ice fall about 20m further up Easy Gully from that route. Climb the ice onto a steep ramp, which leads to a snow field. Go via short steps and snow fields to a short steep chimney, then more snow, into a shallow icy chimney. Climb this, crux, to easy ground and the top.

The Last Post 240m V,5***

TW Patey and RF Brooke, 5 March 1962

An excellent ice route up the left-hand of the major faults. Climb the impressive initial ice fall, starting about half-way up Easy Gully. Above, snow fields lead to the next ice fall, which is climbed in two pitches. Easy snow then leads to the final ice fall, above which easy ground leads to the top. A variation that takes the left-hand side of the initial ice fall, the right-hand side of the second, and avoids the final ice fall on the left can be climbed at grade IV,4.

Post Horn Gallop 650m IV,4

TW Patey and RF Brooke, 28 February 1962

The third part of the girdle. Start by climbing the first pitch of The Last Post variation to a ledge and follow this into the South Post below its second main pitch. Go up a short way and right onto a broad ledge, which leads into the Centre Post below its big ice pitch. Follow the ordinary route and continue diagonally to a spectacular ledge crossing the North Post. Continue into the snow bowl of Staghorn Gully.

South Post Direct **450m V,4****

TW Patey and RF Brooke, 5 March 1962

The second post from the left starts with an impressive ice fall, which is climbed to easier ground. This leads to the next ice pitch, which is climbed diagonally from left to right (crux). Above, the gully and more ice leads to the top. The grade can be reduced to Grade III if the initial ice fall is avoided on the right by climbing diagonally left from the base of Centre Post to join the main route, and the crux pitch is avoided on the left.

Centre Post **400m III****

CM Allan and JHB Bell, 21 March 1937

This is the third fault from the left. The first 250m are straightforward and lead to a huge ice fall. Make a diagonal traverse up the right wall of the gully and climb an ice pitch to the snow field above. This is climbed until a traverse back rejoins the main gully, which is followed to the top.

Centre Post Direct **400m V,5****

B Robertson, F Harper and E Cairns, 22 February 1964

Centre Post Direct takes the huge ice fall direct – the first half being the steepest and the top only slightly easier. It can vary from about 45m to 60m in height, depending on the build-up, and can be very hard early in the season.

North Post **400m V,5****

TW Patey, JH Deacon, GR McLeod and P Danelet, 6 February 1960

The rightmost and narrowest of the posts gives a good route when in condition. Easy snow leads to a steep narrow chimney gully with a chokestone (crux). Above, the gully widens, and a chimney in the left corner eventually leads to a ledge that is followed easily to a large platform on the right. Traverse back left for 25m across the face overlooking the gully. A further 30m of climbing, first rightwards then left, leads to open snow slopes and the top.

Direct Finish **60m VI,5*****

Where the gully widens climb a steep ice fall instead of the chimney in the corner to reach snow ledges of Post Horn Gallop. Above, thinner ice leads to the top.

Postman Pat **290m VII,7****

A Perkins and M Duff, 10 February 1991

A fine hard route combining steep ice and technical mixed climbing. Above the lower section of Staghorn Gully lies a sloping shelf above an overhanging wall. Two icicles sometimes form down this wall. Climb the left-hand icicle to the shelf and head along this to belay below a narrow turf ledge (45m). Traverse left along

Chad Harrison enjoying some steep ice on the first ascent of Postal Strike (photo: Steve Fortune)

this ledge for about 5m until it is possible to climb steeply through the wall (crux) to reach a wide shallow gully (45m). Two pitches then lead to the Post Horn Gallop terrace (100m). Another two pitches up icy runnels and snow slopes lead to the top (100m). In good conditions it is sometimes possible to avoid the traverse left on pitch two by climbing the wall direct on ice.

Postal Strike — 250m VII,6**

C Harrison and S Fortune, 30 January 2010

Another fine route starting up the obvious ice fall up and right of the Postman Pat icicles, then taking a steep and exposed line up the buttress above. Climb the steep ice fall to belay on, or just below, the sloping shelf (40m). Trend up and right to gain a turfy traverse line, and follow this back left past a small groove to gain a large hanging groove. Continue up the left rib of this to belay where the angle eases (50m). Follow the left-facing corner to the big ledge of Post Horn Gallop and traverse left to join and finish up Postman Pat (160m).

Staghorn Gully — 400m III***

CNM Allan, JHB Bell, HM Kelly and H Cooper, 29 April 1934

Where the Post Face bends round into the Inner Corrie there are two parallel gullies in the upper part of the face. These are the South and North Pipes. Staghorn Gully finishes up the latter. It is a justifiably popular route. Start at the foot of North Post and climb a shallow gully, the Shelf, diagonally rightwards to reach these chimneys. The right-hand chimney, the North Pipe, gives a series of short ice pitches leading to a snow bowl and then the top. A more direct variation, which starts up and right of the main route and climbs a shallow gully to gain the North Pipe, can be climbed at the same grade.

South Pipe — 250m IV,4**

JH Deacon and TW Patey, 7 February 1960

Start up the direct start to Staghorn Gully, then climb the South Pipe, which is the left-hand of the parallel chimneys. This gives a fine icy climb.

The Inner Corrie

NN 430 883 — Altitude 900m — North-east facing

This lies between Staghorn Gully and the Window, and is generally less steep and more broken than the other buttresses, but may hold its conditions for longer. The main features of this cliff are, firstly, the large icy corner of The Pumpkin, then the twin ice falls of The Wand and Diadem higher up the cliff. To the right again is the

Eric Pirie starting the North Pipe on Staghorn Gully

prominent gully of Cinderella, then the rocks become somewhat steeper and are bisected by the distinctive curve of Crescent Gully before diminishing in height towards the Window.

The Last Lap — 900m IV,4*

A MacKeith and M Galbraith, 12 February 1966

The final part of the girdle. Climb the Shelf of Staghorn Gully to below the Pipes and traverse right on ledges into The Sash. Descend this to cross below the ice falls of The Wand and Diadem, then go diagonally right onto the snow field. Traverse this and descend into Cinderella, then climb The Prow to a pitch below the top. Move into Crescent Gully and go down to above its ice pitch. Cross the right wall by a spectacular ledge on the vertical wall, then continue across Quasimodo to the Window.

To link Post Horn Gallop to this route, go down The Sash from the snow bowl at the top of Staghorn Gully.

Trespasser Buttress — 300m IV,5**

GN Hunter, H MacInnes, DF Lang and N Quinn, March 1969

The buttress between South Pipe Direct and The Pumpkin has a left-to-right-slanting narrow chimney system. Start at the left corner of the buttress and climb up to

Creag Meagaidh – The Inner Corrie

1 South Pipe IV,4**
2 Trespasser Buttress IV,5**
3 The Pumpkin V,4***
4 The Sash II*
5 The Wand V,5**
6 Diadem IV,4*
7 Glass Slipper III*
8 Cinderella II*
9 The Prow III
10 Crescent Gully II

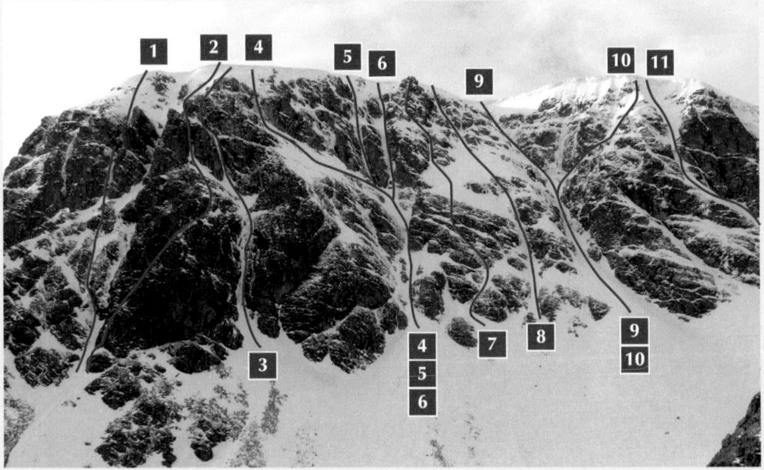

gain the chimney system, which is followed to a snow bay. Move right and climb another chimney to a large overhang. Move right to the Diving Board, an exposed ledge, then continue up easier ground to a large chimney. Climb this, then traverse left to the crest of the upper buttress and follow this. Finish by a small chimney, then easier ground.

The Pumpkin 300m V,4***

R McMillan, GS Peet and N Quinn, 14 April 1968

A classic and very popular ice climb that takes the long right-facing corner right of Trespasser Buttress. The corner is climbed direct to easier ground, above which a left-trending chimney, again difficult, is followed to less demanding climbing and the top.

The Sash 240m II*

TW Patey, RWP Barclay, M Laverty and E Attfield, March 1963

This starts in the narrow gully below the two parallel ice falls and then trends left across the face. Climb the lower gully direct to below the ice, then go up and left on a series of shelves and ledges to reach the plateau.

The Wand 220m V,5**

QT Crichton, DF Lang, GN Hunter and N Quinn, 2 February 1969

The left-hand of the parallel ice falls gives a fine route. Climb The Sash to the ice, then climb the ice close to the corner. Above the ice, a choice of lines leads to the top.

Diadem 220m IV,4*

J Brown and TW Patey, 19 February 1964

The right-hand and easier of the two ice falls is approached via The Sash. Climb the initial ice fall, then go up to a long iced corner, which is followed to easier ground and then the top.

Fairy Godmother 220m III*

MG Geddes and NG Rayner, 27 December 1970

Between the gullies of The Sash and Cinderella is a buttress with a large central snow field that gives a varied climb. Start halfway between The Sash and the narrow initial chimney of Glass Slipper and climb a right-sloping ramp for a pitch. Work up and left by walls and ramps to the central snow field. Climb the obvious short gully, which is left of the three faults above the snow field. Go leftwards up a ramp to above Diadem and finish by the steep tower.

Glass Slipper 220m III*

I MacEacheran and J Knight, March 1964

Start at the right of the buttress at a narrow chimney that leads in two pitches to the snow field. Above this climb the central of three breaks, with one ice pitch to the plateau.

Cinderella 220m II*

W Tout and TW Patey, February 1963

The prominent gully in the centre of the face is climbed direct. It can have a very large cornice, which can be a real avalanche danger.

The Prow 220m III

D Pyper and M Main, March 1963

Climb Cinderella to mid-height, then go right on a ramp to the crest of the buttress. Climb this to the top. The cornice can be large and difficult.

The Ugly Sister 210m III

MG Geddes and NC Rayner, 27 December 1970

Lies on the buttress between Cinderella and Crescent Gully. Climb a ramp sloping up left to a saddle, then go up the crest for about 6m. Traverse right to a better line going left to the crest, and finish up this to a sometimes large cornice.

Crescent Gully 210m II

J Clarkson and RJ Tanton, 17 February 1958

The curving gully on the buttress left of the Window. Climb a diminishing snow line going slightly left. An ice pitch then leads to the upper snowy amphitheatre.

Quasimodo 210m III

RS Burnett and A MacKeith, 22 January 1966

Lies on the right of Crescent Gully. Start up a narrow gully and ramp, which curves left below an overhanging chimney. Where it fades out, traverse right round awkward bulges above the chimney for a pitch. Climb the spur, then snow on the left to the top.

Longfellow 210m II

R MacMillan and GS Peet, 2 March 1968

This route takes the narrow gully right of Crescent Gully. Climb the gully for about 60m, then go right, then left, over a short wall to gain a groove system on the left. Climb this to the crest of the buttress, then the top.

APPENDIX A

Index of Routes: Cairngorms North

APPENDIX B

Index of Routes: Cairngorms South

APPENDIX C

Index of Routes: Creag Meagaidh

LISTING OF CICERONE GUIDES

BRITISH ISLES CHALLENGES, COLLECTIONS AND ACTIVITIES

The End to End Trail
The Mountains of England and Wales
1 Wales & 2 England
The National Trails
The Relative Hills of Britain
The Ridges of England, Wales and Ireland
The UK Trailwalker's Handbook
The UK's County Tops
Three Peaks, Ten Tors

MOUNTAIN LITERATURE

Unjustifiable Risk?

UK CYCLING

Border Country Cycle Routes
Cycling in the Peak District
Lands End to John O'Groats Cycle Guide
Mountain Biking in the Lake District
Mountain Biking on the South Downs
The C2C Cycle Route
The Lancashire Cycleway

SCOTLAND

Backpacker's Britain
Central and Southern Scottish Highlands
Northern Scotland
Ben Nevis and Glen Coe
North to the Cape
Not the West Highland Way
Scotland's Best Small Mountains
Scotland's Far West
Scotland's Mountain Ridges
Scrambles in Lochaber
The Ayrshire and Arran Coastal Paths
The Border Country
The Great Glen Way
The Isle of Mull
The Isle of Skye
The Pentland Hills: A Walker's Guide
The Southern Upland Way
The Speyside Way
The West Highland Way
Walking in Scotland's Far North
Walking in the Cairngorms
Walking in the Hebrides
Walking in the Ochils, Campsie Fells and Lomond Hills
Walking in Torridon
Walking Loch Lomond and the Trossachs
Walking on Harris and Lewis
Walking on Jura, Islay and Colonsay
Walking on the Isle of Arran
Walking on the Orkney and Shetland Isles
Walking the Galloway Hills
Walking the Lowther Hills
Walking the Munros
1 Southern, Central and Western Highlands
2 Northern Highlands and the Cairngorms
Winter Climbs Ben Nevis and Glen Coe
Winter Climbs in the Cairngorms
World Mountain Ranges: Scotland

NORTHERN ENGLAND TRAILS

A Northern Coast to Coast Walk
Backpacker's Britain
Northern England
Hadrian's Wall Path
The Dales Way
The Pennine Way
The Spirit of Hadrian's Wall

NORTH EAST ENGLAND, YORKSHIRE DALES AND PENNINES

Historic Walks in North Yorkshire
South Pennine Walks
The Cleveland Way and the Yorkshire Wolds Way
The North York Moors
The Reivers Way
The Teesdale Way
The Yorkshire Dales Angler's Guide
The Yorkshire Dales
North and East
South and West
Walking in County Durham
Walking in Northumberland
Walking in the North Pennines
Walking in the Wolds
Walks in Dales Country
Walks in the Yorkshire Dales
Walks on the North York Moors – Books 1 & 2

NORTH WEST ENGLAND AND THE ISLE OF MAN

Historic Walks in Cheshire
Isle of Man Coastal Path
The Isle of Man
The Ribble Way
Walking in Cumbria's Eden Valley
Walking in Lancashire
Walking in the Forest of Bowland and Pendle
Walking on the West Pennine Moors
Walks in Lancashire Witch Country
Walks in Ribble Country
Walks in Silverdale and Arnside
Walks in the Forest of Bowland

LAKE DISTRICT

Coniston Copper Mines
Great Mountain Days in the Lake District
Lake District Winter Climbs
Lakeland Fellranger
The Central Fells
The Mid-Western Fells
The Near Eastern Fells

The North-Western Wells
The Southern Fells
The Western Fells
Roads and Tracks of the Lake District
Rocky Rambler's Wild Walks
Scrambles in the Lake District
North & South
Short Walks in Lakeland
1 South Lakeland
2 North Lakeland
3 West Lakeland
The Cumbria Coastal Way
The Cumbria Way and the Allerdale Ramble
Tour of the Lake District

DERBYSHIRE, PEAK DISTRICT AND MIDLANDS

High Peak Walks
The Star Family Walks
Walking in Derbyshire
White Peak Walks
The Northern Dales
The Southern Dales

SOUTHERN ENGLAND

A Walker's Guide to the Isle of Wight
London – The definitive walking guide
The Cotswold Way
The Greater Ridgeway
The North Downs Way
The South Downs Way
The South West Coast Path
The Thames Path
Walking in Berkshire
Walking in Kent
Walking in Sussex
Walking in the Isles of Scilly
Walking in the Thames Valley
Walking on Dartmoor
Walking on Guernsey
Walking on Jersey
Walks in the South Downs National Park

WALES AND WELSH BORDERS

Backpacker's Britain – Wales
Glyndwr's Way
Great Mountain Days in Snowdonia
Hillwalking in Snowdonia
Hillwalking in Wales Vols 1 & 2
Offa's Dyke Path
Ridges of Snowdonia
Scrambles in Snowdonia
The Ascent of Snowdon
The Lleyn Peninsula Coastal Path
The Pembrokeshire Coastal Path
The Shropshire Hills
The Wye Valley Walk
Walking in Pembrokeshire
Walking on the Brecon Beacons
Welsh Winter Climbs

INTERNATIONAL CHALLENGES, COLLECTIONS AND ACTIVITIES

Canyoning
Europe's High Points
The Via Francigena (Canterbury to Rome): Part 1

EUROPEAN CYCLING

Cycle Touring in France
Cycle Touring in Ireland
Cycle Touring in Spain
Cycle Touring in Switzerland
Cycling in the French Alps
Cycling the Canal du Midi
Cycling the River Loire
The Danube Cycleway
The Grand Traverse of the Massif Central
The Way of St James

AFRICA

Climbing in the Moroccan Anti-Atlas
Kilimanjaro: A Complete Trekker's Guide
Mountaineering in the Moroccan High Atlas
Trekking in the Atlas Mountains
Walking in the Drakensberg

ALPS – CROSS-BORDER ROUTES

100 Hut Walks in the Alps
Across the Eastern Alps: E5
Alpine Points of VIew
Alpine Ski Mountaineering
1 Western Alps
2 Central and Eastern Alps
Chamonix to Zermatt
Snowshoeing
Tour of Mont Blanc
Tour of Monte Rosa
Tour of the Matterhorn
Trekking in the Alps
Walking in the Alps
Walks and Treks in the Maritime Alps

PYRENEES AND FRANCE/ SPAIN CROSS-BORDER ROUTES

Rock Climbs in The Pyrenees
The GR10 Trail
The Mountains of Andorra
The Pyrenean Haute Route
The Pyrenees
The Way of St James France & Spain
Through the Spanish Pyrenees: GR11
Walks and Climbs in the Pyrenees

AUSTRIA

Trekking in Austria's Hohe Tauern
Trekking in the Stubai Alps
Trekking in the Zillertal Alps
Walking in Austria

EASTERN EUROPE

The High Tatras
The Mountains of Romania
Walking in Bulgaria's National Parks
Walking in Hungary

FRANCE

Ecrins National Park
GR20: Corsica
Mont Blanc Walks
Mountain Adventures in the Maurienne
The Cathar Way

The GR5 Trail
The Robert Louis Stevenson Trail
Tour of the Oisans: The GR54
Tour of the Queyras
Tour of the Vanoise
Trekking in the Vosges and Jura
Vanoise Ski Touring
Walking in Provence
Walking in the Cathar Region
Walking in the Cevennes
Walking in the Dordogne
Walking in the Haute Savoie North & South
Walking in the Languedoc
Walking in the Tarentaise and Beaufortain Alps
Walking on Corsica

GERMANY

Germany's Romantic Road
Walking in the Bavarian Alps
Walking in the Harz Mountains
Walking the River Rhine Trail

HIMALAYA

Annapurna: A Trekker's Guide
Bhutan
Everest: A Trekker's Guide
Garhwal and Kumaon: A Trekker's and Visitor's Guide
Kangchenjunga: A Trekker's Guide
Langtang with Gosainkund and Helambu: A Trekker's Guide
Manaslu: A Trekker's Guide
The Mount Kailash Trek

IRELAND

Irish Coastal Walks
The Irish Coast to Coast Walk
The Mountains of Ireland

ITALY

Gran Paradiso
Italy's Sibillini National Park
Shorter Walks in the Dolomites
Through the Italian Alps
Trekking in the Apennines
Trekking in the Dolomites
Via Ferratas of the Italian Dolomites: Vols 1 & 2
Walking in Abruzzo
Walking in Sardinia
Walking in Sicily
Walking in the Central Italian Alps
Walking in the Dolomites
Walking in Tuscany
Walking on the Amalfi Coast

MEDITERRANEAN

Jordan – Walks, Treks, Caves, Climbs and Canyons
The Ala Dag
The High Mountains of Crete
The Mountains of Greece
Treks and Climbs in Wadi Rum, Jordan
Walking in Malta
Western Crete

NORTH AMERICA

British Columbia
The Grand Canyon
The John Muir Trail
The Pacific Crest Trail

SOUTH AMERICA

Aconcagua and the Southern Andes
Torres del Paine

SCANDINAVIA

Trekking in Greenland
Walking in Norway

SLOVENIA, CROATIA AND MONTENEGRO

The Julian Alps of Slovenia
The Mountains of Montenegro
Trekking in Slovenia
Walking in Croatia

SPAIN AND PORTUGAL

Costa Blanca Walks 1 West & 2 East
Mountain Walking in Southern Catalunya
The Mountains of Central Spain
Trekking through Mallorca
Walking in Madeira
Walking in Mallorca
Walking in the Algarve
Walking in the Canary Islands 2 East
Walking in the Cordillera Cantabrica
Walking in the Sierra Nevada
Walking on La Gomera and El Hierro
Walking on La Palma
Walking on Tenerife
Walking the GR7 in Andalucia
Walks and Climbs in the Picos de Europa

SWITZERLAND

Alpine Pass Route
Central Switzerland
The Bernese Alps
Tour of the Jungfrau Region
Walking in the Valais
Walking in Ticino
Walks in the Engadine

TECHNIQUES

Geocaching in the UK
Indoor Climbing
Lightweight Camping
Map and Compass
Mountain Weather
Moveable Feasts
Outdoor Photography
Rock Climbing
Sport Climbing
The Book of the Bivvy
The Hillwalker's Guide to Mountaineering
The Hillwalker's Manual

MINI GUIDES

Avalanche!
Navigating with a GPS
Navigation
Pocket First Aid and Wilderness Medicine
Snow

For full information on all our guides, and to order books and eBooks, visit our website: **www.cicerone.co.uk**.

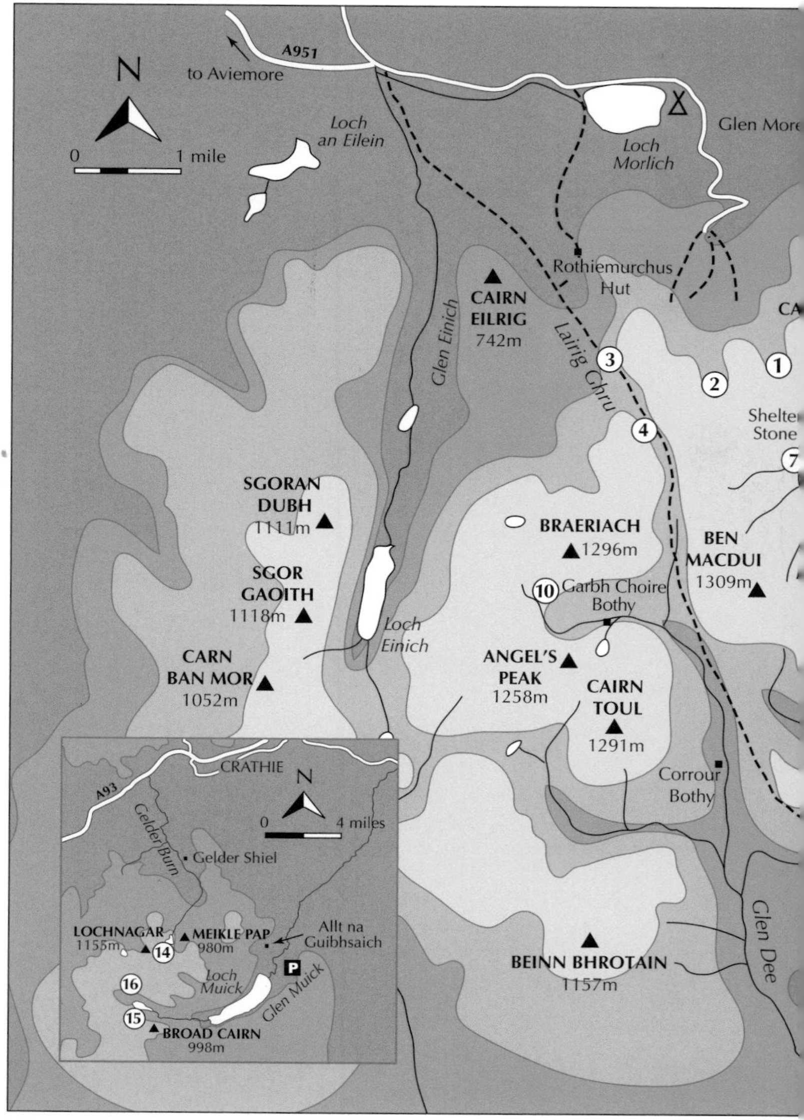
A951
to Aviemore
N
0
1 mile
Loch an Eilein
Loch Morlich
Glen More
Rothiemurchus Hut
CAIRN EILRIG
742m
Glen Einich
Lairig Ghru
3
1
2
4
Shelte
Stone
7
SGORAN DUBH
1111m
BRAERIACH
1296m
BEN MACDUI
1309m
SGOR GAOITH
1118m
10
Garbh Choire Bothy
Loch Einich
CARN BAN MOR
1052m
ANGEL'S PEAK
1258m
CAIRN TOUL
1291m
Corrour Bothy
BEINN BHROTAIN
1157m
Glen Dee
CRATHIE
A93
0
4 miles
Gelder Burn
Gelder Shiel
LOCHNAGAR
1155m
MEIKLE PAP
980m
14
Allt na Guibhsaich
P
16
Loch Muick
Glen Muick
15
BROAD CAIRN
998m